Defensive Coordinator's Football Handbook

Leo Hand

© 2015 Coaches Choice. All rights reserved. Printed in the United States.

No part of this book may be reproduced, stored in a retrieval system or transmitted, in any form or by any means, electronic, mechanical, photocopying, recording, or otherwise, without the prior permission of Coaches Choice. Throughout this book, the masculine shall be deemed to include the feminine and vice versa.

ISBN: 978-1-60679-330-5
Library of Congress Control Number: 2014959916
Cover design: Cheery & Reggie Sugabo
Book layout: Cheery Sugabo
Front cover photo: © Dean M. Beattie/ZUMA Wire

Coaches Choice
P.O. Box 1828
Monterey, CA 93942
www.coacheschoice.com

Dedication

For Coach Jim Murphy, a mentor, a friend, and a truly great football coach.

Acknowledgments

- Thanks to the finest human being that I have ever known, the matriarch of our family and the most wonderful wife that any man could ever hope for. *Ayoo aniinish'ni, Ke alth nos bah.*
- Thanks to our children for their love, understanding, and support.
- Thanks to my parents, Dorothy and Leo Hand, who insisted that their non-academically motivated son graduate from college.
- Thanks to some of the great men who helped foster my love for the game and teach me its most important lessons, my high school and college coaches: Hunk Vadas, Bill Guerrera, Jack Harten, John McVey, George Perles, Ron Blaylock, and Al Koenski.
- Thanks to all of the coaches, principals and athletic directors who have helped me make a living doing a job that I truly love.
- Thanks to all of the associate coaches that I have worked with through the years.
- Thanks to all of the fine young men that I have been privileged to coach.
- Thanks to the many young men who never got a lot of playing time, but attended practice each day, always gave 100 percent, and made the team and those who did get to play better.
- Thanks to my many Zuni, Navajo, and Apache friends and in-laws who have taught me to be a better human being.
- Thanks to James Peterson, Kristi Huelsing, Megan Comstock, and all of the wonderful people at Coaches Choice for their help and support.

Contents

Dedication		3
Acknowledgments		4
Introduction		6
Chapter 1:	Contemporary Offensive Overview	9
Chapter 2:	Identifying Offensive Formations	19
Chapter 3:	Developing a Comprehensive System of Multiplicity	27
Chapter 4:	Base Reads, Reactions, and Techniques of Defensive Linemen	31
Chapter 5:	Base Run Reads, Reactions, and Techniques of Linebackers	65
Chapter 6:	Creating Multiple Even Eight-Man Fronts	71
Chapter 7:	Creating Multiple Even Seven-Man Fronts	83
Chapter 8:	Creating Multiple Odd Eight-Man Fronts	95
Chapter 9:	Creating Multiple Odd Seven-Man Fronts	107
Chapter 10:	Establishing Run Responsibilities for the Defensive Secondary	119
Chapter 11:	Defending the Contemporary Run Game	133
Chapter 12:	Man-to-Man Pass Coverage Techniques	149
Chapter 13:	Man-to-Man Pass Coverages	163
Chapter 14:	Zone and Combo Coverage Techniques and Assignments	179
Chapter 15:	Stunt Strategies and Techniques	195
Chapter 16:	Enhancing Fronts and Coverages With Stunts and Twists	205
Chapter 17:	Preparing to Win	217
Appendix A:	Motivation	225
Appendix B:	One Dozen Suggestions for Longevity in the Coaching Profession	243
About the Author		247

Introduction

Woody Hayes had an unlisted telephone number. As a young coach in Long Beach, California, during the early 1970s, I frequently called Coach Hays to ask his advice regarding various aspects of the game. No matter how busy he was, Coach Hayes always took the time to answer my questions. I'll never forget the first time I called him to inquire about the mechanics of running the outside veer from an I formation. After he finished explaining the mechanics to me, he asked me to repeat everything he said. I had been so excited about the opportunity to personally speak with one of football's greatest coaches that I missed some of the key points that he had described. After listening to my feeble attempt to reiterate his words, Coach Hayes told me to pay closer attention because he was going to start again and explain the entire process to me one more time. After he finished his second explanation, I was able to repeat everything that he said. In subsequent conversations, I can assure you that I paid close attention to everything that Coach Hayes said the first time he said it.

It was also during the early 1970s that I began attending spring practice at USC. John Robinson was the head coach at that time, and he and his staff were very accommodating to high school coaches. We were allowed to walk around on the field during practice, watch coaches teach, stand next to the huddle, attend staff meetings, watch film, and so forth. It was a fantastic learning experience, and for four years, I never missed a spring practice at USC. I also began writing college and pro coaches, asking their advice about various topics, and most of them responded with detailed information regarding my questions. Through the years, I have continued seeking the advice of those much wiser than myself, and I have seldom been disappointed.

The reason that I have begun this book in this way is to explain the enormous debt that I owe to the many great men who have unselfishly shared their knowledge with me. Albert Einstein once said, "A hundred times every day I remind myself that my inner and outer lives are based on the labors of other men, living and dead, and that I must exert myself in order to give in the same measure as I have received and am still receiving." This book, and all of the others that I have written, is an attempt to repay that debt. Hopefully, it will assist others as they teach the strategies, tactics, and skills of the greatest game of all.

What You'll Find in This Book

- An overview of contemporary offensive trends and the forerunner strategies and techniques that spawned them
- A system for identifying offensive formations and personnel groupings
- A simple system, with universal application, for creating multiple defensive fronts and secondary coverages
- The base reads, reactions, and techniques for all 15 alignments that a defensive lineman can be positioned in
- The base reads, reactions, and techniques for linebackers
- A synopsis of the responsibilities and techniques necessary to install 20 different odd and even eight-man fronts
- A summation of the responsibilities and techniques necessary to install 20 different odd and even seven-man fronts
- The run responsibilities and techniques for both three-deep and four-deep secondaries
- The strategies and tactics necessary to stop 19 of today's most potent running plays
- An explanation of the adjustments and techniques necessary to install seven variations of man-to-man pass coverages versus 10 different contemporary offensive formations
- An explanation of the adjustments and techniques necessary to install five variations of zone and combo pass coverages versus 10 different cotemporary offensive formations
- Twelve different stunt strategies that enable your defense to actually attack the offense
- A distinctly different system of phonetic nomenclature that enables any coach to merge multiple stunt maneuvers into a single stunt and then succinctly and expeditiously communicate the stunt to his players
- Sample pass coverage/stunt menus for: the 3-3-5, 4-2-5, bear 46, 3-4, 4-3, and weak eagle defenses
- Suggestions for grading player performance and developing scouting reports and practice plans
- 101 quotes, poems, and anecdotes that can be used to motivate and inspire your players
- 12 suggestions for obtaining longevity in the coaching profession

CHAPTER 1
Contemporary Offensive Overview

I once interviewed a potential candidate for a defensive coordinator position. When I began asking him questions about various offenses, he replied that he didn't know anything about offense; he said that he was strictly a defensive coach. The interview ended immediately because it is impossible for any coach to defend something that he doesn't understand. The purpose of this chapter is to first go back in time and explore the roots of contemporary offenses, and then discuss some of the present-day trends that have evolved from these roots. In doing so, it is hoped that the reader will gain a better understanding of the offensive strategies and tactics that he must defend.

Contemporary Offensive Roots

The old cliché "There's nothing new in football" is as true today as it was 50 years ago. The contemporary offenses that coaches are presently seeing are not new, revolutionary, or space-age; they're essentially discarded remnants that have been recycled, tweaked, and renamed. This journey will begin with the single wing, an offense that dates back to the early 1900s.

The Single Wing

Pop Warner is credited with the most sophisticated development of this offense. The player who received the snap from the center was referred to as the tailback. He was positioned anywhere from four to five yards behind the center. Although he was the passer, he was primarily chosen for his ability as a running back. The player aligned in the backfield near the quarterback was referred to as the fullback, and the player positioned near the line of scrimmage behind the strongside offensive tackle was called the blocking back (Diagram 1-1). The single wing passing game was primarily a play-action attack. The strength of this offense was its ability to outnumber the defense at the point of attack. In its early stages, the single wing was primarily a power attack featuring sweeps, traps, and off-tackle plays toward the unbalanced side of the formation, and reverses and counter plays toward the weakside. Many variations evolved. Some of these were the double wing, the short punt, the A formation, and the Notre Dame box. Without a doubt, the most significant development to ever evolve from the single wing was the spinner series (Diagram 1-2). In their book *Scoring Power With the Winged T Offense*, Evashevski and Nelson refer to the spinner series as "the finest series in single wing football, or all football for that matter."

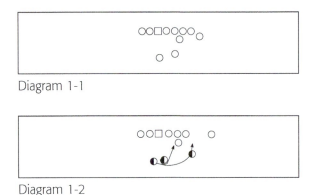

Diagram 1-1

Diagram 1-2

In this series, the fullback is positioned close to the tailback so that either he or the tailback can receive the snap. The wingback's backfield alignment places him in an ideal position to run counters and reverses. The spinner series is commenced by snapping the ball to the fullback, who makes a complete spin. As he spins, he may hand the ball to the tailback or wingback, or he may keep it. Because play-action passes were also incorporated into the series, the spinner series became an explosive multidimensional series that attacked all sectors of the defense with both power and misdirection. Contemporary offenses have been influenced by the single wing in the following ways:

- The single wing established the shotgun as a viable method of transferring the ball from the center into the backfield.
- The single wing tailback is the forefather of the modern "wildcat."
- Today wide receivers are seen running jet motion and either being handed the ball (jet sweep) or being faked to. If the quarterback fakes the jet sweep, he will either keep it or run a play involving the aceback. Metaphorically, today's quarterback becomes the fullback of the spinner series; the wide receiver becomes the tailback, and the aceback becomes the wingback.
- Lastly, coaches today are running a facsimile of the single spinner series from variations of the spread formation.

The Empty Formation

Dutch Meyer was the head coach at TCU from 1934 until 1952. During his tenure, he compiled a 109-79-13 record, won a national championship and three Southwest Conference championships, and his teams appeared in seven bowl games. In 1952, Prentice Hall published his book *Spread Formation Football*. Diagram 1-3 illustrates the primary formation featured in this book. From this formation, Coach Meyer delineates over 100 pass and run plays. Coach Meyer is, without a doubt, the father of the modern spread offense.

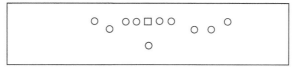

Diagram 1-3

Man-in-Motion T Formation

Historians tell us that the T formation was football's first formation, but its popularity was short-lived. It was quickly replaced by Pop Warner's single wing and its many variations. One coach, despite a great deal of criticism, held fast to the T. That coach was George Halas, head coach of the Chicago Bears. In 1940, Halas's Bears won the NFL championship by beating the Washington Redskins 73-0. The T immediately became football's state-of-the-art offense and remained so for decades. In 1941, Clark Shaughnessy of Stanford University, Ralph Jones of Lake Forest College, and George Halas published a book titled *The Modern T Formation With Man-in-Motion*. In the book's introduction, they describe the offense as a "boxing type of offense" in which "pass plays should be used as the unexpected sock." This offense's contribution to our contemporary style of play is that it did emphasize the importance of throwing the football and stretching the field horizontally.

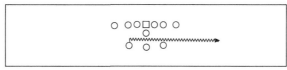

Diagram 1-4

The Split-T

Don Faurot introduced the split-T to college football in 1941 and changed traditional T formation football in two major ways: he used large line splits, and the main staple of his running game was the option. Both Faurot and his former assistant, Bud Wilkinson, achieved extraordinary success with the split-T by amassing a combined win/loss record of 322-125-17 at different schools. In his 1979 book, PB: *The Paul Brown Story*, Coach Brown states: "The split-T helped revolutionize college football, and some of its principles, such as the wishbone and veer formations that are in vogue today." Most contemporary offenses now employ large line splits and incorporate some type of option play in their running game.

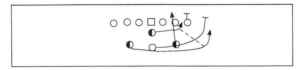

Diagram 1-5

The I Formation

Tom Nugent introduced the football world to the I formation in 1950 while coaching at Virginia Military Institute. During the 2012 football season, the zone read from the pistol formation became the hottest new addition to the spread offensive playbook. The fervor created by this new trend was a result of the defensive havoc created by the San Francisco 49ers quarterback, Colin Kaepernick. Chris Ault, former coach of the University of Nevada, was Kaepernick's college coach and creator of the pistol formation. Before contriving the pistol, Ault was an I formation coach. The pistol is, therefore, an offspring of the I. Furthermore, the zone read and the pistol are not synonymous. The pistol is a formation, and the zone read is a play—a play that Ault did not initially install the into his pistol offense. It was only during his second season with the pistol that Ault installed the read into the offense. The pistol has created many new problems for the defense that the standard shotgun backfield set did not. Designating strength versus a 2x2 receiver set that employs a pistol backfield is the first of these problems. But probably the biggest problem is created by the alignment of the running back. Because the running back is positioned in the center of the formation, all of the plays in which he receives the ball can be run to either side of the formation. With the standard shotgun, plays to the running back are much more predictable.

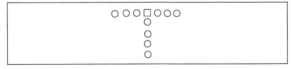

Diagram 1-6

Wing-T

Coach David Nelson began experimenting with the wing-T when he was head coach at the University of Maine in 1949 and continued to develop it when he became the head coach at the University of Delaware in 1951. In many ways, the wing-T is a spinoff of the single wing spinner series. It is a comprehensive attack that organizes passes and runs into sequential play packages that attack all sectors of the defense. Furthermore, it attempts to force defenders to play assignment football while befuddling their assignments with "damned if I do/damned if I don't" conflicts. Although somewhat limited by their formations, most modern spread offenses have attempted to incorporate basic wing-T principles into their attack with sequential play organization that attacks all sectors of a defense and by double binding defenders.

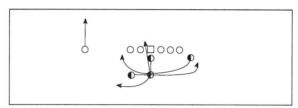

Diagram 1-7

Run-and-Shoot

In 1965, Parker Publishing Company published Glen "Tiger" Ellison's book *Run-and-Shoot Football: Offense of the Future*. In this book, Coach Ellison narrates the story of how the town of Middletown, Ohio, was saved from suffering its first losing football season in its history by the invention of a no-huddle offense, which he dubbed the "lonesome polecat" (because it stunk). From the lonesome polecat, which Ellison described as "insanity," evolved the run-and-shoot offense. The original offense described in the book highlighted a four-receiver aceback set that featured a great deal of motion. Probably the most innovative aspect of the offense was that the receivers adjusted their routes as they were running them based upon the reaction of the defense. This may not have been the first example of what is now referred to as sight adjustment in the modern passing game, but it certainly was the most electrifying. It should also be noted that Coach Ellison's "Frontside Gangster" series featured the quarterback/aceback speed option which is a staple in almost every modern spread offense.

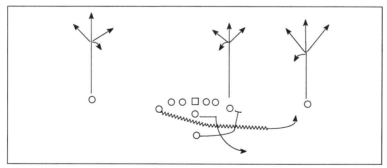

Diagram 1-8

The Multiple Formation Pro Passing Game

Without a doubt, the development of the pro passing game by early pioneers such as Sid Gillman, Don Coryell, and Bill Walsh has had the biggest influence on contemporary offensive football.

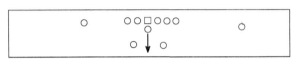

Diagram 1-9

The Houston Veer

Although many coaches contributed to the development the veer offense, probably Bill Yeoman is the one that was most instrumental. The veer is a triple option that leaves two defenders at the end of the line unblocked. The triple option, which is actually three plays in one, features a dive, a quarterback keep, and a pitch. The #2 defender at the end of the line is read by the quarterback. If this defender does not tackle the dive back, the quarterback will give the ball. If #2 does tackle dive back, the quarterback will pull the ball and continue down the line and option #1. The quarterback will pitch the ball if #1 attempts to tackle him; otherwise, he will keep the ball. Many contemporary offenses now run some or all facets of the veer. When executed from a four-receiver set, the quarterback will have the option of pitching the ball to a wide receiver who may or may not be sent into motion. The veer is one of the most explosive running plays in football because it forces the defense to play assignment football.

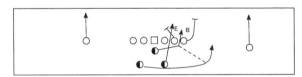

Diagram 1-10

The Midline Option

The midline evolved because defensive teams eventually became adept at defending the veer. The midline may involve a pitch, but usually it is a double option in which the quarterback will either give the ball to the dive back or keep it. Most option teams will run both the veer and the midline. Usually, they prefer to run the midline toward a defensive lineman who is aligned on the outside shade of the playside guard and run the veer in the direction of a defensive linemen aligned on the outside shoulder of the playside tackle. Many contemporary offenses have packaged the veer and midline and achieved great results. It is extremely difficult for any defense to stop these plays unless their preparation has included many practice repetitions, which is virtually impossible to accomplish in a single week.

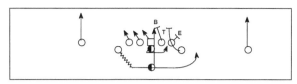
Diagram 1-11

The Fly

Although the fly or jet sweep has been around since the 1950s, Mark Speckman has done more to popularize this play than any other coach. For over 30 years, Speckman has not only used the jet sweep as the staple of his offense, but he has also packaged the play with other pass/run schemes to create an excellent way of not only attacking a defense's perimeter, but also an effective way of attacking all sectors of the defense. Today, almost all contemporary offenses at every level of competition use some form of the jet sweep.

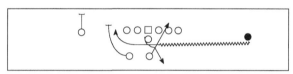
Diagram 1-12

Contemporary Offensive Trends

Having presented the roots of the contemporary offense, it is now appropriate to discuss 12 offensive trends that a defensive coordinator is most likely to encounter. Each trend will be followed with a comment by the author.

Attempting to Force the Defense to Defend the Entire Field

Coaches should remember that plays are seldom initiated from the middle of the field. At least 80 percent of the time, a play originates on a hash mark or within four yards of a hash. When a play is initiated from one of the hash marks, the defense is confronted with defending an unbalanced field. The wideside of the field is 35.6 yards in high school and 33.3 yards in college. The shortside of the field is 17.8 yards in high school and 20 yards in college. Defensive coordinators must, therefore, analyze the tendencies of how the offense is positioning personnel and utilizing space in their play calling.

The Use of Four-Receiver Sets for the Purpose of Allowing Skilled Players to Operate in Space

Allowing skilled players to operate in space is one of the obvious advantages of four-receiver sets; however, all four receivers probably do not possess the same level of athleticism. Some may even be operating on semi-flat tires and/or possess mediocre hands. This is especially true at the high school level. Therefore, it is important that defensive coaches analyze which receivers are the go-to guys and make certain that these players get the utmost attention when devising defensive game plans.

Using Spread Formations in an Attempt to Limit the Number of Defensive Fronts a Team Is Capable of Employing

The defense is still capable of loading the box with at least six defenders and sometimes even seven defenders versus poor passing teams. The positioning of these defenders in countless alignments is not only possible, but prevalent versus the spread.

Using Spread Formations in an Attempt to Make It More Difficult for a Defense to Disguise Blitzes

Spread formations do not deter the disguise of inside blitzes. A four-wide formation may make it more difficult for a defense to disguise a wideside blitz from the edge, but shortside blitzes from the edge are easily disguised. This is especially true for defenses employing a four-deep secondary.

Attempting to Enhance Pass Protection by Positioning the Quarterback in the Gun

Enhancing pass protection is one of the main advantages of the gun, especially when the quarterback is employing a one-step drop and delivering the ball expeditiously. In this situation, it is extremely difficult for the defense to pressure the quarterback; consequently, it far better to concentrate on maximum coverage and/or jamming receivers.

Attempting to Pressure the Defense by Not Huddling

At one time, no-huddle offenses caused a great deal of confusion for defenses that attempted to huddle, but by now, all defenses should be no-huddle defenses. There are two types of no-huddle offenses. The first type is a hurry-up type. This type attempts to create personnel mismatches by making rapid substitutions and to limit defensive front, coverage, and blitz strategies. This tactic can be averted by devoting adequate practice time to making rapid defensive play calls and substitutions that ensure proper match-ups. Another goal of the hurry-up no-huddle is to wear out a defense. This should never occur if the defense is properly conditioned. The hurry-up no-huddle tactic often ends up being a double-edged sword for many offensive teams. It is effective when the offense is consistently moving the chains and putting points on the scoreboard, but if the offense ends up with too many three-and-outs, they put undue pressure on their own defense by denying them adequate time to rest.

The second type of no-huddle offense is the slow-paced no-huddle. This type lines up in its offensive formation and then waits for the defense to adjust. Either the quarterback or a coach will then call a play based upon his evaluation of the pre-snap read given by the defense. Although this tactic benefits the offense, it also benefits the defense because 15 or more seconds will usually expire from the time the offense assumes its formation until the ball is snapped. This time lapse affords the defense extra time to signal in their call, make adequate adjustments, and dupe the offense by disguising their pre-snap read.

Many Spread Coaches Have Adopted the Offensive Philosophy That: "The Defense Can Stop the Run, and It Can Stop the Pass, But Can It Stop Both?"

This challenge an extremely difficult for any defensive coordinator when the offense possesses both an explosive run and pass attack. The decisive question, however, is: can the offense effectively do both? At the high school level, the answer is often no. The offense may have a great passing game, but their running game may be limited, or vice versa. It is the defensive coordinator's responsibility to make certain that his defense shuts down the things that the offense does well and force it into doing what it doesn't do as well.

The Tendency of Spread Teams to Rely Upon the Quarterback as a Major Factor in Their Run Offense

This tendency is the great catch-22 of the spread offense. If the quarterback is a great passer, is it worth the risk of using him as a running back? If he's not a great passer, most of the problems in defending the spread are greatly reduced. In an attempt to keep their quarterback out of harm's way, many coaches are now involving their wide receivers in the run game with jet sweeps, fake jet sweeps, and reverses.

The Use of Multiple Formations and Motions in an Attempt to Force Defensive Adjustments and Mistakes

This tactic is more effective versus zone coverages than it is versus man coverages. Because of the effectiveness of this tactic, it necessary for defensive coaches to spend considerable practice time making certain that their formation adjustments are not only sound, but that highest priority is given to ideal personnel match-ups.

The Utilization of Spread Formations That Remove Defenders From the Box Leaving Linemen With Fewer Defenders to Block

The number of defenders that are removed from the box will be dependent upon the offense's ability to pass the ball to their spread receivers. Also, because there are fewer offensive players remaining in the box, it is not necessary to have as many defenders positioned in the box.

Using Spread Formations for the Purpose of Making Pre-Snap Coverages Easier for the Quarterback to Read

Both pre-snap and post-snap coverage disguises are directly related to the creativity of the coach that designed them and the players that execute them. Offensive formations only play a minor role in this matter.

Spread Formations That Are a Conglomeration of Many Different Styles of Offense

After examining the roots of present-day offenses, it becomes apparent that they are an amalgamation of the best elements of offenses of the past. In order for a defense coach to adequately defend any strategy or tactic, he must first understand it. It is, therefore, imperative that defensive coaches must have a thorough understanding of both the offenses of the past and present in order to deal with the offenses of the future—a future that may occur as soon as their next game.

CHAPTER 2
Identifying Offensive Formations

Personnel Groupings

As the offense takes the field, and as it makes substitutions during a series, it is imperative that the defensive coordinator identifies the personnel grouping that is on the field. An error in identifying the personnel grouping may result in a mismatch that lights up the scoreboard. Personnel groupings are identified by two-digit numbers in the following manner:
- The first digit designates the number of running backs in the backfield.
- The second digit identifies the number of tight ends in the formation.
- Consequently, if one running back is in the formation and no tight ends, the personnel grouping would be 10 personnel. If two running backs are in the formation and one tight end, the personnel grouping would be 21 personnel. If no running backs are in the backfield, the first digit is 0; therefore, if the backfield is empty and there is one tight end, the personnel grouping is 01 personnel, and if there are no tight ends, the personnel grouping is 00 personnel.

Identifying Backfield Sets

As the offense breaks the huddle and begins to assume their formation, loud chatter should commence among the members of the defense. This chatter should not only involve formation identification, but it should also involve communicating personnel placement and formation/personnel tendencies. It is the responsibility of the linebackers to identify the alignment of the running backs as the offense assumes its formation. Diagrams 2-1A through 2-1H illustrate eight of the most common contemporary backfield alignments:

- Gun right (Diagram 2-1A)
- Gun left (Diagram 2-1B)
- Gun pistol (Diagram 2-1C)
- Ace (Diagram 2-1D)
- Sniff left-gun right (Diagram 2-1E)
- Deuce left (Diagram 2-1F)
- Deuce split (Diagram 2-1G)
- Diamond (Diagram 2-1H)

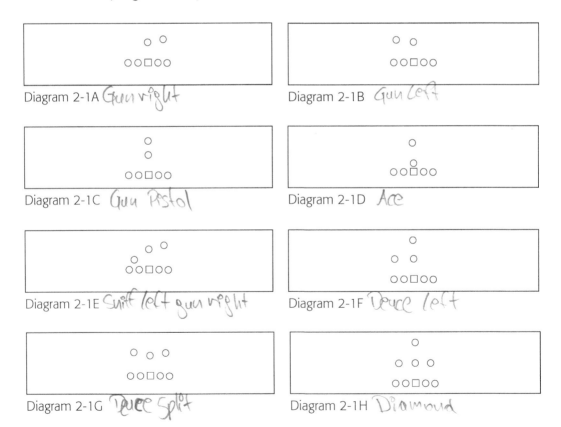

If no backs are in the backfield, the linebackers will make an empty call.

Identifying Receiver Alignments

As receivers assume their positions, the defensive backs will identify the alignment of the receivers by a two-digit number in the following manner:

- The first digit designates the number of eligible receivers aligned to the left of center.
- The second digit identifies the number of eligible receivers aligned to the right of center.
- Consequently, if two receivers are to the left and two receivers to the right, the call would be 22. If three receivers are to the left and one receiver to the right, the number would be 31.
- The defensive backs will also identify the presence of a tight end. For example, if one tight end is to the left and three wide receivers to the right, the call would be 13 tight left.
- If no running backs are in the backfield, the defensive backs will make one of four possible calls (excluding tight end designations): 32, 23, 41, or 14.

Putting It All Together

Diagrams 2-2A through 2-2L illustrate one dozen examples of how the system of formation identification works. These 12 diagrams will follow the following format:

- First, the personnel grouping will be identified.
- Next, the backfield alignment will be identified.
- Lastly, the call alignment of the receivers will be identified.

As you read these examples, remember that only two calls are made on the field, the backfield set and the receiver alignment. The personnel grouping is not a call that is made on the field; it is information that the defensive coordinator must know in order to insure the appropriate match up of his defensive personnel with that of the offense.

- 10 personnel, pistol, 22 (Diagram 2-2A)
- 10 personnel, gun left, 31 (Diagram 2-2B)
- 10 personnel, gun right, 13 (Diagram 2-2C)
- 11 personnel, gun right, 22 tight left (Diagram 2-2D)
- 11 personnel, gun left, 31 tight right (Diagram 2-2E)
- 11 personnel, ace, 13 tight left (Diagram 2-2F)
- 20 personnel, deuce left, 21 (Diagram 2-2G)
- 21 personnel, gun right/sniff left, 21 tight left (Diagram 2-2H)
- 30 personnel, diamond, 30 (Diagram 2-2I)
- 02 personnel, empty, 32 double tight (Diagram 2-2J)
- 00 personnel, empty, 23 (Diagram 2-2K)
- 00 personnel, empty, 41 (Diagram 2-2L)

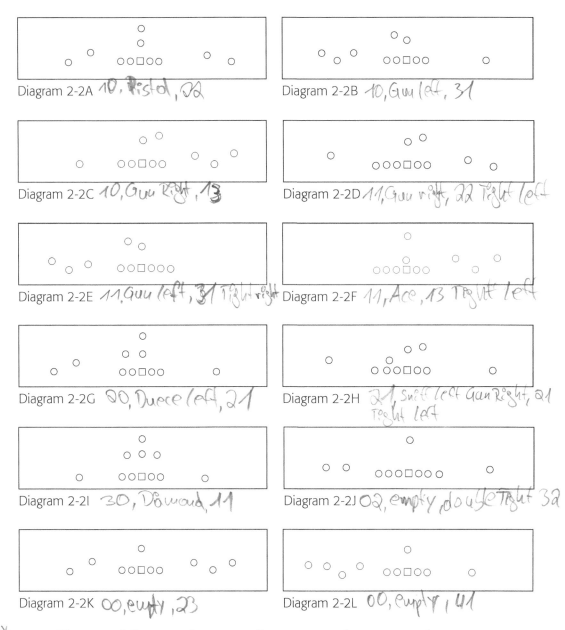

Diagram 2-2A 10, Pistol, 02
Diagram 2-2B 10, Guu left, 31
Diagram 2-2C 10, Guu Right, 13
Diagram 2-2D 11, Guu right, 22 Tight left
Diagram 2-2E 11, Guu left, 31 Tight right
Diagram 2-2F 11, Ace, 13 Tight left
Diagram 2-2G 00, Duece left, 21
Diagram 2-2H 21, Sniff left Gun Right, 01 Tight left
Diagram 2-2I 30, Diamond, 11
Diagram 2-2J 02, empty double Tight 32
Diagram 2-2K 00, empty, 23
Diagram 2-2L 00, empty, 41

Dealing With Motion and Unusual Formations

A number of sophisticated systems can be used for identifying motion. Most of them involve identifying a particular player, such as the flanker or running back, and then designating a particular type of motion with that player. For example, if the flanker, who most coaches identify as Z, were to run a particular motion, the motion might be identified as zoom, zig, or zap. These systems are necessary for offensive communication, and were also helpful tools for defensive communication when offensive formations were fairly standard. But, attempting to identify contemporary formations, featuring four and five wide receivers, can be quite complicated with these systems. Only three motions are significant in today's game and need to be identified: backfield motion, fly motion, and flap motion.

Backfield Motion

Backfield motion changes both the backfield call and receiver alignment call. The initial call (prior to motion) for the alignment illustrated in Diagram 2-3 is deuce left 21. As the motion occurs, the call should change to pistol 22.

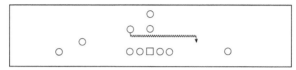

Diagram 2-3

Fly Motion

Fly motion changes the backfield alignment as the motioned receiver is in the backfield (making the alignment a two-back set); as the receiver leaves the backfield and enters the perimeter, the receiver alignment changes from 22 to 31 (Diagram 2-4). Attempting to communicate all of this information would be unduly complicated and cause a great deal of confusion; therefore, it is much simpler to simply make the call fly left (or right).

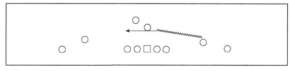

Diagram 2-4

Flap Motion

Flap and fly motion are very similar, but they're sometimes difficult for players to identify during the course of a game. Fly motion occurs between the line of scrimmage and the quarterback. Its purpose is to: run the jet sweep, fake the jet sweep, and run a different running play, fake the jet sweep, add an extra receiver via motion, and pass, and run a receiver across the formation without faking the jet sweep in an attempt to enhance a pass play or to use the motioned receiver as an extra blocker. Flap motion sends a receiver into the backfield, behind the quarterback (Diagram 2-5). It is primarily used to: add an extra running to the formation, or fake a running play that doesn't involve the motion receiver and then throw a pass to him. The second purpose is often very successful because defenses are often deceived by the run fake and lose track of the motioned receiver. Like fly motion, flap motion should be identified by a simple flap right (or left) call.

Diagram 2-5

Detached Linemen

Although not yet a trend, a number of coaches sometimes position offensive linemen into the perimeter. They do this to either confuse the defense or to provide wide receivers with extra blockers for quick screen passes. In Diagram 2-6, both the #2 player to the left and the #3 player to the right are ineligible and should be wearing a jersey numbers in the range of 50 to 79. A few years ago, two coaches from Piedmont High School in California—Kurt Bryan and Steve Humphries—found a loophole in the scrimmage kick rule that allowed the two previously noted ineligible players to wear legal receiver jersey numbers, providing the quarterback was at least seven yards deep. They called their offense the "A-11 offense" and used it for a couple of seasons. Eventually, the loophole was closed, and the A-11 offense can only be used if the detached linemen wear the appropriate jersey numbers (50 to 79). It is important for defensive coordinators to remember that in dealing with formations that utilize detached linemen that they must match strength with strength and not get outmanned by extra blockers in the perimeter.

Diagram 2-6

The Lonesome Polecat

The lonesome polecat is the precursor of the run-and-shoot offense which was devised by Tiger Ellison at Middleton High School. It is very similar to the swinging gate formation that was created in the 1930s. Both the swinging gate and the polecat are now primarily used as pre-shift formations in PAT situations. If the defense doesn't make sound adjustments, the offense will immediately snap the ball to the quarterback and attempt a two-point conversion. If the defense does adjust properly, the offense will then shift into their PAT formation and kick the extra point. Because of the similarity of the swinging gate and the polecat, specific attention will be given to the latter. Like all formations, the polecat features five eligible receivers. Players identified in Diagram 2-7 as #4 and #5 are positioned off the line, which makes the center an eligible receiver.

Diagram 2-7

The deciding factor on whether to kick the extra point or go for two requires the quarterback to simply count the number of defenders aligned opposite the wall in front of #1. If fewer than five defenders are positioned opposite the wall, the quarterback will immediately throw the ball to #1. The quarterback may also have the option of throwing to one of the other receivers if the defense didn't cover that receiver, but usually most teams use the polecat to throw the quick screen to #1. If a defensive coordinator is confronted by a team that uses the polecat more frequently, his first priority is to prevent the quick screen to #1, his second priority is to make certain that all eligible receivers are covered, and his last priority is to contain and pressure the quarterback.

CHAPTER 3
Developing a Comprehensive System of Multiplicity

When I began coaching 45 years ago, I assumed that every coach had at his disposal an all-inclusive system that would enable his offensive linemen to know exactly who to block no matter how a defense lined up. I was wrong. After considerable research, I quickly learned that this was a problematic area for all coaches—even those in the NFL. Through the years, I have also learned that every defensive front has both specific strengths and weaknesses, and if a coach attempts to play only one front or one coverage for an entire game, a smart offensive coordinator will eventually discover and exploit the weakness. The purpose of this chapter is to lay the foundation for the implementation of a comprehensive system multiple fronts.

The Numbering System

Some coaches credit Bear Bryant with the invention of the numbering system; others claim Bum Phillips as the inventor. No matter who invented the first numbering system or how it has been altered through the years, all numbering systems have one inherent problem: there are 15 possible positions in which defensive linemen can line up in, and there are only 9 single-digit numbers. In an attempt to remedy this situation, I have developed a numbering system that uses letters in conjunction with the nine single-digit numbers. This system is illustrated in Diagram 3-1.

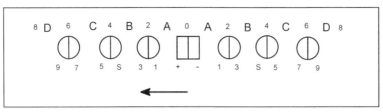

Diagram 3-1

Three of the four letters in this system are used to signify universal A, B, and C gap responsibilities. The letter "S" is the only other letter used, and it is used to signify an inside shade alignment on the offensive tackle.

A Systematic Lettering of Personnel

In order to achieve multiplicity without creating a great deal of confusion, it is advantageous to have a system that provides permanent letters and names for the nine possible positions in which skilled defenders may line up. Obviously, this entire lettering system can be tweaked by any coach so that it fits his particular situations. Diagram 3-2 illustrates the system that will be used throughout this book.

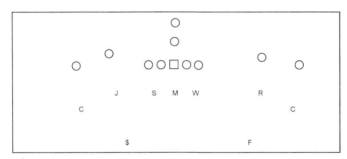

Diagram 3-2

The following are the names representing each position and the types of personnel that would be used for that position:

- *C (Cornerback):* These two players are the traditional cornerback type that would be used in any defensive scheme.
- *J and R (Joker and Rover):* In an eight-man front, these two players are the hybrid outside linebacker/strong safety type. In a seven-man front, they are usually typical outside linebackers. Versus teams that pass a great deal or in obvious passing situations, defensive backs may be substituted for J and R.
- *S, M, and W (Sam, Mike, and Will):* These players are the classic type of inside linebacker used in any defensive scheme.
- *$ and F (Dollar and Free):* These players are archetypal safeties; dollar is the strong safety, and F is the free safety.

An additional advantage for designating a letter for each position is that it generates a simplified system for communicating stunt assignments. For example, when Sam is assigned to stunt, the following are the names that would be used for the gaps that he is assigned to stunt into:

- A gap: Say
- B gap: Stab
- C gap: Stick
- D gap: Sod

Creating Multiple Fronts Using Three Defensive Linemen

When three defensive linemen are used, they are referred to as the nose and the two ends. A three-digit number is used to create both a seven-man and an eight-man front that employs three defensive linemen. The three digits identify where the three defensive linemen should line up. Diagram 3-3A illustrates an eight-man front. The name of this defense is 404 because both ends are positioned in a 4 alignment and the nose is in a 0 alignment. Diagram 3-3B illustrates a seven-man front. The name of this defense is 505 because the two ends are aligned in 5 techniques and the nose is in a 0. Using this system, a defensive coordinator can easily switch from an eight-man front (404) to a seven-man front (505) by simply substituting dollar for Mike.

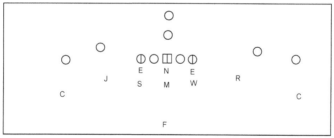

Diagram 3-3A

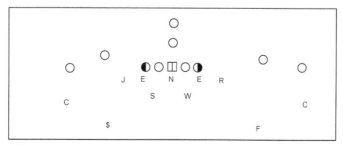

Diagram 3-3B

Creating Multiple Fronts Using Four Defensive Linemen

When four defensive linemen are used, they are referred to as the tackles and the ends. A two-digit number, specifying where the two tackles line up, is used to create both a seven-man and an eight-man front that employs four defensive linemen. Diagram 3-4A illustrates an eight-man front. The name of this defense is 31 because the left tackle is line up in a 3 and the right tackle is lined up in a 1. Diagram 3-4B illustrates a seven-man front. The name of this defense is 22 because the two tackles are aligned in 2 techniques.

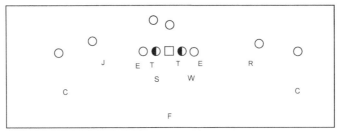

Diagram 3-4A

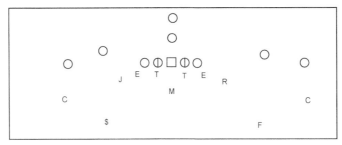

Diagram 3-4B

CHAPTER 4
Base Reads, Reactions, and Techniques of Defensive Linemen

Basic Fundamental vs. Run and Pass

Formulating a Defensive Line Philosophy

A defensive lineman's stance, initial steps, and techniques are dependent upon the defensive line philosophy. The two basic philosophies are: read or attack. Both philosophies have been used successfully at all levels of competition. It is up to the defensive coordinator to decide which philosophy best suits his personnel and which will be most effective versus his opponents.

Both the read and the attack philosophy begin with defensive linemen controlling the line of scrimmage and dominating offensive blockers. The read philosophy is more concerned with attacking offensive blockers, reading and reacting to blocking schemes and pursuing the ball along the line of scrimmage. An attacking philosophy is based on penetrating the line of scrimmage and reading on the run.

Stance

A defensive lineman should position his feet no wider than his shoulders. If an attack philosophy is employed, the lineman's stance will resemble that of a sprinter—a narrow stance with a significant stagger of his feet. A read philosophy lineman's stance will be more conventional; his feet will be approximately shoulder-width apart and either parallel or slightly staggered. The attack defender will position his buttocks higher than his shoulders, whereas the read defender's buttocks and shoulders will be parallel. Both defenders will focus on the helmet screws of their opposing offensive linemen and keep the movement of the ball in their periphery. In an obvious passing down, the read defender's stance will duplicate that of the attack defender.

Initial Movement

It is vital that a defensive lineman explodes out of his stance as the ball is snapped. An attack defender will usually stagger the foot toward the direction of his gap responsibility. In other words, a player playing a 3 technique on the left side of the line would stagger his left foot and make his first step with his left foot. The opposite is true of a read defender. A read defender aligned in a similar position as just described will stagger his right foot and take a short jab step with his left foot as the ball is snapped.

As the ball is snapped, the defender (both read and attack) should explode out of his stance by pushing off his front foot and attacking the blocker with a violent hand shiver, using the heels of his hands. As contact is made, the defender will continue to keep his feet moving. In executing the hand shiver, the defender's thumbs should be pointed upward and his palms out. Normally, the defender's target will be inside the numbers on the blocker's jersey. If the blocker's approach is low, the defender may not be able to strike the blocker's numbers. He will then strike the blocker's shoulder pads. Pad level is vital. It is imperative that the defender's pad level is lower than that of the blocker. As he attacks the blocker, the defender will roll his hips and try to gain separation from the blocker with a bench press technique. Throughout this process, it is important that the defender first concentrates on the screws of the defender's helmet and defeats the blocker. A defender often gets knocked off his feet because he is mainly focusing on the backfield action and paying limited attention to the blocker.

Escape From a Run Block

After defeating the blocker and finding the ball, the defender must now shed the blocker and begin his path to the ball. Probably the two most effective ways of shedding a run blocker are: the rip and the pull release. When executing the rip release, the defender will first use his playside arm to force the blocker's playside shoulder backward. He will then get low and violently rip his trail arm under the extended arms of the blocker. It is vital that the defender gets his hips past the blocker's hips as he rips with his trail arm.

When executing the pull release, the defender will again use his playside arm to force the blocker's playside shoulder backward. The defender will then use his trail arm to grab the top of the blocker's backside shoulder. The defender will then violently pull the blocker's backside shoulder downward. This will force the blocker's shoulders parallel to the line of scrimmage. It is important while executing this technique that the defender keeps the blocker's body extended and away from his own body. When executing either technique, it is vital that the defender remains extremely aggressive and keeps his feet moving.

Pass Rush Techniques

A variety of pass rush moves can be used to pressure and sack the quarterback. Before discussing any of these moves, it is first important that the defender understands that he must concentrate on controlling one half of the blocker's body. When doing this, he must pressure the blocker, maintain contact with the blocker, and most importantly attempt to destroy the blocker's balance. The following are four techniques that a defender may use to destroy a blocker's balance and set up an effective pass rush move:

- *Shoulder club:* The blocker will use his outside arm to deliver a blow to the shoulder of the blocker.
- *Hand slap:* This move is similar to the club with the exception that the defender will strike the blocker's shoulder pad with the heel of his hand in a similar motion that a boxer would use when throwing a hook.
- *Grab-and-jerk:* The defender will firmly grab the blocker's jersey (usually on the shoulder joints) and then pull the blocker either sideways or forward, depending upon the body position of the blocker.
- *Rip up:* The defender will use his arm, hand, and shoulder in a rip up motion underneath the blocker's armpit and shoulder.

In executing any of these techniques, it is imperative that the defender's execution extremely quick and is aggressive. It is also vital that the defender maintains position in his pass rush lane, sees the quarterback, and keeps his feet moving.

The following are three techniques that a defender may use to defeat a blocker when rushing the quarterback:

- *Rip:* This move can be set up by a shoulder club, a hand slap, or a rip up. It can also be executed by having the defender use his near hand to lift the near hand of the blocker. As he lifts, the defender will simultaneously rip under the blocker's outside shoulder with his trail arm and leg in a similar manner that was described in run block escape. It is vital that the defender gets his hips past the blocker during the rip. This is an effective technique when the defender is the same height or shorter than the blocker.
- *Arm over:* This move is most effective when the blocker has a forward lean and is usually set up by a grab and downward pull. Tall defenders usually favor this technique. In executing the arm over, the defender will actually punch over the blocker's outside shoulder with his far arm (similar to a boxer's right cross). As the defender's punch clears the blocker's shoulder, the defender will simultaneously step with his trail leg and get his hips past the blocker. It is important that the defender uses his punch arm to press against the blocker's back as he moves his hips past the blocker.
- *Bull rush:* This move is most effective versus a high or soft blocker and also as a change of pace. This technique involves having the defender use his power and momentum to drive the blocker into the quarterback's lap. It is important that the defender maintains a good forward lean as he progresses toward the quarterback. It is also important that the defender does not rely upon this move as his only technique because he will encounter defenders that he will be unable to overpower.

Other principles must be included in any discussion of pass rush techniques:
- Urgency and desire are probably the two most important elements of a successful pass rush.
- Defenders must be taught both the importance and the methods of using a blocker's momentum and body position to their advantage.
- A defender should never leave his feet when rushing the quarterback because he will become vulnerable to a scramble.
- A defender should get his hands up when he is facing the quarterback and the quarterback is beginning his throwing motion. If the defender is not facing the quarterback, he should not get his hands up; he should run through the quarterback.
- The first objective of a pass rusher is to sack the quarterback. Obviously, a sack will not always occur. Pass rushers must also understand that they have an important role in pressuring the quarterback by impairing his vision and preventing him from throwing on rhythm.
- When confronted by a screen pass, defenders must be taught the importance of changing direction, sprinting to the ball, and preventing a long run.

READS, REACTIONS, AND TECHNIQUES OF EACH DEFENSIVE ALIGNMENT

Minus Technique

Stance and Alignment

The defender lines up on the weakside of the formation with his inside eye aligned on the outside eye of the center in a three- or four-point stance.

Responsibilities

Run toward: Weakside A gap
Run away: Squeezes the A gap, and pursues from an inside-out position.
Pass: Rushes the weakside A gap.

Keys

Primary: Center, weakside guard
Secondary: Backfield flow

Important Techniques/Concepts

The defender's target is the center's outside eye. He will employ a crush technique by attacking the center with his hands (inside lockout). He will keep his shoulders square. It is important that he recognizes that a pulling guard indicates the point of attack.

Key Blocks

Center drive block (Diagram 4-1A): The defender must knock the center back, stay square, and locate the ball.

Guard/center double-team (Diagram 4-1B): The defender must attack the guard, stay low, and not get driven back. As a last resort, the defender will drop his outside hip and plug the A gap by rolling outside.

Center reach block (Diagram 4-1C): The defender must control the center's outside shoulder, keep his own shoulders parallel to the line, and plug the A gap. He can't get hooked.

Weak zone (Diagram 4-1D): The defender will play it like a center hook block and control the center's outside shoulder.

Strong zone—center/weak guard combo (Diagram 4-1E): The defender will squeeze inside and jam the center's near hip and prevent the center from releasing to the second level. He will simultaneously flatten out and pursue the ball.

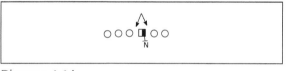

Diagram 4-1A

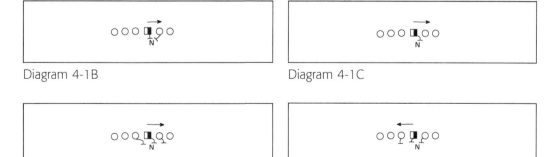

Diagram 4-1B

Diagram 4-1C

Diagram 4-1D

Diagram 4-1E

Center blocks strong/reach block by guard (Diagram 4-1F): The defender will release pressure from the center and control the outside shoulder of the guard. He will work across the guard's face and pursue the ball from an inside-out position.

Guard pulls strong/center turnout (Diagram 4-1G): The defender should beat the center's block, penetrate across the line of scrimmage, and follow the guard to the point of attack. If defender is unable to penetrate, he should flatten across the center's face and pursue the ball from an inside-out position.

Guard pulls weak/center reach blocks (Diagram 4-1H): The defender must control the center's outside shoulder, attempt to gain penetration, and get into the guard's hip pocket.

Pass (Diagram 4-1I): The defender will rush the weakside A gap.

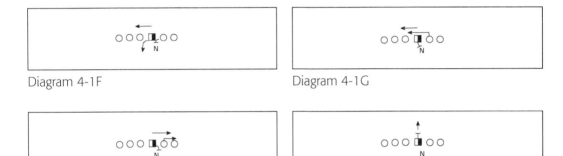

Diagram 4-1F

Diagram 4-1G

Diagram 4-1H

Diagram 4-1I

0 Technique

Stance and Alignment

Crowd the football in a three- or four-point stance, nose-to-nose with the center. Minimum to no stagger of the feet.

Responsibilities

Run: Playside A gap
Pass: Rushes either A gap (may vary, depending upon the scheme).

Keys

Primary: Center, ball movement
Secondary: Both guards

Important Techniques/Concepts

Target: Crush technique: The defender attacks the center with both hands—inside lockout. He then takes a short jab step in the direction of the play, controls the center's playside shoulder, keeps his own shoulders square to the line of scrimmage, and secures the playside A gap. It is vital that the defender remembers that pulling guards indicate the point of attack.

Key Blocks

The center drive blocks—runs directly at the defender (Diagram 4-2A): The defender knocks the center back, continues to drive his feet, and crushes the center into the backfield. The defender controls the center's block, stays square, doesn't pick a side, and waits for the ballcarrier to commit.

The center/guard double-team (Diagram 4-2B): The defender attacks the guard, stays low, and doesn't get driven back. As a last resort, he drops his outside hip and rolls into and plugs the A gap.

The center reach blocks, one or both guards pull (Diagram 4-2C): The defender controls the center's playside shoulder. He initially keeps his own shoulders parallel to the line of scrimmage and then turns them slightly toward the outside as he works his hips into the playside A gap. The defender then pursues the ball from an inside-out position. It is vital that the nose doesn't get hooked.

The center/backside guard zone combo zone (Diagram 4-2D): The defender plays the center's block like a hook block. It is vital that he jams the center and prevents the center from releasing to the next level to block a linebacker.

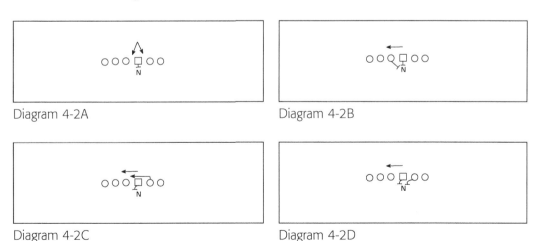

Diagram 4-2A

Diagram 4-2B

Diagram 4-2C

Diagram 4-2D

The center blocks away, the guard down blocks (Diagram 4-2E): The defender releases pressure from the center and focuses his attention on the guard. If the defender's crush technique has enabled him to beat the guard's head across the line of scrimmage, he continues to penetrate the line and makes the play in the backfield. On the other hand, if the guard's head is in front of the nose, the defender attacks the guard, controls the guard's outside shoulder, secures the playside A gap, and then pursues flat along the line of scrimmage.

The center pass blocks (Diagram 4-2F): The defender rushes either A gap.

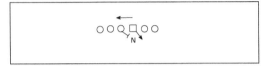

Diagram 4-2E   Diagram 4-2F

Plus Technique

Stance and Alignment

The defender lines up on the strongside of the formation with his inside eye aligned on the outside eye of the center in a three- or four-point stance.

Responsibilities

Run toward: Strongside A gap
Run away: Squeezes the A gap, and pursues from an inside-out position.
Pass: Rushes the strongside A gap.

Keys

Primary: Center, strongside guard
Secondary: Strongside guard, backfield flow

Important Techniques/Concepts

The defender's target is the center's outside eye. He will employ a crush technique by attacking the center with his hands (inside lockout). He will keep his shoulders square. It is important that he recognizes that a pulling guard indicates the point of attack.

Key Blocks

Center drive block (Diagram 4-3A): The defender must knock the center back, stay square, and locate the ball.

Guard/center double-team (Diagram 4-3B): The defender must attack the guard, stay low, and not get driven back. As a last resort, the defender will drop his outside hip and plug the A gap by rolling outside.

Center reach block (Diagram 4-3C): The defender must control the center's outside shoulder, keep his own shoulders parallel, and plug the A gap. He can't get hooked.

Weak zone—strongside guard/center combo (Diagram 4-3D): The defender will jam the center's near hip and prevent the center from releasing to the second level. He will simultaneously flatten down the line and pursue the ball from an inside-out position.

Center blocks weak/down block by guard (Diagram 4-3E): The defender will release pressure from the center and control the outside shoulder of the guard. He will work across the guard's face and pursue the ball from an inside-out position.

Strongside guard pulls weak/center turnout (Diagram 4-3F): The defender should beat the center's block, penetrate across the line of scrimmage, and follow the guard to the point of attack. If defender is unable to penetrate, he should flatten across center's face and pursue the ball from an inside-out position.

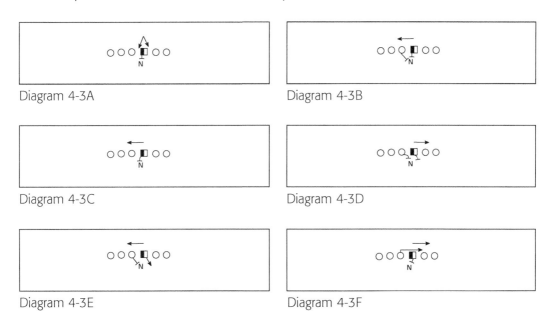

Diagram 4-3A

Diagram 4-3B

Diagram 4-3C

Diagram 4-3D

Diagram 4-3E

Diagram 4-3F

Strongside guard pulls strong/center reach blocks (Diagram 4-3G): The defender must control the center's outside shoulder, attempt to gain penetration, and follow the guard to the point of attack.

Pass (Diagram 4-3H): The defender will rush the strongside A gap.

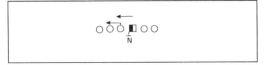

Diagram 4-3G

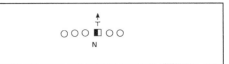

Diagram 4-3H

1 Technique

Stance and Alignment

The defender lines up with his outside eye pointed at the inside eye of the guard in a three- or four-point stance.

Responsibilities

Run toward: Secures the A gap and pursues the ball from an inside-out position.
Run away: Secures the A gap, and trails the play from an inside-out position.
Pass: Rushes the A gap.

Keys

Primary: Guard is the defender's visual key.
Secondary: Center is his pressure key.

Important Techniques/Concepts

Defender gets off the ball on movement, immediately attack the guard with his hands (inside lockout), keeps his shoulders square, reads and reacts to the guard's head, finds the ball and makes the tackle.

Key Blocks

The guard drive blocks (Diagram 4-4A): Defender attacks the guard, knocks the guard backward, secures the A gap, finds the ball, and makes the tackle.

Guard/center zone—run toward (Diagram 4-4B): Defender reacts to the guard's movement, jams the guard and prevents the guard from releasing to the second level. He avoids or defeats the center's block, and pursues the ball from an inside-out position.

The guard reach blocks—run away (Diagram 4-4C): Defender reacts to the guard's head, secures the A gap as he moves in the direction of the ball. Pursues the ballcarrier from an inside-out position.

Guard pulls outside, the center reach blocks (Diagram 4-4D): Defender avoids or defeats the center's block and follows the guard to the point of attack.

The guard pulls outside, the center blocks away (Diagram 4-4E): This is a trap. Defender will close inside and trap the trapper with an inside forearm rip. It is imperative that the defender does not penetrate the line of scrimmage any deeper than the heel line.

The guard pulls inside, the center blocks the defender (Diagram 4-4F): If the defender beats the center's face across the line, he will pursue the play behind the line. If not, he will cross the center's face and pursue the ball along the line.

Guard pass blocks (Diagram 4-4G): Defender will rush through the A gap.

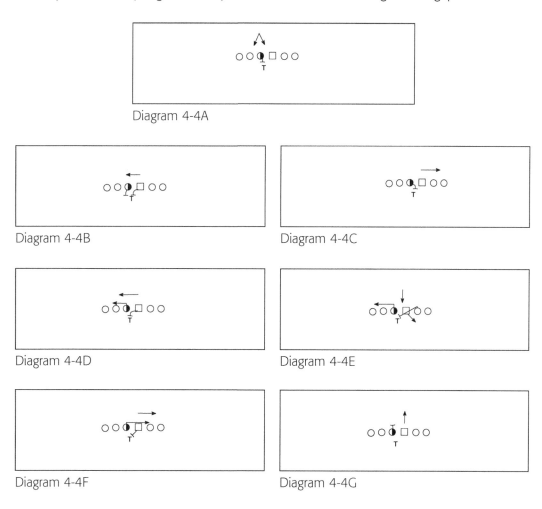

2 Technique

Stance and Alignment

Crowds the ball in a three- or four-point stance, nose-to-nose with the guard. Minimum to no stagger of the feet.

Responsibilities

Run: Defender is a two-gap player. When aligned on the strongside, he is responsible for the B gap when plays are directed toward the strongside and the A gap when plays are directed toward the weakside. When aligned on the weakside, he is responsible for the A gap when plays are directed toward the strongside and the B gap when plays are directed toward the weakside.

Pass: Rushes either the A or B gap. When a 22 scheme is employed, one 2 technique defender will rush the A gap, and the other will rush the B gap.

Keys

Primary: Guard, ball movement
Secondary: Center and tackle

Important Techniques/Concepts

Crush technique: The defender attacks the guard with both hands—inside lockout. He then takes a short jab step in the direction of the play, controls the guard's playside shoulder, keep his own shoulders square to the line of scrimmage, and secures the playside gap.

Key Blocks

The guard drive blocks—runs directly at the defender (Diagram 4-5A): The defender knocks the guard back, continues to drive his feet, and crushes the guard into the backfield. The defender controls the guard's block, stays square, doesn't pick a side, and waits for the ballcarrier to commit.

The guard reach blocks (Diagram 4-5B): The defender controls the guard's playside shoulder. He initially keeps his own shoulders parallel to the line of scrimmage and then turns them slightly toward the outside as he works his hips into the playside gap. The defender then pursues the ball from an inside-out position. It is vital that the defender doesn't get hooked.

Diagram 4-5A   Diagram 4-5B

Guard/center strongside zone (Diagram 4-5C): The defender plays the guard's block like a hook block. It is vital that he jams the guard and prevents the guard from releasing to the next level to block a linebacker.

Guard/tackle weakside zone (Diagram 4-5D): The defender plays the guard's block like a hook block. It is vital that he jams the guard and prevents the guard from releasing to the next level to block a linebacker.

The guard/tackle double-team (Diagram 4-5E): The defender attacks the tackle, stays low, and does not get driven back. As a last resort, he drops his outside hip and rolls into and plugs the B gap.

The guard/tackle kiss block (Diagram 4-5F): The defender must force a double-team and prevent the tackle from releasing to the next level to block a linebacker.

The guard pulls outside, the tackle cracks (Diagram 4-5G): The defender should penetrate the line of scrimmage if he's beaten the tackle's head; otherwise, he should, secure the B gap, flatten across the tackle's face, and pursue the ball from an inside-out position.

The guard blocks inside, no outside pressure (Diagram 4-5H): This block is a trap. The defender must trap the trapper with his inside forearm and squeeze the ballcarrier inside.

The guard/tackle fold (Diagram 4-5I): The defender should penetrate the line of scrimmage if he's beaten the tackle's head; otherwise, he should, secure the B gap, flatten across the tackle's face, and pursue the ball from an inside-out position.

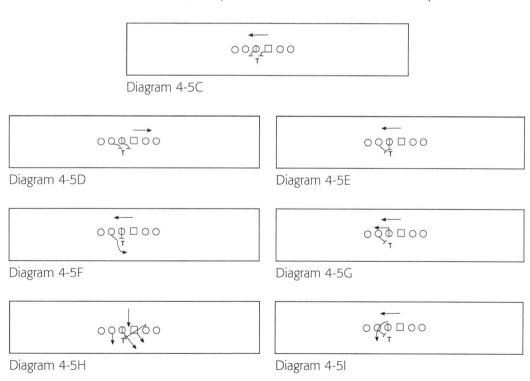

Diagram 4-5C

Diagram 4-5D

Diagram 4-5E

Diagram 4-5F

Diagram 4-5G

Diagram 4-5H

Diagram 4-5I

The guard pulls outside, no outside pressure (Diagram 4-5J): This is also a trap. The defender must trap the trapper with his inside forearm and squeeze the ballcarrier inside.

The guard pulls inside, the tackle reaches (Diagram 4-5K): The defender must avoid the tackle's block get in the guard's hip pocket and follow him to the point of attack.

The guard pulls inside, the center blocks the 2 technique (Diagram 4-5L): If the defender has beaten the center's head across the line of scrimmage, he gets in the guard's hip pocket and follows him to the point of attack. If the center's head is in front of the defender, the defender attacks the center, controls his playside shoulder, flattens across his face, and pursues down the line.

The guard pass blocks (Diagram 4-5M): The defender rushes his assigned A or B gap.

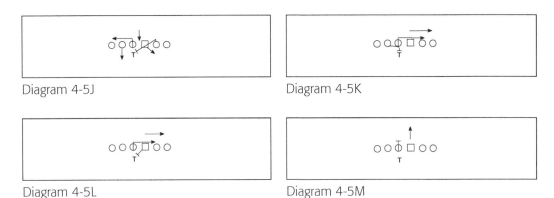

Diagram 4-5J

Diagram 4-5K

Diagram 4-5L

Diagram 4-5M

3 Technique

Stance and Alignment

Three- or four-point stance. The defender's inside foot should be pointed slightly inside of the offensive guard's outside foot.

Responsibilities

Run toward: B gap
Run away: Squeezes the backside A gap and pursues the ball from an inside-out position.
Pass: B gap rush

Keys

Primary: Guard, ball movement
Secondary: Tackle, pulling linemen

Important Techniques/Concepts:

The 3 technique is an aggressive read-on-the-run technique in which the defender's target is the outside shoulder of the offensive guard. The defender attacks his target with his hands underneath the pads of the blocker. He must also maintain outside leverage, keep his shoulders square to the line of scrimmage, secure the B gap, and not get hooked by the guard.

Key Blocks

The guard drive blocks (Diagram 4-6A): The defender must read the guard's head, fight pressure, and secure the B gap before pursuing to another area.

The guard hook blocks (Diagram 4-6B): The defender controls the guard's outside shoulder. He initially keeps his shoulders parallel to the line of scrimmage and then turns them slightly toward the inside as he works his hips into the playside B gap. The defender then pursues the ball from an inside-out position. It is vital that the defender doesn't get hooked.

The guard turnout blocks, flow away (Diagram 4-6C): The defender must squeeze the backside A gap with the guard's body and look for cutback as he pursues flat down the line.

The guard/tackle double-team (Diagram 4-6D): The defender attacks the tackle, stays low, and does not get driven back. As a last resort, he drops his outside hip and rolls into and plugs the B gap.

The guard/tackle kiss block (Diagram 4-6E): The defender must force a double-team and prevent the tackle from releasing to the next level to block a linebacker.

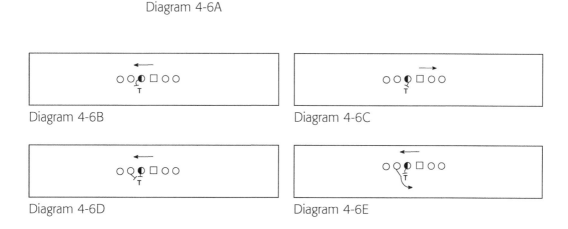

Diagram 4-6A

Diagram 4-6B

Diagram 4-6C

Diagram 4-6D

Diagram 4-6E

The guard/tackle zone, flow away (Diagram 4-6F): Versus this scheme, it is imperative that the guard is prevented from working to the second level. The defender must, therefore, jam the guard and flatten the guard's shoulders parallel to the line of scrimmage as he pursues the ball.

The guard/center zone, flow toward (Diagram 4-6G): The defender plays the guard's block like a hook block. It is vital that he jams the guard and prevents the guard from releasing to the next level to block a linebacker.

The guard blocks inside, the tackle cracks (Diagram 4-6H): The defender must first jam the guard and then fight outside pressure. If he has beaten the tackle's head across the line, he continues to penetrate and tackles the ballcarrier in the backfield. If the tackle's head is in front of him, he controls the blocker's outside shoulder, flattens across the blocker's face, and pursues the ball from an inside-out position.

The guard blocks inside, no outside pressure (Diagram 4-6I): This block is a trap. The defender must trap the trapper with his outside forearm and spill the play outside.

The guard/tackle fold (Diagram 4-6J): The defender should penetrate the line of scrimmage if he's beaten the tackle's head; otherwise, he should, secure the B gap, flatten across the tackle's face, and pursue the ball from an inside-out position.

The guard pulls outside, no outside pressure (Diagram 4-6K): This block is a trap. The defender must trap the trapper with his outside forearm and spill the play outside.

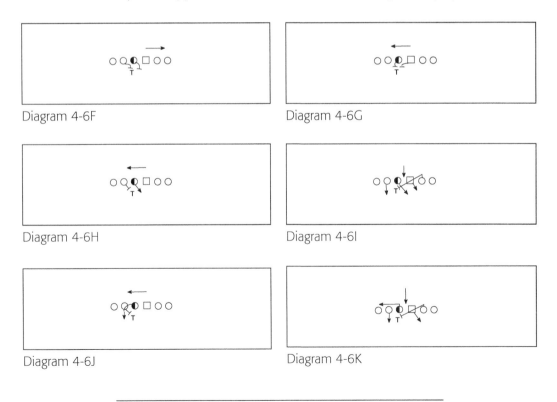

Diagram 4-6F

Diagram 4-6G

Diagram 4-6H

Diagram 4-6I

Diagram 4-6J

Diagram 4-6K

The guard pulls inside, the tackle cuts off (Diagram 4-6L): The defender must get in the guard's hip pocket and follow him to the point of attack.

The guard pulls inside, the center blocks the 3 technique (Diagram 4-6M): If the defender has beaten the center's head across the line of scrimmage, he gets in the guard's hip pocket and follows him to the point of attack. If the center's head is in front of the defender, the defender attacks the center, controls his playside shoulder, flattens across his face, and pursues down the line.

The guard pass blocks (Diagram 4-6N): The defender rushes the B gap.

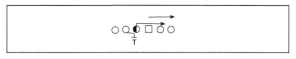

Diagram 4-6L

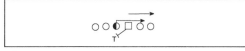

Diagram 4-6M

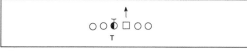

Diagram 4-6N

S Technique

Stance and Alignment

The defender lines up with his outside eye pointed at the inside eye of the tackle in a three- or four-point stance.

Responsibilities

Run toward: Secures the B gap, squeezes inside plays, and pursues outside plays from an inside-out position.
Run away: Secures the B gap, and trails the play from an inside-out position.
Pass: Rushes the B gap.

Keys

Primary: Tackle is defender's visual key.
Secondary: Guard is his pressure key.

Important Techniques/Concepts

Defender gets off the ball on movement, immediately attack the tackle with his hands (inside lockout), keeps his shoulders square, reads and reacts to the tackle's head, finds the ball, and makes the tackle.

Key Blocks

The tackle drive blocks (Diagram 4-7A): Defender attacks the tackle and keeps his shoulders parallel the line as he fights pressure. Secures and the B gap, finds the ball, and reacts in the play's direction.

Outside zone–guard/tackle combo (Diagram 4-7B): Defender jams the tackle and prevents him from releasing to the second level. He then avoids or defeats the guard's block as he locates and pursues the ball.

Fan block–tackle blocks out, guard blocks defender (Diagram 4-7C): The play will be directed inside of the defender; he must defeat the guard's block and make certain that the B gap is secured as he closes inside.

Tackle blocks out, guard blocks inside (Diagram 4-7D): This is a trap. Defender will close inside and trap the trapper with an inside forearm rip.

Tackle reach blocks the defender–play is away (Diagram 4-7E): Defender will immediately squeeze the B gap and pursue the play along the heel line if he has beaten the tackle's head across the line of scrimmage. If he hasn't beaten the tackle's head across the line, he will keep his shoulders square as he slides along the line and watches for cutback.

Tackle pass blocks (Diagram 4-7F): The defender will rush the quarterback through the B gap.

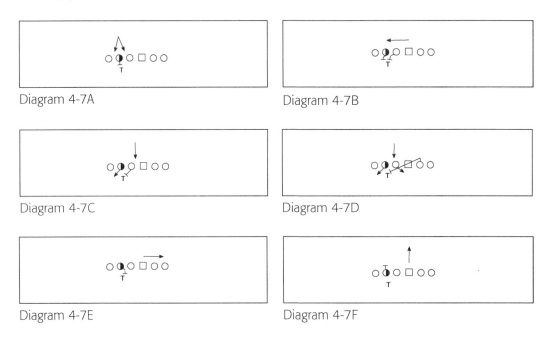

Diagram 4-7A

Diagram 4-7B

Diagram 4-7C

Diagram 4-7D

Diagram 4-7E

Diagram 4-7F

4 Technique

Strong tackle is illustrated for this alignment.

Stance and Alignment

Crowds the ball in a three- or four-point stance, nose-to-nose with the tackle. Minimum to no stagger of the feet.

Responsibilities

Run: Defender is a two-gap player. He is responsible for the C gap when plays are directed to his outside and the B gap when plays are directed to his inside.
Pass: Rushes the C gap and contains the quarterback.

Keys

Primary: Tackle, ball movement
Secondary: Guard (tight end if a tight end is aligned to defender's outside)

Important Techniques/Concepts

Target: Crush technique: The defender attacks the tackle with both hands—inside lockout. He then takes a short jab step in the direction of the play, controls the tackle's playside shoulder, keeps his own shoulders square to the line of scrimmage, and secures the playside gap.

Key Blocks

Tackle drive block (Diagram 4-8A): The defender must defeat the tackle's block, fight pressure, and pursue the ball.

Tackle hook block (Diagram 4-8B): The defender must keep his shoulders parallel to the line of scrimmage, plug the gap in the direction of the play, and pursue the ball.

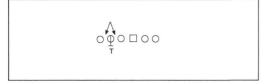

Diagram 4-8A

Diagram 4-8B

Tackle/tight end double-team (Diagram 4-8C): The defender must attack the tight end and not get driven back. As a last resort, he should drop his outside hip and roll into and plug the C gap.

Strong or weak zone (Diagram 4-8D): The defender must play the tackle's block like a hook block and prevent the tackle from releasing to the second level.

Tackle blocks inside/tight end cracks (Diagram 4-8E): The defender must first jam the tackle, release pressure, and then flatten across tight end's face.

Tackle blocks inside/no outside pressure (Diagram 4-8F): This is a trap. The defender must jam the tackle and squeeze the B gap. He will attack whomever blocks him with an inside forearm, maintain outside leverage on the blocker, and force the play inside.

Tackle pulls inside (Diagram 4-8G): This is most likely a counter trey. The defender must get in the tackle's hip pocket and follow him to the point of attack (unless he is the player assigned to tackle the quarterback).

Tackle pulls outside (Diagram 4-8H): If there is a tight end and the tight end cracks on the defender, he must fight outside pressure and flatten across the tight end's face. If the tight end doesn't crack, the play is either a quick pitch or a trap. The defender must read the backfield action and trap the trapper if the play is a trap. If the play is a quick pitch, the defender will pursue flat down the line.

Tackle pass blocks (Diagram 4-8I): The defender must pressure and contain the quarterback.

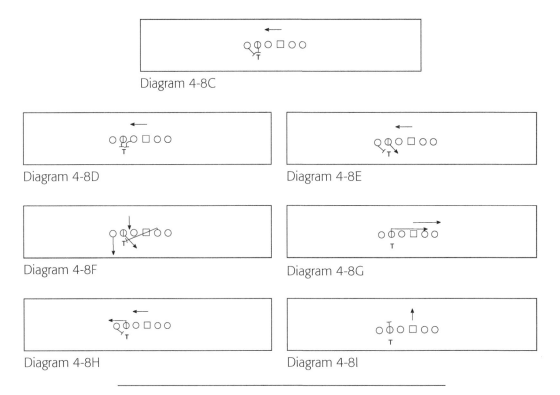

Diagram 4-8C

Diagram 4-8D

Diagram 4-8E

Diagram 4-8F

Diagram 4-8G

Diagram 4-8H

Diagram 4-8I

5 Technique

Strongside end illustrated for this alignment.

Stance and Alignment

Three- or four-point stance; the defender's inside foot should split the offensive tackle's stance. Some players may have to widen and position their inside foot slightly inside the outside foot of the offensive tackle.

Responsibilities

Run toward: C gap
Run away: Squeezes the B gap, then pursues the ball.
Pass: Contains the quarterback.

Keys

Primary: Tackle, ball movement
Secondary: Tight end, near back, pulling linemen

Important Techniques/Concepts

The defender's target is the guard's outside shoulder. He must maintain outside leverage, secure the C gap, and not get hooked by the tackle.

Key Blocks

Tackle drive block (Diagram 4-9A): The defender must read the tackle's head, fight pressure, and secure the C gap before pursuing the ball.

Tackle reach blocks (Diagram 4-9B): The defender must maintain outside leverage, keep his shoulders parallel to the line of scrimmage, and plug the C gap by getting his hips into the hole.

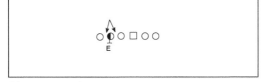

Diagram 4-9A

Diagram 4-9B

Tackle turnout block (Diagram 4-9C): The defender must squeeze the B gap with the tackle's body and look for a cutback as he pursues flat down the line.

Tackle/tight end double-team (Diagram 4-9D): The defender must attack the tight end and not get driven back. As a last resort, he should drop his outside hip and roll into and plug the C gap.

Strong zone guard/tackle combo (Diagram 4-9E): The defender must play the tackle's block like a hook block.

Tackle blocks inside/tight end cracks (Diagram 4-9F): The defender must first jam the tackle, release pressure, and then flatten across tight end's face.

Tackle blocks inside/no outside pressure (Diagram 4-9G): This is a trap. The defender must jam the tackle and squeeze the B gap. He will attack whomever blocks him with an inside forearm. He must force the play inside.

Tackle pulls inside (Diagram 4-9H): This is most likely a counter trey. The defender must get in the tackle's hip pocket and follow him to the point of attack (unless he is the player assigned to tackle the quarterback).

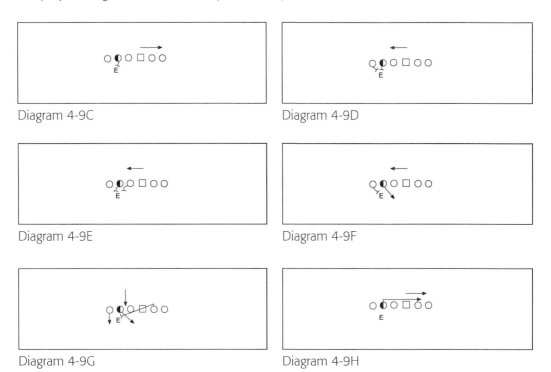

Diagram 4-9C

Diagram 4-9D

Diagram 4-9E

Diagram 4-9F

Diagram 4-9G

Diagram 4-9H

Tackle pulls outside (Diagram 4-9I): If there is a tight end and the tight end cracks on the defender, he must fight outside pressure and flatten across the tight end's face. If the tight end doesn't crack, the play is either a quick pitch or a trap. The defender must read the backfield action and trap the trapper if the play is a trap. If the play is a quick pitch, the defender will pursue flat down the line. If the defender attempts to stop a quick pitch by penetrating across the line, he will almost always end up chasing air.

Tackle pass blocks (Diagram 4-9J): The defender must pressure and contain the quarterback.

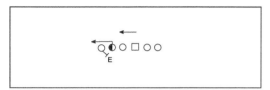

Diagram 4-9I

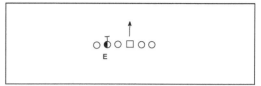

Diagram 4-9J

6 Technique

Stance and Alignment

Only used versus a tight end. If no tight end is present, the defender will play a ghost 7 technique. Crowds the ball in a three- or four-point stance. Feet parallel or slight stagger of the inside foot. Nose-to-nose with the tight end.

Responsibilities

Run toward: C gap
Run away: The defender first looks for bootleg. If none, the defender trails the play along the heel line, checking for reverse, counter, or cutback.
Pass: Contains rush.

Keys

Primary: The tight end is the defender's visual key and the offensive tackle is his pressure key.
Secondary: Near back, pulling linemen

Important Techniques

A 6 technique is primarily used to assist the defender in getting a good jam on the tight end and to put him in a better position to help secure the D gap on runs into the perimeter. Defender must immediately get his hands on the tight end, jam and control the tight end, and not get driven back.

Key Blocks

The tight end blocks the 6 technique, the tackle blocks inside—off-tackle run (Diagram 4-10A): Defender must attack the tight end, defeat the tight end's block and not get driven back. Defender must make certain that the C gap is secure, fight pressure, locate the ball, and make the tackle.

The tight end blocks the 6 technique, the tackle blocks inside—outside run (Diagram 4-10B): The defender must control the tight end, make certain that the C gap is secured, and then work across the tight end's face, and pursue the ball from an inside-out position.

The tight end releases, the tackle blocks the 6 technique—inside iso (Diagram 4-10C): Defender must maintain outside leverage and use the tackle's body to squeeze the play inside. He must be prepared for the ballcarrier to bounce the play outside as he squeezes inside.

The tight end releases, the tackle blocks the 6 technique—weakside run (Diagram 4-10D): The defender must fight through or avoid the tackle's block as he penetrates the line of scrimmage. He must first look for bootleg. If none, he trails the play along the heel line, checking for counter, cutback, and reverse.

The tight end releases, the tackle blocks inside, the near back kicks out the 6 technique—C gap run (Diagram 4-10E): The defender must squeeze the C gap, attack the back with his inside forearm, maintain outside leverage, and force the play inside. It is important that the defender does not penetrate across the line of scrimmage and create an alley for the ballcarrier.

The tight end releases, the tackle reach blocks the 6 technique—outside run (Diagram 4-10F): The defender must first jam the tight end and squeeze the C gap. He will then control the tackle's outside shoulder, maintain outside leverage, force the play outside, and pursue the ball from an inside-out position.

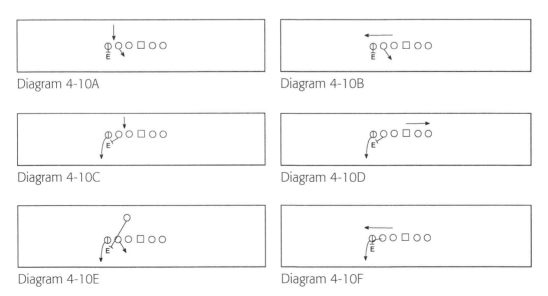

Diagram 4-10A

Diagram 4-10B

Diagram 4-10C

Diagram 4-10D

Diagram 4-10E

Diagram 4-10F

The tight end releases, the tackle blocks inside, an offensive lineman traps the 6 technique—C gap run (Diagram 4-10G): The defender jams the tight end and secure the C gap by squeezing back inside. He will then attack the blocker on the line of scrimmage with his inside forearm, maintain outside leverage, and force the play inside. In the case of a counter trey (both the guard and the tackle pull), it is important that the defender cut blocks the guard and thereby prevents the tackle from leading through the hole.

The tight end releases, the tackle blocks inside—weakside run (Diagram 4-10H): The defender must first look for bootleg. If none, he trails the play along the heel line, checking for counter, cutback, and reverse.

The tight end releases/passes (Diagram 4-10I): The defender must pressure and contain the quarterback.

Diagram 4-10G

Diagram 4-10H   Diagram 4-10I

7 Technique

Stance and Alignment

Three- or four-point stance, inside shade of the tight end.

Responsibilities

Run toward: C gap
Run away: The defender first looks for bootleg. If none, the defender trails the play along the heel line, checking for reverse, counter, or cutback.
Pass: Contains rush.

Keys

Primary: The tight end is the defender's pressure key and the offensive tackle is his visual key.
Secondary: Near back, pulling linemen

Important Techniques

The defender immediately gets his hands on the tight end, and jams him. He must not get driven back or crushed inside

Key Blocks

The tight end blocks the 7 technique, the tackle blocks inside—off-tackle run (Diagram 4-11A): The defender must control the tight end, plug the C gap, and force the play outside.

The tight end blocks the 7 technique, the tackle blocks inside—outside run (Diagram 4-11B): The defender must control the tight end, secure the C gap, work across the tight end's face, and pursue the ball from an inside-out position.

The tight end releases, the tackle blocks the 7 technique—inside iso (Diagram 4-11C): Defender must use the tackle's body to squeeze the play inside, maintain outside leverage, and be prepared for the ballcarrier to bounce the play outside.

The tight end releases, the tackle blocks the 7 technique—weakside run (Diagram 4-11D): The defender must fight through or avoid the tackle's block as he penetrates the line of scrimmage. He must first look for bootleg. If none, he trails the play along the heel line, checking for counter, cutback, and reverse.

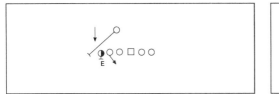

Diagram 4-11A

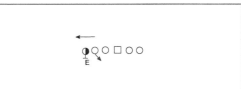

Diagram 4-11B

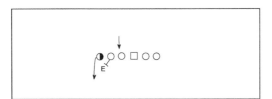

Diagram 4-11C

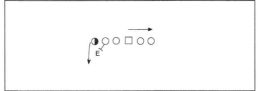

Diagram 4-11D

The tight end releases, the tackle blocks inside, the near back kicks out the 7 technique—C gap run (Diagram 4-11E): The defender must squeeze the C gap, attack the back with his inside forearm, maintain outside leverage, and force the play inside. It is important that the defender does not penetrate across the line of scrimmage and create an alley for the ballcarrier.

The tight end releases, the tackle reach blocks the 7 technique—outside run (Diagram 4-11F): The defender must first secure the C gap, force the play outside, and pursue the ball from an inside-out position. It is vital that the defender controls the tackle's outside shoulder.

The tight end releases, the tackle blocks inside, an offensive lineman traps the 7 technique—C gap run (Diagram 4-11G): The defender must attack the blocker on the line of scrimmage with his inside forearm, maintain outside leverage, and force the play inside. In the case of a counter trey (both the guard and the tackle pull), it is important that the defender cut blocks the guard and thereby prevents the tackle from leading through the hole.

The tight end releases, the tackle blocks inside—weakside run (Diagram 4-11H): The defender must first look for bootleg. If none, he trails the play along the heel line, checking for counter, cutback, and reverse.

The tight end releases/passes (Diagram 4-11I): The defender must pressure and contain the quarterback.

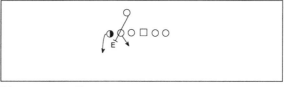

Diagram 4-11E

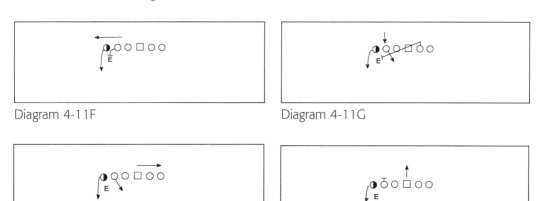

Diagram 4-11F

Diagram 4-11G

Diagram 4-11H

Diagram 4-11I

Ghost 7 Technique

Stance and Alignment

Two- or three-point stance. Outside foot back, one yard outside of the tackle.

Responsibilities

Run toward: C gap. Depending upon the specific scheme, the end may or may not have containment responsibility.
Run away: The defender first looks for bootleg. If none, he trails the play along the heel line, checking for reverse, counter, or cutback.
Pass: Contains rush.

Keys

Primary: The offensive tackle to the near back
Secondary: The pulling linemen

Important Techniques

The defender employs a jet technique and quickly penetrates the line of scrimmage (to the heel line). He maintains outside leverage on blocks by the offensive tackle or the near back and never gets hooked.

Key Blocks

The tackle reach blocks the 7 technique—outside run (Diagram 4-12A): The defender must beat the tackle's head across the line of scrimmage and not get hooked. If he has eluded the tackle's block, he should continue toward the ballcarrier and make the tackle in the backfield. If blocked, he must maintain outside leverage by controlling the tackle's outside shoulder. The defender's first priority is to secure the C gap.

The tackle blocks the 7 technique—inside iso (Diagram 4-12B): The defender must use the tackle's body to squeeze the play inside, maintain outside leverage, and be prepared for the ballcarrier to bounce the play outside.

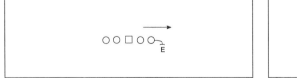

Diagram 4-12A

Diagram 4-12B

The tackle blocks the 7 technique—run away (Diagram 4-12C): The defender must fight through or avoid the tackle's block as he penetrates the line of scrimmage. He must first look for bootleg. If none, he trails the play along the heel line, checking for counter, cutback, and reverse.

The tackle blocks inside, the near back kicks out the 7 technique—C gap run (Diagram 4-12D): The defender must squeeze the C gap, attack the back with his inside forearm, maintain outside leverage, and force the play inside. It is important that he does not penetrate too deeply across the line of scrimmage and create an alley for the ballcarrier.

The tackle blocks inside, an offensive lineman traps the 7 technique—C gap run (Diagram 4-12E): The defender must attack the blocker on the line of scrimmage with his inside forearm, maintain outside leverage, and force the play inside. In the case of a counter trey (both the guard and the tackle pull), it is important that the end cut blocks the guard and thereby prevents the tackle from leading through the hole.

The tackle pulls toward center—run away (Diagram 4-12F): The defender must first look for bootleg. If none, he defeats the fullback's block and hen trails the play along the heel line, checking for counter, cutback, and reverse.

The tackle pass blocks—pass (Diagram 4-12G): The defender must contain rush.

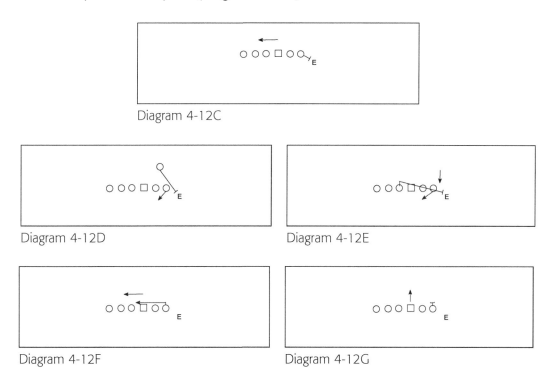

Diagram 4-12C

Diagram 4-12D

Diagram 4-12E

Diagram 4-12F

Diagram 4-12G

9 Technique

Stance and Alignment

Three- or four-point stance. The defender's inside foot is in the middle of the tight end's stance. Some defenders may have to widen to a position in which their inside foot is slightly inside of tight end's outside foot.

Responsibilities

Run toward: D gap
Run away: Trails the play along the heel line.
Pass: Rushes and contains the quarterback.

Keys

Primary: Tight end
Secondary: Near back, pulling linemen, the ball

Important Techniques

The defender must maintain outside leverage and not get driven back or hooked. He will attack the tight end with his hands and use a forearm rip when taking on a running back or pulling lineman. When dealing with a cut block, the defender must use his hands, sprawl, and immediately ricochet off the ground.

Key Blocks

Tight end reach blocks (Diagram 4-13A): The defender will immediately get his hands on the tight end and lock him out. He must control the tight end's outside shoulder and secure the D gap.

Tight end turnout block, inside run into either the B or C gap (Diagram 4-13B): The defender will create a stalemate and squeeze the C gap with the tight end's body while maintaining outside leverage on the ball.

Diagram 4-13A   Diagram 4-13B

Tight end releases, near back kickout block (Diagram 4-13C): As the defender jams the tight end, he must see the near back out of his periphery. The defender must close back inside and seal the C gap. He will attack the blocker with an inside forearm, and force the play inside. It is important that the defender does not penetrate across the line of scrimmage and create an alley for the ballcarrier.

Tight end releases, flow away (Diagram 4-13D): Defender will first check for bootleg before he chases along the heel line, checking for counter, cutback, or reverse.

Tight end blocks inside (Diagram 4-13E): The defender must jam the tight end's outside hip and squeeze the C gap. He will then attack the blocker (near back or pulling lineman) with his inside shoulder and spill the play outside.

Tight end releases/pass (Diagram 4-13F): Defender will rush and contain the quarterback.

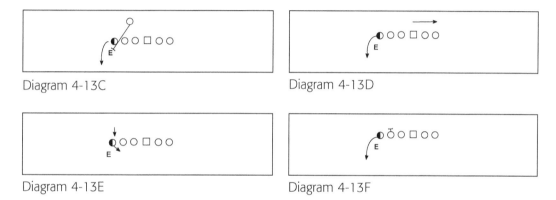

Diagram 4-13C

Diagram 4-13D

Diagram 4-13E

Diagram 4-13F

8 Technique

Stance and Alignment

Defender will line up approximately one yard outside of the tight end in a two-, three-, or four-point stance (depending upon preference).

Responsibilities

Run toward: Contains perimeter runs.
Run away: The defender first looks for bootleg. If none, the defender trails the play along the heel line, checking for reverse, counter, or cutback.
Pass: Contains rush.

Keys

Primary: The tight end
Secondary: Near back, pulling linemen

Important Techniques

The defender will explode upfield and aggressively penetrate the line of scrimmage at the snap. He must contain the quarterback and all perimeter runs. As he penetrates the line, he will react to the movements of the near back and pulling linemen. The defender must keep his outside leg and arm free as he maintains outside leverage on blockers.

Key Blocks

Reach block by the tight end—outside run (Diagram 4-14A): Defender can never be hooked by the tight end. He must avoid or ricochet of the block and contain the ballcarrier.

Turnout block by the tight end—inside run (Diagram 4-14B): Defender must defeat the tight end's block as he squeezes and condenses the play. At all times he must maintain outside leverage on the ballcarrier.

Tight end blocks inside, defender is blocked by a running back or offensive lineman (Diagram 4-14C): Defender will contain and squeeze the play inside as he maintains outside leverage on the blocker.

Tight end releases, flow away (Diagram 4-14D): Defender will chase along the heel line, checking for bootleg, counter, cutback, or reverse.

Tight releases, pass (Diagram 4-14E): Defender will contain rush.

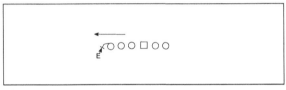

Diagram 4-14A

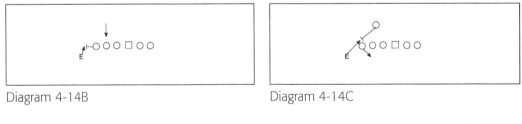

Diagram 4-14B

Diagram 4-14C

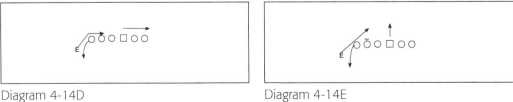

Diagram 4-14D

Diagram 4-14E

A, B, and C Gap Techniques

Defenders aligned in the gaps will crowd the line of scrimmage and explode across the line at the snap. Their initial penetration should be no deeper than the heal line. As they identify the play, they may gain depth if they are able to stop the play in the backfield. Their basic reads and reactions are identical to the following techniques:

- A gap player: Same as a 1 technique.
- B gap player: Same as an S technique.
- C gap player: Same as a 7 technique.

CHAPTER 5
Base Run Reads, Reactions, and Techniques of Linebackers

This chapter deals exclusively in linebacker techniques versus the run. Linebacker techniques versus the pass will be dealt with in a later chapter. Chapter 4 delineated the specific reads, reactions, and techniques for defensive linemen aligned in a 6, 7, or 9 alignment. A linebacker positioned in one of these alignments would follow the same guidelines when defending the run. The only difference is that of the stance. The linebacker's stance is obviously a two-point stance rather than a three- or four-point stance. The one linebacker run technique not synonymous with technique described in Chapter 4 is that of the 8 technique.

OUTSIDE LINEBACKERS

Loose 8 Technique

Stance and Alignment

It is assumed that this player is either an outside linebacker or a hybrid strong safety/linebacker. The defender lines up in a two-point stance. His inside foot is slightly staggered back. Depending upon the down-and-distance situation and offensive tendency, the defender may line up anywhere from one to five yards deep and two to five yards outside of the tight end. When he is aligned close to the receiver, the defender will tilt outside at a 45-degree angle; otherwise, he will keep his shoulders parallel to the line of scrimmage.

Responsibilities

Run toward: Comes up quickly and secures the D gap.
Run away: Sinks and checks for throwback, counter, bootleg, and reverse before pursuing.
Pass: Depends upon coverage.

Keys

Primary: Tight end, ball movement
Secondary: Near back, pulling linemen

Important Techniques

Versus most contemporary offenses, the defender is both a linebacker and defensive back; he must be able to play opposite a tight end and also in space. He must be able to instantly read and react to the tight end's movements. Versus a run in which the tight end blocks inside, he must close the seam between himself and the tight end and force the play inside. When the tight end releases, he must jam the tight end and simultaneously read the near back. If the near back's movements indicate run, the player must restrict the D gap, squeeze the play inside, and be prepared for the ball to bounce outside. If the play is pass, his technique varies depending upon the coverage.

Reactions to Key Blocks

The tight end blocks inside; the near back kicks out the defender—off-tackle play: The defender must fill tight to tight end's block and seal off any inside seams. It is important that the player does not penetrate the line and open up a seam for the ballcarrier to slip through. He must attack the blocker with an inside forearm, maintain outside leverage on the blocker, force the play inside, and be prepared to react outside.

The tight end blocks inside; the near back hook blocks the defender—sweep: The defender closes inside and begins to penetrate the line of scrimmage to the heel line as he attacks the near back. He must keep his shoulders parallel to the line of scrimmage as he strikes the near back with an inside forearm. He must then force the ballcarrier inside or wide and deep, ricochet off the back's block, and tackle the ballcarrier.

The tight end blocks the defender; the near back blocks the 7 technique—inside power: The defender must jam the tight end and use the tight end's body to squeeze the play inside. The defender should maintain outside leverage on the tight end's block and expect the ballcarrier to bounce outside.

The tight end blocks the defender; the near back blocks inside—inside iso: The defender must jam the tight end and use the tight end's body to squeeze the play inside. He should maintain outside leverage on the tight end's block and expect the ballcarrier to bounce outside.

The tight end releases and hook blocks the defender—sweep or stretch play: The defender must jam the tight end and maintain outside leverage on the tight end's block by attacking it with his inside forearm and keeping his outside leg back. He must then ricochet off the block and make the tackle.

The tight end releases—flow away: The defender must jam the tight end and check for throwback, counter, bootleg, and reverse during his jam. Once he is absolutely certain that the play is a run, he may then pursue the ball.

The tight end releases; the near back pass blocks: The play is pass. The defender's responsibility depends upon coverage.

INSIDE LINEBACKERS

Stance

Inside linebackers will line up in a balanced two-point stance with their feet shoulder-width (or slightly wider than shoulder-width) apart. Their weight should be on the balls of their feet, and their toes should be pointed straight ahead or turned in slightly. They will get into a good football position by bending at the hips, not at the waist. Their hands will hang loosely in front of their body.

Two-Gap Players

Unlike defensive linemen, most of whom are required to defend only one gap, linebackers are required to defend two gaps. Linebackers must defend a specific gap when a running play is directed toward their side of the ball and a different gap when a run is directed in the opposite direction. In order to communicate a linebacker's two-gap responsibility, some coaches use a system involving two numbers. The first number designates the linebacker's responsibility when runs are directed toward his side of the ball, and the second number designates his responsibility when runs are directed away from his side of the ball. Coaches who use the numbering system number the gaps in this way: the A gap is #1; the B gap is #2, the C gap is #3; and the D gap is #4. Other coaches, prefer to use the universal A, B, C, D gap lettering system in designating two-gap responsibilities.

Diagram 5-1 illustrates a plus 3 defensive alignment. This seven-man front is a variation of the 4-3 defense that derives its name from the position of the two defensive tackles. The left tackle is positioned in a plus alignment, and the right tackle is positioned in a 3 alignment. The Mike linebacker is responsible for the strongside B gap versus strongside runs and the weakside A gap versus weakside runs. Rover is responsible for the weakside D gap versus weakside runs and the weakside A gap versus strongside runs. In the numbering system, Mike's responsibility would be referred to as 21, and Rover's responsibility would be 41. In the letter system, Mike is a B-A player, and Rover is a D-A player. I have found both the numbering and lettering system to be somewhat confusing for Rover because neither system specifies the exact A gap (weakside or strongside) that Rover must secure versus strongside plays. In an attempt to make the system more exact, I have merged the two systems. My amalgamated system, and the one that will be used throughout the remainder of the book, consists of using letters on the side of the ball in which a linebacker is aligned and numbers on the opposite side of the ball. Diagram 5-2A illustrates how this system functions for Mike, and Diagram 5-2B illustrates how it functions for Rover.

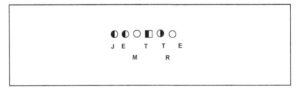

Diagram 5-1

Diagram 5-2A   Diagram 5-2B

Using the amalgamated system, Mike's gap responsibility becomes B-1, and Rover's becomes D-A. Occasionally, a linebacker will not have a specific gap responsibility because all of the gaps are being secured by other defenders. When this occurs, the defender's gap responsibility will be referred to as 0. A linebacker who was responsible for securing the B gap versus run directed toward his side of the line, but doesn't have a specific gap to secure versus runs toward the other side of the line would be referred to as a B-0 linebacker.

Reads and Keys

This topic is sometimes debated among linebacker coaches. Some coaches believe a linebacker's best key is the offensive line. Others believe in keying or cross-keying the running backs. Because peripheral vision is one of the key requisites needed to be a linebacker, most linebackers can become masters of simultaneously reading both the blocking scheme and backfield flow if they are taught and drilled to read backfield flow through the offensive line. In order to assist his players in developing this skill, a coach needs to set up a drill in which his linebackers must fit into their assigned gap responsibility by reacting to both the blocking scheme and the flow of a single running back. Diagrams 5-3A through 5-3D illustrate four examples of how this drill could be implemented.

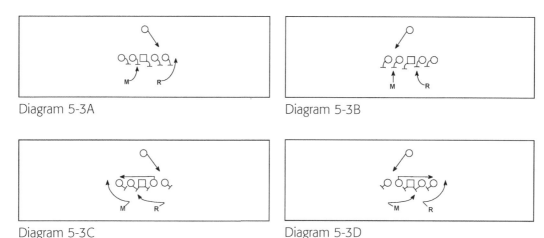

Diagram 5-3A

Diagram 5-3B

Diagram 5-3C

Diagram 5-3D

Movement

As the ball is snapped, the linebacker should take a short six-inch jab step toward the direction of the play. This step should be downhill and directly at the linebacker's playside gap responsibility. Next, he will run downhill and secure this gap. In securing the gap, it is imperative that the linebacker keeps his shoulders parallel and attacks potential blockers as close to the line of scrimmage as possible. His objective is to assist in building an impenetrable wall. If the ballcarrier moves outside of his assigned gap, the linebacker will shuffle down the line, keep his shoulders parallel to the line, and pursue the ball from an inside-out position. It is important that the linebacker does not cross his feet as he is shuffling. On quick-developing outside plays, the linebacker may be required to turn and run in the play's direction; however, it is still important for the linebacker to maintain an inside-out pursuit angle on the ballcarrier.

Defeating Offensive Blockers

The linebacker will follow very similar guidelines as a defensive lineman when attacking and escaping from the block of an offensive linemen:
- Contacts the blocker with both feet securely on the ground.
- Concentrates on the screws of the blocker's helmet as contact is made.
- Attacks the blocker with a violent hand shiver, using the heels of the hands (thumbs up, palms out).
- Maintains a pad level lower than that of the blocker.

- Rolls the hips as contact is made, and tries to gain separation from the blocker with a bench press technique.
- Releases contact from the block by employing either a rip or pull-and-release technique.
- Maintains intense aggressiveness, and keeps the feet moving.

Linebackers will frequently be required to defeat the block of a running back. If the back's pad level is high, the linebacker will attack the block with a forearm shiver. When executing this technique, the linebacker will step with his inside foot toward the middle of the blocker. He will then drive his forearm in an upward movement underneath the pads of the blocker. As contact is made, the linebacker will explode his hips and drive through the blocker. He will also simultaneously punch the outside shoulder of the blocker with his free hand as he controls and gains separation form the blocker.

When confronted with a cut block, the linebacker will focus both of his eyes on the head on the head and shoulders of the blocker. He will attack the blocker with both hands and press the blocker to the ground. It will be necessary for the blocker to give ground in order to gain ground. As he gives ground, the linebacker will gain separation from the block and then be free to pursue the ball. The primary reason why most linebackers are unsuccessful versus the cut block is that they do not focus on the blocker. Instead, they focus on the ballcarrier, which allows the blocker to get into the linebacker's legs.

CHAPTER 6
Creating Multiple Even Eight-Man Fronts

Chapters 6 through 9 present 40 multiple defensive fronts that can be employed using the information that has been presented thus far in this book. Each front includes an illustration and clear, concise delineations of all of the techniques and responsibilities assigned to each of the defensive linemen and linebackers involved.

Chapter 6 presents 10 multiple eight-man fronts. All 10 fronts are "even fronts" (even fronts utilize two defensive tackles and two defensive ends). Each front's name is dependent upon the alignment of the two tackles. If, for example, the strongside tackle is aligned in a 3 technique and the weakside tackle is aligned in a 1 technique, the defense is named 31. The 10 fronts presented in Chapter 6 are used in conjunction with three-deep secondaries. Coverages, techniques, and responsibilities for the defensive secondary are detailed in later chapters.

It should also be noted that the assumption is made in Chapters 6 through 9 that six defenders will remain in the box versus 10 personnel (which may not be true of all pass coverages). It is therefore important to remember which defenders stay in the box and which defenders adjust. In Chapter 6, Joker and Rover are the adjusters.

Defensive Alignment: 11

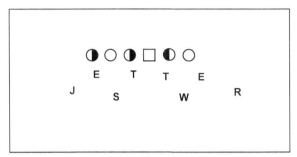

Diagram 6-1

Joker: Plays a loose 8 technique versus 21, 22, 11, and 12 personnel. Adjusts to a 9 technique versus 30, 31, and 32 personnel. Adjusts according to coverage versus 20 and 10 personnel.

Left Strongside End: Plays a 7 technique versus 21, 22, 11, 12, 31 and 32 personnel. Adjusts to a ghost 7 technique versus 10, 20, and 30 personnel. *Keys:* (1) the tight end, (2) the tackle, (3) the running back, (4) pulling linemen. *Responsibilities:* Secures the C gap versus strongside run, and trails weakside runs along the heel line looking for bootleg, reverse, counter, or cutback.

Left Strongside Tackle: Plays a 1 technique. *Keys:* (1) guard, (2) center. *Responsibilities:* Secures the A gap versus strongside runs, and pursues weakside runs from an inside-out position.

Sam: Plays a B-0 technique. *Keys:* Backfield flow through the offensive line. *Responsibilities:* Secures the B gap versus strongside run, and pursues weakside runs from an inside-out position.

Will: Plays a B-0 technique. Keys: Backfield flow through the offensive line. Responsibilities: Secures the B gap versus weakside run, and pursues strongside runs from an inside-out position.

Right Weakside Tackle: Plays a 1 technique. *Keys:* (1) guard, (2) center. *Responsibilities:* Secures the A gap versus weakside runs and pursues strongside runs from an inside-out position.

Right Weakside End: Plays a ghost 7 technique versus 10, 20, 30, 21, and 11 personnel. Adjusts to a 7 technique versus 12, 22, and 32 personnel. *Keys:* (1) the tackle, (2) the running back, (3) pulling linemen. *Responsibilities:* Secures the C gap versus weakside run, and trails strongside runs along the heel line, looking for bootleg, reverse, counter, or cutback.

Rover: Plays a loose 8 technique versus 21 and 22 personnel. Adjusts to a 9 technique versus 30, 31, and 32 personnel. Adjusts according to coverage versus 11, 12, 20, and 10 personnel.

Defensive Alignment: 22

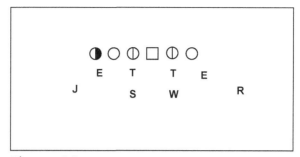

Diagram 6-2

Joker: Plays a loose 8 technique versus 21, 22, 11, and 12 personnel. Adjusts to a 9 technique versus 30, 31, and 32 personnel. Adjusts according to coverage versus 20 and 10 personnel.

Left Strongside End: Plays a 7 technique versus 21, 22, 11, 12, 31, and 32 personnel. Adjusts to a ghost 7 technique versus 10, 20, and 30 personnel. *Keys:* (1) the tight end, (2) the tackle, (3) the running back, (4) pulling linemen. *Responsibilities:* Secures the C gap versus strongside run, and trails weakside runs along the heel line, looking for bootleg, reverse, counter, or cutback.

Left Strongside Tackle: Plays a 2 technique. Defender is a two-gap player. *Keys:* (1) guard, (2) ball, (3) center, (4) tackle. *Responsibilities:* Secures the B gap versus strongside run, the A gap versus weakside run.

Sam: Plays a 0-1 technique. *Keys:* Backfield flow through the offensive line. *Responsibilities:* Pursues strongside run from an inside-out position, and secures the 1 gap versus weakside run.

Will: Plays a 0-1 technique. *Keys:* Backfield flow through the offensive line. *Responsibilities:* Pursues weakside run from an inside-out position, and secures the 1 gap versus strongside run.

Right Weakside Tackle: Plays a 2 technique. Defender is a two-gap player. *Keys:* (1) guard, (2) ball, (3) center, (4) tackle. *Responsibilities:* Secures the B gap versus weakside run, the A gap versus strongside run.

Right Weakside End: Plays a ghost 7 technique versus 10, 20, 30, 21, and 11 personnel. Adjusts to a 7 technique versus 12, 22, and 32 personnel. *Keys:* (1) the tackle, (2) the running back, (3) pulling linemen. *Responsibilities:* Secures the C gap versus weakside run, and trails strongside runs along the heel line, looking for bootleg, reverse, counter, or cutback.

Rover: Plays a loose 8 technique versus 21 and 22 personnel. Adjusts to a 9 technique versus 30, 31, and 32 personnel. Adjusts according to coverage versus 11, 12, 20, and 10 personnel.

Defensive Alignment: 33

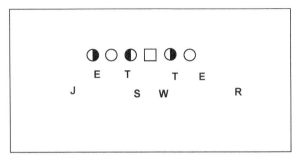

Diagram 6-3

Joker: Plays a loose 8 technique versus 21, 22, 11, and 12 personnel. Adjusts to a 9 technique versus 30, 31, and 32 personnel. Adjusts according to coverage versus 20 and 10 personnel.

Left Strongside End: Plays a 7 technique versus 21, 22, 11, 12, 31, and 32 personnel. Adjusts to a ghost 7 technique versus 10, 20, and 30 personnel. *Keys:* (1) the tight end, (2) the tackle, (3) the running back, (4) pulling linemen. *Responsibilities:* Secures the C gap versus strongside run, and trails weakside runs along the heel line, looking for bootleg, reverse, counter, or cutback.

Left Strongside Tackle: Plays a 3 technique. *Keys:* (1) guard, (2) ball, (3) tackle, (4) pulling linemen. *Responsibilities:* Secures the B gap versus strongside run, and squeezes the A gap as he pursues the ball from an inside-out position versus weakside run.

Sam: Plays an A-1 technique. *Keys:* Backfield flow through the offensive line. *Responsibilities:* Secures the A gap before pursuing strongside run from an inside-out position, and secures the 1 gap versus weakside run.

Will: Plays an A-1 technique. *Keys:* Backfield flow through the offensive line. *Responsibilities:* Secures the A gap before pursuing weakside run from an inside-out position and secures the 1 gap versus strongside run.

Right Weakside Tackle: Plays a 3 technique. *Keys:* (1) guard, (2) ball, (3) tackle, (4) pulling linemen. *Responsibilities:* Secures the B gap versus weakside run and squeezes the A gap as he pursues the ball from an inside-out position versus strongside run.

Right Weakside End: Plays a ghost 7 technique versus 10, 20, 30, 21, and 11 personnel. Adjusts to a 7 technique versus 12, 22, and 32 personnel. *Keys:* (1) the tackle, (2) the running back, (3) pulling linemen. *Responsibilities:* Secures the C gap versus weakside run, and trails strongside runs along the heel line looking for bootleg, reverse, counter, or cutback.

Rover: Plays a loose 8 technique versus 21 and 22 personnel. Adjusts to a 9 technique versus 30, 31, and 32 personnel. Adjusts according to coverage versus 11, 12, 20, and 10 personnel.

Defensive Alignment: 31

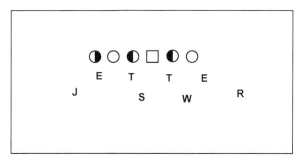

Diagram 6-4

Joker: Plays a loose 8 technique versus 21, 22, 11, and 12 personnel. Adjusts to a 9 technique versus 30, 31, and 32 personnel. Adjusts according to coverage versus 20 and 10 personnel.

Left Strongside End: Plays a 7 technique versus 21, 22, 11, 12, 31, and 32 personnel. Adjusts to a ghost 7 technique versus 10, 20, and 30 personnel. *Keys:* (1) the tight end, (2) the tackle, (3) the running back, (4) pulling linemen. *Responsibilities:* Secures the C gap versus strongside run, and trails weakside runs along the heel line, looking for bootleg, reverse, counter, or cutback.

Left Strongside Tackle: Plays a 3 technique. *Keys:* (1) guard, (2) ball, (3) tackle, (4) pulling linemen. *Responsibilities:* Secures the B gap versus strongside run, and squeezes the A gap as he pursues the ball from an inside-out position versus weakside run.

Sam: Plays an A-0 technique. *Keys:* Backfield flow through the offensive line. *Responsibilities:* Secures the A gap before pursuing strongside run from an inside-out position, and pursues weakside run from an inside-out position.

Will: Plays a B-1 technique. *Keys:* Backfield flow through the offensive line. *Responsibilities:* Pursues the B gap versus weakside run, and secures the 1 gap versus strongside run.

Right Weakside Tackle: Plays a 1 technique. *Keys:* (1) guard, (2) center. *Responsibilities:* Secures the A gap versus weakside runs, and pursues strongside runs from an inside-out position.

Right Weakside End: Plays a ghost 7 technique versus 10, 20, 30, 21, and 11 personnel. Adjusts to a 7 technique versus 12, 22, and 32 personnel. *Keys:* (1) the tackle, (2) the running back, (3) pulling linemen. *Responsibilities:* Secures the C gap versus weakside run, and trails strongside runs along the heel line, looking for bootleg, reverse, counter, or cutback.

Rover: Plays a loose 8 technique versus 21 and 22 personnel. Adjusts to a 9 technique versus 30, 31, and 32 personnel. Adjusts according to coverage versus 11, 12, 20, and 10 personnel.

Defensive Alignment: 13

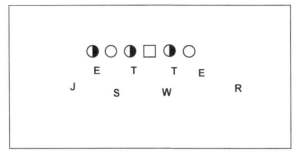

Diagram 6-5

Joker: Plays a loose 8 technique versus 21, 22, 11, and 12 personnel. Adjusts to a 9 technique versus 30, 31, and 32 personnel. Adjusts according to coverage versus 20 and 10 personnel.

Left Strongside End: Plays a 7 technique versus 21, 22, 11, 12, 31, and 32 personnel. Adjusts to a ghost 7 technique versus 10, 20, and 30 personnel. *Keys:* (1) the tight end, (2) the tackle, (3) the running back, (4) pulling linemen. *Responsibilities:* Secures the C gap versus strongside run, and trails weakside runs along the heel line, looking for bootleg, reverse, counter, or cutback.

Left Strongside Tackle: Plays a 1 technique. *Keys:* (1) guard, (2) center. *Responsibilities:* Secures the A gap versus strongside runs, and pursues weakside runs from an inside-out position.

Sam: Plays a B-1 technique. *Keys:* Backfield flow through the offensive line. *Responsibilities:* Secures the B gap versus strongside run, and secures the 1 gap versus weakside run.

Will: Plays an A-0 technique. *Keys:* Backfield flow through the offensive line. *Responsibilities:* Secures the A gap versus weakside run, and pursues strongside run from an inside-out position.

Right Weakside Tackle: Plays a 3 technique. *Keys:* (1) guard, (2) ball, (3) tackle, (4) pulling linemen. *Responsibilities:* Secures the B gap versus weakside run, and squeezes the A gap as he pursues the ball from an inside-out position versus strongside run.

Right Weakside End: Plays a ghost 7 technique versus 10, 20, 30, 21 and 11 personnel. Adjusts to a 7 technique versus 12, 22, and 32 personnel. *Keys:* (1) the tackle, (2) the running back, (3) pulling linemen. *Responsibilities:* Secures the C gap versus weakside run, and trails strongside runs along the heel line, looking for bootleg, reverse, counter, or cutback.

Rover: Plays a loose 8 technique versus 21 and 22 personnel. Adjusts to a 9 technique versus 30, 31, and 32 personnel. Adjusts according to coverage versus 11, 12, 20, and 10 personnel.

Defensive Alignment: BA

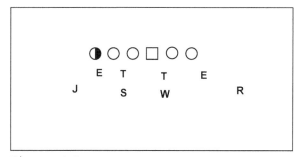

Diagram 6-6

Joker: Plays a loose 8 technique versus 21, 22, 11, and 12 personnel. Adjusts to a 9 technique versus 30, 31, and 32 personnel. Adjusts according to coverage versus 20 and 10 personnel.

Left Strongside End: Plays a 7 technique versus 21, 22, 11, 12, 31, and 32 personnel. Adjusts to a ghost 7 technique versus 10, 20, and 30 personnel. *Keys:* (1) the tight end, (2) the tackle, (3) the running back, (4) pulling linemen. *Responsibilities:* Secures the C gap versus strongside run, and trails weakside runs along the heel line, looking for bootleg, reverse, counter, or cutback.

Left Strongside Tackle: Plays a B technique. *Keys:* (1) tackle, (2) guard, and (3) ball. *Responsibilities:* Secures the B gap versus strongside runs, and pursues weakside runs from an inside-out position.

Sam: Plays a 0-A technique. *Keys:* Backfield flow through the offensive line. *Responsibilities:* Pursues strongside runs from an inside-out position after checking for A gap isolations. Secures the A gap versus weakside run.

Will: Plays a B-1 technique. *Keys:* Backfield flow through the offensive line. *Responsibilities:* Secures the B gap versus weakside run and the 1 gap versus strongside run.

Right Weakside Tackle: Plays an A technique. *Keys:* (1) guard, (2) center, and (ball). *Responsibilities:* Secures the A gap versus weakside runs, and pursues strongside runs from an inside-out position.

Right Weakside End: Plays a ghost 7 technique versus 10, 20, 30, 21, and 11 personnel. Adjusts to a 7 technique versus 12, 22, and 32 personnel. *Keys:* (1) the tackle, (2) the running back, (3) pulling linemen. *Responsibilities:* Secures the C gap versus weakside run, and trails strongside runs along the heel line, looking for bootleg, reverse, counter, or cutback.

Rover: Plays a loose 8 technique versus 21 and 22 personnel. Adjusts to a 9 technique versus 30, 31, and 32 personnel. Adjusts according to coverage versus 11, 12, 20, and 10 personnel.

Defensive Alignment: AB

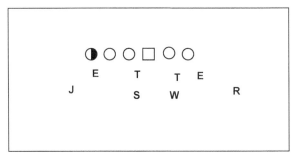

Diagram 6-7

Joker: Plays a loose 8 technique versus 21, 22, 11, and 12 personnel. Adjusts to a 9 technique versus 30, 31, and 32 personnel. Adjusts according to coverage versus 20 and 10 personnel.

Left Strongside End: Plays a 7 technique versus 21, 22, 11, 12, 31, and 32 personnel. Adjusts to a ghost 7 technique versus 10, 20, and 30 personnel. *Keys:* (1) the tight end, (2) the tackle, (3) the running back, (4) pulling linemen. *Responsibilities:* Secures the C gap versus strongside run, and trails weakside runs along the heel line, looking for bootleg, reverse, counter, or cutback.

Left Strongside Tackle: Plays an A technique. *Keys:* (1) guard, (2) center, and (ball). *Responsibilities:* Secures the A gap versus strongside runs, and pursues weakside runs from an inside-out position.

Sam: Plays a B-1 technique. *Keys:* Backfield flow through the offensive line. *Responsibilities:* Secures the B gap versus strongside run and the 1 gap versus weakside run.

Will: Plays a 0-A technique. *Keys:* Backfield flow through the offensive line. *Responsibilities:* Pursues weakside runs from an inside-out position after checking for A gap isolations. Secures the A gap versus strongside run.

Right Weakside Tackle: Plays a B technique. *Keys:* (1) tackle, (2) guard, and (3) ball. *Responsibilities:* Secures the B gap versus weakside runs, and pursues strongside runs from an inside-out position.

Right Weakside End: Plays a ghost 7 technique versus 10, 20, 30, 21, and 11 personnel. Adjusts to a 7 technique versus 12, 22, and 32 personnel. *Keys:* (1) the tackle, (2) the running back, (3) pulling linemen. *Responsibilities:* Secures the C gap versus weakside run, and trails strongside runs along the heel line, looking for bootleg, reverse, counter, or cutback.

Rover: Plays a loose 8 technique versus 21 and 22 personnel. Adjusts to a 9 technique versus 30, 31, and 32 personnel. Adjusts according to coverage versus 11, 12, 20, and 10 personnel.

Defensive Alignment: Minus 3

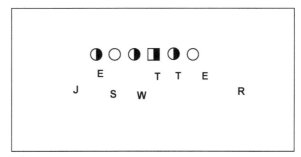

Diagram 6-8

Joker: Plays a loose 8 technique versus 21, 22, 11, and 12 personnel. Adjusts to a 9 technique versus 30, 31, and 32 personnel. Adjusts according to coverage versus 20 and 10 personnel.

Left Strongside End: Plays a 7 technique versus 21, 22, 11, 12, 31, and 32 personnel. Adjusts to a ghost 7 technique versus 10, 20, and 30 personnel. *Keys:* (1) the tight end, (2) the tackle, (3) the running back, (4) pulling linemen. *Responsibilities:* Secures the C gap versus strongside run, and trails weakside runs along the heel line, looking for bootleg, reverse, counter, or cutback.

Left Strongside Tackle: Plays a minus technique. *Keys:* (1) center, (2) weakside guard, (3) ball. *Responsibilities:* Secures the weakside A gap versus both strongside and weakside runs.

Sam: Plays a B-A technique. *Keys:* Backfield flow through the offensive line. *Responsibilities:* Secures the B gap versus strongside run and the A gap versus weakside run.

Will: Plays an A-0 technique. *Keys:* Backfield flow through the offensive line. *Responsibilities:* Secures the A gap versus strongside run, and pursues weakside run from an inside-out position.

Right Weakside Tackle: Plays a 3 technique. *Keys:* (1) guard, (2) ball, (3) tackle, (4) pulling linemen. *Responsibilities:* Secures the B gap versus weakside run, and squeezes the A gap as he pursues the ball from an inside-out position versus strongside run.

Right Weakside End: Plays a ghost 7 technique versus 10, 20, 30, 21, and 11 personnel. Adjusts to a 7 technique versus 12, 22, and 32 personnel. *Keys:* (1) the tackle, (2) the running back, (3) pulling linemen. *Responsibilities:* Secures the C gap versus weakside run, and trails strongside runs along the heel line, looking for bootleg, reverse, counter, or cutback.

Rover: Plays a loose 8 technique versus 21 and 22 personnel. Adjusts to a 9 technique versus 30, 31, and 32 personnel. Adjusts according to coverage versus 11, 12, 20, and 10 personnel.

Defensive Alignment: S0

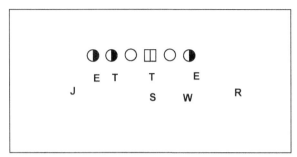

Diagram 6-9

Joker: Plays a loose 8 technique versus 21, 22, 11, and 12 personnel. Adjusts to a 9 technique versus 30, 31, and 32 personnel. Adjusts according to coverage versus 20 and 10 personnel.

Left Strongside End: Plays a 7 technique versus 21, 22, 11, 12, 31, and 32 personnel. Adjusts to a ghost 7 technique versus 10, 20, and 30 personnel. *Keys:* (1) the tight end, (2) the tackle, (3) the running back, (4) pulling linemen. *Responsibilities:* Secures the C gap versus strongside run, and trails weakside runs along the heel line, looking for bootleg, reverse, counter, or cutback.

Left Strongside Tackle: Plays an S technique. *Keys:* (1) tackle, (2) guard, (3) ball. *Responsibilities:* Secures the B gap versus strongside plays, and pursues weakside plays from an inside-out position.

Sam: Plays a 0-0 technique. *Keys:* Backfield flow through the offensive line. *Responsibilities:* Pursues both strongside and weakside runs from an inside-out position.

Will: Plays a bobtail-A technique. *Keys:* (1) tackle, (2) ball. *Responsibilities:* Bobtails weakside runs with the right end. Reacts to the movement of the offensive tackle. If the tackle blocks the defensive end, Will secures the B gap. If the tackle attempts to block Will, the defender will scrape outside and secure the C gap. Secures the A gap versus strongside run.

Right Weakside Tackle: Plays a 0 technique. *Keys:* (1) center, (2) both guards, (3) ball. *Responsibilities:* Executes a crush technique, and secures the playside A gap versus run.

Right Weakside End: Plays a 5 technique. *Keys:* (1) tackle, (2) ball. *Responsibilities:* Bobtails weakside runs with Will. If blocked by the tackle, the end will secure the C gap. If the tackle attempts to block Will, the end will squeeze inside and secure the B gap. Chases strongside runs along the heel line, checking for counter, reverse, and bootleg.

Rover: Plays a loose 8 technique versus 21 and 22 personnel. Adjusts to a 9 technique versus 30, 31, and 32 personnel. Adjusts according to coverage versus 11, 12, 20, and 10 personnel.

Defensive Alignment: Plus Minus

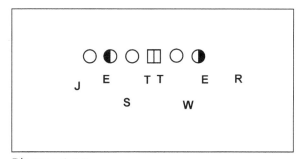

Diagram 6-10

Joker: Plays a loose 8 technique versus 21, 22, 11, and 12 personnel. Adjusts to a 9 technique versus 30, 31, and 32 personnel. Adjusts according to coverage versus 20 and 10 personnel.

Left Strongside End: Plays a 5 technique. *Keys:* (1) tackle, (2) ball. *Responsibilities:* Secures the C gap versus strongside run. Chases weakside runs along the heel line checking for counter, reverse, and bootleg.

Left Strongside Tackle: Plays a plus technique. *Keys:* (1) center, (2) weakside guard, (3) ball. *Responsibilities:* Crushes the center, and secures the strongside A gap versus both strongside and weakside runs.

Sam: Plays a B-0 technique. *Keys:* Backfield flow through the offensive line. *Responsibilities:* Secures the B gap versus strongside run, and pursues weakside runs from an inside-out position.

Will: Plays a B-0 technique. *Keys:* Backfield flow through the offensive line. *Responsibilities:* Secures the B gap versus weakside run, and pursues strongside runs from an inside-out position.

Right Weakside Tackle: Plays a minus technique. *Keys:* (1) center, (2) weakside guard, (3) ball. *Responsibilities:* Crushes the center, and secures the weakside A gap versus both strongside and weakside runs.

Right Weakside End: Plays a 5 technique. *Keys:* (1) tackle, (2) ball. *Responsibilities:* Secures the C gap versus weakside run. Chases strongside runs along the heel line, checking for counter, reverse, and bootleg.

Rover: Plays a loose 8 technique versus 21 and 22 personnel. Adjusts to a 9 technique versus 30, 31, and 32 personnel. Adjusts according to coverage versus 11, 12, 20, and 10 personnel.

CHAPTER 7
Creating Multiple Even Seven-Man Fronts

Chapter 7 presents 10 multiple seven-man fronts. All 10 fronts are "even fronts." Like the even eight-man fronts of Chapter 6, each front's name is dependent upon the alignment of the two tackles. The 10 fronts presented in this chapter are used in conjunction with four-deep secondaries. Versus 10 personnel, Rover is the adjuster for seven of the 10 defenses, and Joker will adjust for the following fronts: Plus 3 Weak Eagle, 03 Weak Eagle, and AB.

Note the absence of Sam and Will and the presence of Mike in the diagram for each of the seven-man fronts. Usually, either Sam or Will is taken out of the game and an additional defensive back, dollar, is substituted into the game when switching from an eight-man front to a seven-man front. Coaches that frequently make this type of switch will usually continue designating the remaining linebacker as either Sam or Will. The designation of Mike is used in this chapter for coaches that stay in seven-man fronts and do not switch back and forth.

Defensive Alignment: 11

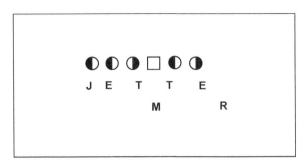

Diagram 7-1

Joker: Plays a 9 technique versus 11, 12, 20, 21, 22, 30, 31, and 32 personnel. Keys: (1) tight end, (2) near back, (3) pulling linemen, (4) ball. Responsibilities: Secures the D gap versus strongside run, and checks for bootleg, counter, and reverse versus weakside run.

Left Strongside End: Plays a 5 technique. Keys: (1) tackle, (2) ball. Responsibilities: Secures the C gap versus strongside run. Chases weakside runs along the heel line, checking for counter, reverse, and bootleg.

Left Strongside Tackle: Plays a 1 technique. Keys: (1) guard, (2) center. Responsibilities: Secures the A gap versus strongside runs and pursues weakside runs from an inside-out position.

Mike: Plays a B-B technique. Keys: Backfield flow through the offensive line. Responsibilities: Secures the B gap versus both strongside and weakside runs.

Right Weakside Tackle: Plays a 1 technique. Keys: (1) guard, (2) center. Responsibilities: Secures the A gap versus weakside runs and pursues strongside runs from an inside-out position.

Right Weakside End: Plays a 5 technique. Keys: (1) tackle, (2) ball. Responsibilities: Secures the C gap versus weakside run. Chases strongside runs along the heel line, checking for counter, reverse, and bootleg.

Rover: Plays a 9 technique versus 12, 20, 21, 22, 30, 31, and 32 personnel. Adjusts according to coverage versus 11 and 10 personnel.

Defensive Alignment: 22

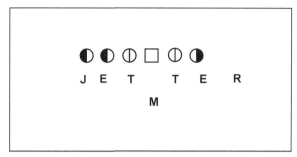

Diagram 7-2

Joker: Plays a 9 technique versus 11, 12, 20, 21, 22, 30, 31, and 32 personnel. Keys: (1) tight end, (2) near back, (3) pulling linemen, (4) ball. Responsibilities: Secures the D gap versus strongside run, and checks for bootleg, counter, and reverse versus weakside run.

Left Strongside End: Plays a 5 technique. Keys: (1) tackle, (2) ball. Responsibilities: Secures the C gap versus strongside run. Chases weakside runs along the heel line, checking for counter, reverse, and bootleg.

Left Strongside Tackle: Plays a 2 technique. Defender is a two-gap player. Keys: (1) guard, (2) ball, (3) center, (4) tackle. Responsibilities: Secures the B gap versus strongside run, the A gap versus weakside run.

Mike: Plays an A-A technique. Keys: Backfield flow through the offensive line. Responsibilities: Secures the A gap versus both strongside and weakside runs.

Right Weakside Tackle: Plays a 2 technique. Defender is a two-gap player. Keys: (1) guard, (2) ball, (3) center, (4) tackle. Responsibilities: Secures the B gap versus weakside run, the A gap versus strongside run.

Right Weakside End: Plays a 5 technique. Keys: (1) tackle, (2) ball. Responsibilities: Secures the C gap versus weakside run. Chases strongside runs along the heel line, checking for counter, reverse, and bootleg.

Rover: Plays a 9 technique versus 12, 20, 21, 22, 30, 31, and 32 personnel. Adjusts according to coverage versus 11 and 10 personnel.

Defensive Alignment: 31

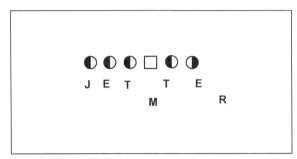

Diagram 7-3

Joker: Plays a 9 technique versus 11, 12, 20, 21, 22, 30, 31, and 32 personnel. *Keys:* (1) tight end, (2) near back, (3) pulling linemen, (4) ball. *Responsibilities:* Secures the D gap versus strongside run, and checks for bootleg, counter, and reverse versus weakside run.

Left Strongside End: Plays a 5 technique. *Keys:* (1) tackle, (2) ball. *Responsibilities:* Secures the C gap versus strongside run. Chases weakside runs along the heel line, checking for counter, reverse, and bootleg.

Left Strongside Tackle: Plays a 3 technique. *Keys:* (1) guard, (2) ball, (3) tackle, (4) pulling linemen. *Responsibilities:* Secures the B gap versus strongside run, and squeezes the A gap as he pursues the ball from an inside-out position versus weakside run.

Mike: Plays an A-2 technique. *Keys:* Backfield flow through the offensive line. *Responsibilities:* Secures the A gap before pursuing strongside run and the B gap versus weakside run.

Right Weakside Tackle: Plays a 1 technique. *Keys:* (1) guard, (2) center. *Responsibilities:* Secures the A gap versus weakside runs, and pursues strongside runs from an inside-out position.

Right Weakside End: Plays a 5 technique. *Keys:* (1) tackle, (2) ball. *Responsibilities:* Secures the C gap versus weakside run. Chases strongside runs along the heel line, checking for counter, reverse, and bootleg.

Rover: Plays a 9 technique versus 12, 20, 21, 22, 30, 31, and 32 personnel. Adjusts according to coverage versus 11 and 10 personnel.

Defensive Alignment: 03

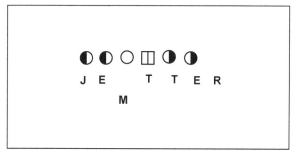

Diagram 7-4

Joker: Plays a 9 technique versus 11, 12, 20, 21, 22, 30, 31, and 32 personnel. *Keys:* (1) tight end, (2) near back, (3) pulling linemen, (4) ball. *Responsibilities:* Secures the D gap versus strongside run, and checks for bootleg, counter, and reverse versus weakside run.

Left Strongside End: Plays a 5 technique. *Keys:* (1) tackle, (2) ball. *Responsibilities:* Secures the C gap versus strongside run. Chases weakside runs along the heel line, checking for counter, reverse, and bootleg.

Left Strongside Tackle: Plays a 0 technique. *Keys:* (1) center, (2) both guards, (3) ball. *Responsibilities:* Executes a crush technique and secures the playside A gap versus both strongside and weakside runs.

Mike: Plays a B-A technique. *Keys:* Backfield flow through the offensive line. *Responsibilities:* Secures the B gap versus strongside run, and checks the A gap before pursuing weakside runs from an inside-out position.

Right Weakside Tackle: Plays a 3 technique. *Keys:* (1) guard, (2) ball, (3) tackle, (4) pulling linemen. *Responsibilities:* Secures the B gap versus weakside run, and squeezes the A gap as he pursues the ball from an inside-out position versus strongside run.

Right Weakside End: Plays a 5 technique. *Keys:* (1) tackle, (2) ball. *Responsibilities:* Secures the C gap versus weakside run. Chases strongside runs along the heel line, checking for counter, reverse, and bootleg.

Rover: Plays a 9 technique versus 12, 20, 21, 22, 30, 31, and 32 personnel. Adjusts according to coverage versus 11 and 10 personnel.

Defensive Alignment: 30

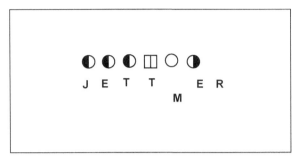

Diagram 7-5

Joker: Plays a 9 technique versus 11, 12, 20, 21, 22, 30, 31, and 32 personnel. *Keys:* (1) tight end, (2) near back, (3) pulling linemen, (4) ball. *Responsibilities:* Secures the D gap versus strongside run, and checks for bootleg, counter, and reverse versus weakside run.

Left Strongside End: Plays a 5 technique. *Keys:* (1) tackle, (2) ball. *Responsibilities:* Secures the C gap versus strongside run. Chases weakside runs along the heel line, checking for counter, reverse, and bootleg.

Left Strongside Tackle: Plays a 3 technique. *Keys:* (1) guard, (2) ball, (3) tackle, (4) pulling linemen. *Responsibilities:* Secures the B gap versus strongside run, and squeezes the A gap as he pursues the ball from an inside-out position versus weakside run.

Mike: Plays a B-0 technique. *Keys:* Backfield flow through the offensive line. *Responsibilities:* Secures the B gap versus weakside run, and pursues strongside runs from an inside-out position.

Right Weakside Tackle: Plays a 0 technique. *Keys:* (1) center, (2) both guards, (3) ball. *Responsibilities:* Executes a crush technique and secures the playside A gap versus both strongside and weakside runs.

Right Weakside End: Plays a 5 technique. *Keys:* (1) tackle, (2) ball. *Responsibilities:* Secures the C gap versus weakside run. Chases strongside runs along the heel line, checking for counter, reverse, and bootleg.

Rover: Plays a 9 technique versus 12, 20, 21, 22, 30, 31, and 32 personnel. Adjusts according to coverage versus 11 and 10 personnel.

Defensive Alignment: Plus 3 Weak Eagle

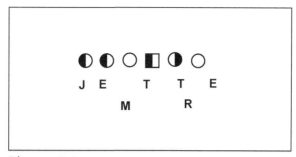

Diagram 7-6

Note: Weakside area of the front is vulnerable versus 22, 12, 30, 31, and 32 personnel. Coaches may compensate for this by rolling their secondary weak, widening Rover and the weak end and assigning Rover C gap responsibility and the end D gap responsibilities, or checking to another defense.

Joker: Plays a 9 technique. *Keys:* (1) tight end, (2) near back, (3) pulling linemen, (4) ball. *Responsibilities:* Secures the D gap versus strongside run, and checks for bootleg, counter, and reverse versus weakside run. May be required to adjust according to coverage versus 20 and 10 personnel.

Left Strongside End: Plays a 5 technique. *Keys:* (1) tackle, (2) ball. *Responsibilities:* Secures the C gap versus strongside run. Chases weakside runs along the heel line, checking for counter, reverse, and bootleg.

Left Strongside Tackle: Plays a plus technique. *Keys:* (1) center, (2) strongside guard, (3) ball. *Responsibilities:* Crushes the center and secures the strongside A gap versus strongside run, and pursues weakside run from an inside-out position.

Mike: Plays a B-1 technique. *Keys:* Backfield flow through the offensive line. *Responsibilities:* Secures the B gap versus strongside run and the weakside A gap versus weakside runs.

Right Weakside Tackle: Plays a 3 technique. *Keys:* (1) guard, (2) ball, (3) tackle, (4) pulling linemen. *Responsibilities:* Secures the B gap versus weakside run, and squeezes the A gap as he pursues the ball from an inside-out position versus strongside run.

Right Weakside End: Plays a ghost 7 technique versus 10, 20, 30, 21, and 11 personnel. *Keys:* (1) tackle, (2) running back, (3) pulling linemen. *Responsibilities:* Secures the C gap versus weakside run, and trails strongside runs along the heel line, looking for reverse, counter, or cutback. See Note versus 22, 12, 30, 31, and 32 personnel.

Rover: Plays an eagle technique. *Responsibilities:* Scrapes outside and secures the D gap versus weakside run, and secures the A gap versus strongside run.

Defensive Alignment: 03 Weak Eagle

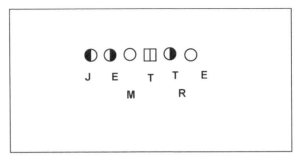

Diagram 7-7

Note: Weakside area of the front is vulnerable versus 22, 12, 30, 31, and 32 personnel. Coaches may compensate for this by rolling their secondary weak, widening Rover and the weak end, and assigning Rover C gap responsibility and the end D gap responsibilities, or checking to another defense.

Joker: Plays a 9 technique versus 21, 22, 11, 30, 31, 32, and 12 personnel. *Keys:* (1) tight end, (2) near back, (3) pulling linemen, (4) ball. *Responsibilities:* Secures the D gap versus strongside run, and checks for bootleg, counter, and reverse versus weakside run.

Left Strongside End: Plays an S technique. *Keys:* (1) tackle, (2) guard, (3) ball. *Responsibilities:* Secures the B gap versus strongside plays, and pursues weakside plays from an inside-out position.

Left Strongside Tackle: Plays a 0 technique. *Keys:* (1) center, (2) both guards, (3) ball. *Responsibilities:* Executes a crush technique, and secures the playside A gap versus both strongside and weakside runs.

Mike: Plays a C-0 technique. *Keys:* Backfield flow through the offensive line. *Responsibilities:* Secures the C gap versus strongside runs and pursues weakside runs from an inside-out position.

Right Weakside Tackle: Plays a 3 technique. *Keys:* (1) guard, (2) ball, (3) tackle, (4) pulling linemen. *Responsibilities:* Secures the B gap versus weakside run, and squeezes the A gap as he pursues the ball from an inside-out position versus strongside run.

Right Weakside End: Plays a ghost 7 technique versus 10, 20, 30, 21, and 11 personnel. *Keys:* (1) tackle, (2) running back, (3) pulling linemen. *Responsibilities:* Secures the C gap versus weakside run, and trails strongside runs along the heel line, looking for reverse, counter, or cutback. See Note versus 22, 12, 30, 31, and 32 personnel.

Rover: Plays an eagle technique. *Responsibilities:* Scrapes outside and secures the D gap versus weakside run, and secures the A gap versus strongside run.

Defensive Alignment: 31 Double Hawk

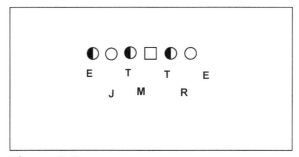

Diagram 7-8

Note: Coverage may dictate checking to an 11 or 22 front versus 10 and 20 personnel. Versus 12, 22, 30, 31, and 32 personnel, Rover and the weak end will widen, and Rover will be reassigned C gap responsibility and the end D gap responsibility.

Joker: Plays a hawk (C-A) technique. *Keys:* (1) tackle, (2) near back, (3) ball. *Responsibilities:* Secures the C gap versus strongside run, the A gap versus weakside run.

Left Strongside End: Plays a 9 technique versus 12, 21, 22, 11, 31, and 32 personnel. *Keys:* (1) tight end, (2) near back, (3) pulling linemen, (4) ball. *Responsibilities:* Secures the D gap versus strongside run, and trails the heel line versus weakside run, checking for bootleg, counter, and reverse. Adjusts to a ghost 7 technique versus 30, 20, and 10 personnel.

Left Strongside Tackle: Plays a 3 technique. *Keys:* (1) guard, (2) ball, (3) tackle, (4) pulling linemen. *Responsibilities:* Secures the B gap versus strongside run, and squeezes the A gap as he pursues the ball from an inside-out position versus weakside run.

Mike: Plays an A-0 technique. *Keys:* Backfield flow through the offensive line. *Responsibilities:* Secures the A gap before pursuing strongside run from an inside-out position, and pursues weakside run from an inside-out position.

Right Weakside Tackle: Plays a 1 technique. *Keys:* (1) guard, (2) center. *Responsibilities:* Secures the A gap versus weakside runs, and pursues strongside runs from an inside-out position.

Right Weakside End: Plays a ghost 7 technique versus 10, 20, 30, 21, and 11 personnel. *Keys:* (1) tackle, (2) running back, (3) pulling linemen. *Responsibilities:* Secures the C gap versus weakside run, and trails strongside runs along the heel line, looking for reverse, counter, or cutback. Adjusts to a 6 technique versus 12, 22, and 32 personnel.

Rover: Plays a hawk (B-0) technique. *Keys:* Backfield flow through the offensive line. *Responsibilities:* Secures the B gap versus weakside run, and pursues strongside run from an inside-out position. Adjusts according to coverage versus 10 and 11 personnel.

Defensive Alignment: 11 Strong Hawk

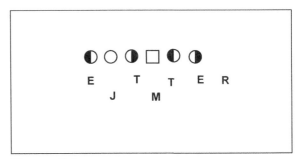

Diagram 7-9

Joker: Plays a C-B technique. *Keys:* (1) tackle, (2) near back, (3) ball. *Responsibilities:* Secures the C gap versus strongside run, the B gap before pursuing versus weakside run from an inside-out position.

Left Strongside End: Plays a 9 technique versus 12, 21, 22, 11, 31, and 32 personnel. *Keys:* (1) tight end, (2) near back, (3) pulling linemen, (4) ball. *Responsibilities:* Secures the D gap versus strongside run, and trails the heel line versus weakside run, checking for bootleg, counter, and reverse. Adjusts to a ghost 7 technique versus 30, 20, and 10 personnel.

Left Strongside Tackle: Plays a 1 technique. *Keys:* (1) guard, (2) center. *Responsibilities:* Secures the A gap versus strongside run, and pursues weakside runs from an inside-out position.

Mike: Plays a B-B technique. Keys: Backfield flow through the offensive line. *Responsibilities:* Secures the B gap versus both strongside and weakside runs.

Right Weakside Tackle: Plays a 1 technique. *Keys:* (1) guard, (2) center. *Responsibilities:* Secures the A gap versus weakside runs, and pursues strongside runs from an inside-out position.

Right Weakside End: Plays a 5 technique. *Keys:* (1) tackle, (2) ball. *Responsibilities:* Secures the C gap versus weakside run. Chases strongside runs along the heel line, checking for counter, reverse, and bootleg.

Rover: Plays a 9 technique versus 12, 20, 21, 22, 30, 31, and 32 personnel. Adjusts according to coverage versus 11 and 10 personnel.

Defensive Alignment: AB

```
  ◐ ◐ ○ □ ◐ ◐
  J  E  T     T  E
           M  R
```
Diagram 7-10

Joker: Plays a 9 technique versus 11, 12, 20, 21, 22, 30, 31, and 32 personnel. *Keys:* (1) tight end, (2) near back, (3) pulling linemen, (4) ball. *Responsibilities:* Secures the D gap versus strongside run, and checks for bootleg, counter, and reverse versus weakside run. May be required to adjust according to coverage versus 10 personnel.

Left Strongside End: Plays a 5 technique. *Keys:* (1) tackle, (2) ball. *Responsibilities:* Secures the C gap versus strongside run. Chases weakside runs along the heel line, checking for counter, reverse, and bootleg.

Left Strongside Tackle: Plays an A technique. *Keys:* (1) guard, (2) center, and (ball). *Responsibilities:* Secures the A gap versus strongside runs, and pursues weakside runs from an inside-out position.

Mike: Plays a B-1 technique. *Keys:* Backfield flow through the offensive line. *Responsibilities:* Secures the B gap versus strongside run, and the weakside A gap versus weakside run.

Right Weakside Tackle: Plays a B technique. *Keys:* (1) tackle, (2) guard, and (3) ball. *Responsibilities:* Secures the B gap versus weakside runs, and pursues strongside runs from an inside-out position.

Right Weakside End: Plays a ghost 7 technique versus 10, 20, 30, 21, and 11 personnel. Adjusts to a 9 technique versus 12, 22, and 32 personnel. *Keys:* (1) tackle, (2) running back, (3) pulling linemen. *Responsibilities:* Secures the C gap versus weakside run, and trails strongside runs along the heel line, looking for reverse, counter, or cutback.

Rover: Plays a D-A technique. *Keys:* Backfield flow through the offensive line. *Responsibilities:* Scrapes outside and secures the D gap versus weakside run, and secures the weakside A gap versus strongside run.

CHAPTER 8
Creating Multiple Odd Eight-Man Fronts

Chapter 8 presents 10 multiple eight-man fronts. All 10 fronts are "odd fronts" (odd eight-man fronts utilize three defensive linemen and three inside linebackers). Each front's name is given a three-digit designation which is dependent upon the alignment of the three defensive linemen. If, for example, the two ends are aligned in 4 techniques and the nose is aligned in a 0 technique, the defense is named 404. The 10 fronts presented in this chapter are used in conjunction with three-deep secondaries. Joker and Rover are the adjusters for all 10 fronts.

Defensive Alignment: 404

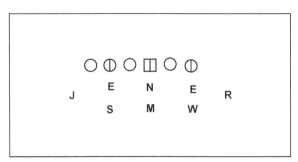

Diagram 8-1

Note: Most coaches who use this defense will slant the three down linemen the majority of the time. The base techniques described would be used mostly as a change-up.

Joker: Plays a loose 8 technique versus 21, 22, 11, and 12 personnel. Adjusts to a 9 technique versus 30, 31, and 32 personnel. Adjusts according to coverage versus 10 and 20 personnel.

Left Strongside End: Plays a 4 technique. *Keys:* (1) tackle, (2) guard, (3) tight end, (4) ball. *Responsibilities:* Employs a two-gap crush technique. Secures the C gap versus strongside run, and the B gap versus weakside flow.

Sam: Plays a D-A technique. *Keys:* Backfield flow through the offensive line. *Responsibilities:* Scrapes into and secures the D gap versus strongside run and secures the A gap versus weakside run.

Nose: Plays a 0 technique. *Keys:* (1) center, (2) both guards, (3) ball. *Responsibilities:* Secures the playside A gap versus both strongside and weakside runs.

Mike: Plays a B-B technique. *Keys:* Backfield flow through the offensive line. *Responsibilities:* Scrapes into and secures the playside B gap versus both strongside and weakside runs.

Will: Plays a D-A technique. *Keys:* Backfield flow through the offensive line. *Responsibilities:* Scrapes into and secures the D gap versus weakside run, and secures the A gap versus strongside run.

Right Weakside End: Plays a 4 technique. *Keys:* (1) tackle, (2) guard, (3) tight end, (4) ball. *Responsibilities:* Employs a two-gap crush technique. Secures the C gap versus weakside run, and the B gap versus strongside run.

Rover: Plays a loose 8 technique versus 12, 21, and 22 personnel. Adjusts to a 9 technique versus 30, 31, and 32 personnel. Adjusts according to coverage versus 10, 11, and 20 personnel.

Defensive Alignment: 505

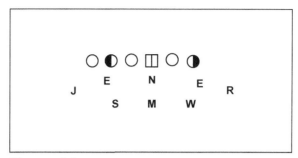

Diagram 8-2

Joker: Plays a loose 8 technique versus 21, 22, 11, and 12 personnel. Adjusts to a 9 technique versus 30, 31, and 32 personnel. Adjusts according to coverage versus 10 and 20 personnel.

Left Strongside End: Plays a 5 technique. *Keys:* (1) tackle, (2) ball. *Responsibilities:* Bobtails strongside runs with Sam. If blocked by the tackle, the end will secure the C gap. If the tackle attempts to block Sam, the end will squeeze inside and secure the B gap. Chases strongside runs along the heel line, checking for counter, reverse, and bootleg.

Sam: Plays a bobtail-A technique. *Keys:* (1) tackle, (2) ball. *Responsibilities:* Bobtails strongside runs with the left strongside end. Reacts to the movement of the offensive tackle. If the tackle blocks the defensive end, Sam will secure the B gap. If the tackle attempts to block Sam, Sam will scrape outside and secure the C gap. Secures the A gap versus weakside run.

Nose: Plays a 0 technique. *Keys:* (1) center, (2) both guards, (3) ball. *Responsibilities:* Secures the playside A gap versus both strongside and weakside run.

Mike: Plays a B-B technique. *Keys:* Backfield flow through the offensive line. *Responsibilities:* Scrapes into and secures the playside B gap versus both strongside and weakside runs.

Will: Plays a bobtail-A technique. *Keys:* (1) tackle, (2) ball. *Responsibilities:* Bobtails weakside runs with the right end. Reacts to the movement of the offensive tackle. If the tackle blocks the defensive end, Will fills the B gap. If the tackle attempts to block Will, Will scrapes outside and secures the C gap. Secures the A gap versus strongside run.

Right Weakside End: Plays a 5 technique. *Keys:* (1) tackle, (2) ball. *Responsibilities:* Bobtails weakside runs with Will. If blocked by the tackle, the end will secure the C gap. If the tackle attempts to block Will, the end will squeeze inside and secure the B gap. Chases strongside runs along the heel line, checking for counter, reverse, and bootleg.

Rover: Plays a loose 8 technique versus 12, 21, and 22 personnel. Adjusts to a 9 technique versus 30, 31, and 32 personnel. Adjusts according to coverage versus 10, 11, and 20 personnel.

Defensive Alignment: S05

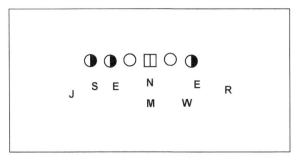

Diagram 8-3

Joker: Plays a loose 8 technique versus 21, 22, 11, and 12 personnel. Adjusts to a 9 technique versus 30, 31, and 32 personnel. Adjusts according to coverage versus 10 and 20 personnel.

Left Strongside End: Plays an S technique. *Keys:* (1) tackle, (2) guard, (3) ball. *Responsibilities:* Secures the B gap versus strongside runs, and pursues weakside runs from an inside-out position.

Sam: Plays a 7 technique versus 21, 22, 11, 12, 31, and 32 personnel. *Keys:* (1) tight end, (2) tackle, (3) running back, (4) pulling linemen. *Responsibilities:* Secures the C gap versus strongside run, and trails weakside runs along the heel line, looking for reverse, counter, or cutback. Adjusts to a ghost 7 technique versus 10, 20, and 30 personnel.

Nose: Plays a 0 technique. *Keys:* (1) center, (2) both guards, (3) ball. *Responsibilities:* Secures the playside A gap versus both strongside and weakside runs.

Mike: Plays a B-B technique. *Keys:* Backfield flow through the offensive line. *Responsibilities:* Scrapes into and secures the playside B gap versus both strongside and weakside runs.

Will: Plays a bobtail-A technique. *Keys:* (1) tackle, (2) ball. *Responsibilities:* Bobtails weakside runs with the right end. Reacts to the movement of the offensive tackle. If the tackle blocks the defensive end, Will fills the B gap. If the tackle attempts to block Will, Will scrapes outside and secures the C gap. Secures the A gap versus strongside run.

Right Weakside End: Plays a 5 technique. *Keys:* (1) tackle, (2) ball. *Responsibilities:* Bobtails weakside runs with Will. If blocked by the tackle, the end will secure the C gap. If the tackle attempts to block Will, the end will squeeze inside and secure the B gap. Chases strongside runs along the heel line, checking for counter, reverse, and bootleg.

Rover: Plays a loose 8 technique versus 12, 21, and 22 personnel. Adjusts to a 9 technique versus 30, 31, and 32 personnel. Adjusts according to coverage versus 10, 11, and 20 personnel.

Defensive Alignment: 503

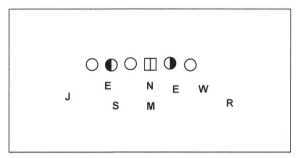

Diagram 8-4

Joker: Plays a loose 8 technique versus 21, 22, 11, and 12 personnel. Adjusts to a 9 technique versus 30, 31, and 32 personnel. Adjusts according to coverage versus 10 and 20 personnel.

Left Strongside End: Plays a 5 technique. *Keys:* (1) tackle, (2) ball. *Responsibilities:* Bobtails strongside runs with Sam. If blocked by the tackle, the end will secure the C gap. If the tackle attempts to block Sam, the end will squeeze inside and secure the B gap. Chases weakside runs along the heel line, checking for counter, reverse, and bootleg.

Sam: Plays a bobtail-A technique. *Keys:* (1) tackle, (2) ball. *Responsibilities:* Bobtails strongside runs with the left strongside end. Reacts to the movement of the offensive tackle. If the tackle blocks the defensive end, Sam will secure the B gap. If the tackle attempts to block Sam, Sam will scrape outside and secure the C gap. Secures the A gap versus strongside run.

Nose: Plays a 0 technique. *Keys:* (1) center, (2) both guards, (3) ball. *Responsibilities:* Secures the playside A gap versus both strongside and weakside runs.

Mike: Plays a B-0 technique. *Keys:* Backfield flow through the offensive line. *Responsibilities:* Scrapes into and secures the playside B gap versus strongside run, and pursues weakside run from an inside-out position.

Will: Plays a ghost 7 technique versus 21, 11, 31, 10, 20, and 30 personnel. Adjusts to a 7 technique versus 22, 12, and 32 personnel. *Keys:* (1) tight end, (2) tackle, (3) running back, (4) pulling linemen. *Responsibilities:* Secures the C gap versus strongside run, and trails weakside runs along the heel line, looking for reverse, counter, or cutback.

Right Weakside End: Plays a 3 technique. *Keys:* (1) guard, (2) ball, (3) tackle, (4) pulling linemen. *Responsibilities:* Secures the B gap versus weakside run, and squeezes the A gap as he pursues the ball from an inside-out position versus strongside run.

Rover: Plays a loose 8 technique versus 12, 21, and 22 personnel. Adjusts to a 9 technique versus 30, 31, and 32 personnel. Adjusts according to coverage versus 10, 11, and 20 personnel.

Defensive Alignment: BA7

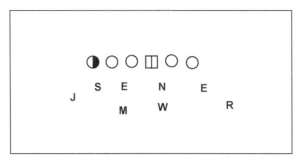

Diagram 8-5

Joker: Plays a loose 8 technique versus 21, 22, 11, and 12 personnel. Adjusts to a 9 technique versus 30, 31, and 32 personnel. Adjusts according to coverage versus 10 and 20 personnel.

Left Strongside End: Plays a B technique. *Keys:* (1) tackle, (2) guard, (3) ball. *Responsibilities:* Secures the B gap versus strongside runs, and pursues weakside runs from an inside-out position.

Sam: Plays a 7 technique versus 21, 11, 31, 22, 12, and 32 personnel. Adjusts to a ghost 7 technique versus a 10, 20, and 30 personnel. *Keys:* (1) tight end, (2) tackle, (3) running back, (4) pulling linemen. *Responsibilities:* Secures the C gap versus strongside run, and trails weakside runs along the heel line, looking for reverse, counter, or cutback.

Nose: Plays an A technique. *Keys:* (1) guard, (2) center, (3) ball. *Responsibilities:* Secures the A gap versus weakside runs and pursues strongside runs from an inside-out position.

Mike: Plays a D-A technique. *Keys:* Backfield flow through the offensive line. *Responsibilities:* Scrapes outside and secures the playside D gap versus strongside run, and secures the A gap versus weakside run.

Will: Plays a B-1 technique. *Keys:* Backfield flow through the offensive line. *Responsibilities:* Scrapes into and secures the weakside B gap versus weakside run, and secures the strongside A gap versus strongside run.

Right Weakside End: Plays a 7 technique versus 22, 12, and 32 personnel. Adjusts to a ghost 7 technique versus 21, 11, 31 10, 20, and 30 personnel. *Keys:* (1) tight end, (2) tackle, (3) running back, (4) pulling linemen. *Responsibilities:* Secures the C gap versus strongside run, and trails weakside runs along the heel line, looking for reverse, counter, or cutback.

Rover: Plays a loose 8 technique versus 12, 21, and 22 personnel. Adjusts to a 9 technique versus 30, 31, and 32 personnel. Adjusts according to coverage versus 10, 11, and 20 personnel.

Defensive Alignment: 303

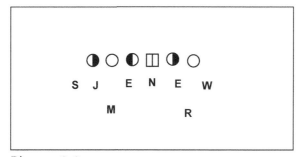

Diagram 8-6

Note: This is a variation of the bear 46, which is primarily a cover 1 defense. The Joker is aligned in a 7 technique because it was felt by the Bears that this was the most advantageous position for covering the tight end.

Joker: Plays a 7 technique and covers the tight end. Adjusts according to coverage versus 10 and 20 personnel.

Left Strongside End: Plays a 3 technique. *Keys:* (1) guard, (2) ball, (3) tackle, (4) pulling linemen. *Responsibilities:* Secures the B gap versus strongside run, and squeezes the A gap as he pursues weakside run from an inside-out position.

Sam: Plays an 8 technique *Keys:* (1) near back, (2) ball, (3) pulling linemen. *Responsibilities:* Rushes from the edge and contains strongside runs. Trails weakside runs along the heel line, looking for reverse, counter, or cutback.

Nose: Plays a two-gap crush technique. *Keys:* (1) guard, (2) center, (ball). *Responsibilities:* Secures the playside A gap versus both strongside and weakside runs.

Mike: Plays a C-A technique. *Keys:* Backfield flow through the offensive line. *Responsibilities:* Secures the C gap versus strongside run and the A gap as he pursues weakside run from an inside-out position.

Will: Plays a ghost 7 technique versus 21, 11, 31, 10, 20, and 30 personnel. Adjusts to a 9 technique versus 22, 12, and 32 personnel. *Keys:* (1) tight end, (2) tackle, (3) running back, (4) pulling linemen. *Responsibilities:* Contains weakside run and trails strongside runs along the heel line, looking for reverse, counter, or cutback.

Right Weakside End: Plays a 3 technique. *Keys:* (1) guard, (2) ball, (3) tackle, (4) pulling linemen. *Responsibilities:* Secures the B gap versus weakside run, and squeezes the A gap as he pursues strongside run from an inside-out position.

Rover: Plays a C-A technique. *Keys:* Backfield flow through the offensive line. *Responsibilities:* Secures the C gap versus weakside run and the A gap as he pursues strongside run from an inside-out position. Adjusts according to coverage versus 11, 12, and 10 personnel.

Defensive Alignment: 5 Plus 3

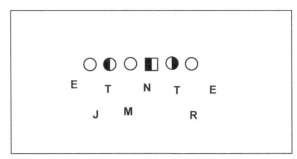

Diagram 8-7

Note: For this variation of the 5-3 defense, both Sam and Will have been replaced by two defensive tackles.

Joker: Lines up opposite the tight end and covers the tight end or drops into coverage versus 21, 22, 11, 31 32, and 12 personnel. Remains in the box and either covers the near back or drops into coverage versus 30 personnel. Adjusts according to coverage versus 20 and 10 personnel.

Left Strongside End: Plays an 8 technique *Keys:* (1) near back, (2) ball, (3) pulling linemen. *Responsibilities:* Rushes from the edge, and contains strongside runs. Trails weakside runs along the heel line looking for reverse, counter, or cutback.

Left Strongside Tackle: Plays a 5 technique. *Keys:* (1) tackle, (2) tight end, (3) ball. *Responsibilities:* Secures the C gap versus strongside run. Pursues weakside run from an inside-out position.

Nose: Plays a plus technique. *Keys:* (1) center, (2) strongside guard, (3) ball. *Responsibilities:* Crushes the center and secure the strongside A gap versus strongside run, squeezes weakside A gap, and pursues weakside run from an inside-out position.

Mike: Plays a B-1 technique. *Keys:* Backfield flow through the offensive line. *Responsibilities:* Secures the B gap versus strongside run and the weakside A gap versus weakside run.

Right Weakside Tackle: Plays a 3 technique. *Keys:* (1) guard, (2) ball, (3) tackle, (4) pulling linemen. *Responsibilities:* Secures the B gap versus weakside run, and squeezes the A gap as he pursues strongside run from an inside-out position.

Right Weakside End: Plays a ghost 7 technique versus 21, 11, 31, 10, 20, and 30 personnel. *Keys:* (1) tight end, (2) tackle, (3) running back, (4) pulling linemen. *Responsibilities:* Contains weakside run and trails strongside runs along the heel line, looking for reverse, counter, or cutback. Adjusts to a 7 technique versus a 12, 22, and 32 personnel.

Rover: Plays a C-A technique versus 20, 21, and 30 personnel. *Keys:* Backfield flow through the offensive line. *Responsibilities:* Secures the C gap versus weakside run, and pursues strongside run from an inside-out position. Adjusts to a loose 8 technique versus 12, 22, and 32 personnel. Adjusts according to coverage versus 11 and 10 personnel.

Defensive Alignment: SOS

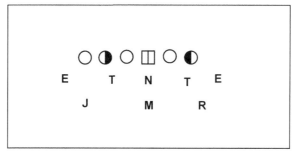

Diagram 8-8

Note: For this variation of the 5-3 defense, both Sam and Will have been replaced by two defensive tackles.

Joker: Lines up opposite the tight end, and covers the tight end or drops into coverage versus 21, 22, 11, 31 32, and 12 personnel. Remains in the box, and either covers the near back or drops into coverage versus 30 personnel. Adjusts according to coverage versus 20 and 10 personnel.

Left Strongside End: Plays an 8 technique *Keys:* (1) near back, (2) ball, (3) pulling linemen. *Responsibilities:* Rushes from the edge, and contains strongside runs. Trails weakside runs along the heel line, looking for reverse, counter, or cutback.

Left Strongside Tackle: Plays an S technique. *Keys:* (1) tackle, (2) guard, (3) ball. *Responsibilities:* Secures the B gap versus strongside plays, and pursues weakside plays from an inside-out position.

Nose: Plays a 0 technique. *Keys:* (1) center, (2) both guards, (3) ball. *Responsibilities:* Secures the playside A gap versus both strongside and weakside runs.

Mike Plays a 0-0 technique. *Keys:* Backfield flow through the offensive line. *Responsibilities:* Pursues both strongside and weakside runs from an inside-out position.

Right Weakside Tackle: Plays an S technique. *Keys:* (1) tackle, (2) guard, (3) ball. *Responsibilities:* Secures the B gap versus weakside run, and pursues strongside run from an inside-out position.

Right Weakside End: Plays a ghost 7 technique versus 21, 11, 31, 10, 20, and 30 personnel. *Keys:* (1) tight end, (2) tackle, (3) running back, (4) pulling linemen. *Responsibilities:* Contains weakside run, and trails strongside runs along the heel line, looking for reverse, counter, or cutback. Adjusts to an 8 technique versus 12, 22, and 32 personnel.

Rover: Plays a C-A technique versus 20, 21, and 30 personal. *Keys:* Backfield flow through the offensive line. *Responsibilities:* Secures the C gap versus weakside run, and pursues strongside run from an inside-out position. Adjusts to a loose 8 technique versus 12, 22, and 32 personnel. Adjusts according to coverage versus 11 and 10 personnel.

Defensive Alignment: 505 Diamond

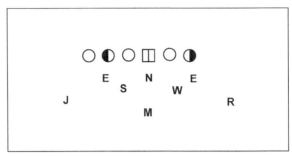

Diagram 8-9

Note: This peculiar defense affords the defense an abundance of stunt and coverage possibilities.

Joker: Plays a loose 8 technique versus 21, 22, 11, and 12 personnel. Adjusts to a 9 technique versus 30, 31, and 32 personnel. Adjusts according to coverage versus 20 and 10 personnel.

Left Strongside End: Plays a 5 technique. *Keys:* (1) tackle, (2) tight end, (3) ball. *Responsibilities:* Secures the C gap versus strongside run. Pursues weakside run from an inside-out position.

Sam: Plays a B-A technique. *Keys:* Backfield flow through the offensive line. *Responsibilities:* Secures the strongside B gap versus strongside run, and checks the strongside A gap before pursuing weakside runs from an inside-out position.

Nose: Plays a 0 technique. *Keys:* (1) center, (2) both guards, (3) ball. *Responsibilities:* Crushes the center, and secures the playside A gap versus both strongside and weakside run.

Mike: Plays a 0-0. *Keys:* backfield flow through the offensive line. *Responsibilities:* Pursues both strongside and weakside runs from an inside-out position.

Will: Plays a B-A technique. *Keys:* Backfield flow through the offensive line. *Responsibilities:* Secures the weakside B gap versus weakside run, and checks the weakside A gap before pursuing strongside runs from an inside-out position.

Right Weakside End: Plays a 5 technique. *Keys:* (1) tackle, (2) tight end, (3) ball. *Responsibilities:* Secures the C gap versus weakside run. Pursues strongside run from an inside-out position.

Rover: Plays a loose 8 technique versus 20, 21, and 22 personnel. Adjusts to a 9 technique versus 30, 31, and 32 personnel. Adjusts according to coverage versus 10, 11, and 12 personnel.

Defensive Alignment: 707

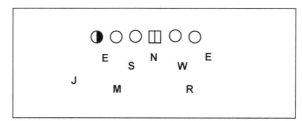

Diagram 8-10

Note: This variation of the double eagle-double flex defense is the author's preferred defense because it is an unusual three-level defense that affords a defensive coordinator a multitude of stunt and coverage possibilities.

Joker: Plays a loose 8 technique versus 21, 22, 11, and 12 personnel. Adjusts to a 9 technique versus 30, 31, and 32 personnel. Adjusts according to coverage versus 20 and 10 personnel.

Left Strongside End: Plays a 7 technique versus 21, 22, 11, 12, 31, and 32 personnel. Adjusts to a ghost 7 technique versus 10, 20, and 30 personnel. *Keys:* (1) tight end, (2) tackle, (3) running back, (4) pulling linemen. *Responsibilities:* Secures the C gap versus strongside run, and trails weakside runs along the heel line, looking for reverse, counter, or cutback.

Sam: Defender is usually involved in some sort of stunt. When assigned to read, he plays a B-A technique. *Keys:* Backfield flow through the offensive line. *Responsibilities:* Secures the strongside B gap versus strongside run, and checks the strongside A gap before pursuing weakside runs from an inside-out position.

Nose: Plays a 0 technique. *Keys:* (1) center, (2) both guards, (3) ball. *Responsibilities:* Crushes the center, and secures the playside A gap versus both strongside and weakside runs.

Mike: Plays a D-0 technique. *Keys:* Backfield flow through the offensive line. *Responsibilities:* Scrapes outside and secures the playside D gap versus strongside run, and pursues weakside run from an inside-out position.

Will: Defender is usually involved in some sort of stunt. When assigned to read, he plays a B-A technique. *Keys:* Backfield flow through the offensive line. *Responsibilities:* Secures the weakside B gap versus weakside run, and checks the weakside A gap before pursuing strongside runs from an inside-out position.

Right Weakside End: Plays a ghost 7 technique versus 10, 20, 30, 21, and 11 personnel. Adjusts to a 7 technique versus 12, 22, and 32 personnel. *Keys:* (1) tackle, (2) running back, (3) pulling linemen. *Responsibilities:* Secures the C gap versus weakside run, and trails strongside runs along the heel line, looking for reverse, counter, or cutback.

Rover: Plays a D-0 technique versus 20, 21, 22, 31, 32, and 30 personnel. *Keys:* Backfield flow through the offensive line. *Responsibilities:* Scrapes outside and secures the playside D gap versus strongside run, and pursues weakside run from an inside-out position. Adjusts according to coverage versus 11, 12, and 10 personnel.

CHAPTER 9
Creating Multiple Odd Seven-Man Fronts

Chapter 9 presents 10 multiple seven-man fronts. All 10 fronts are "odd fronts" (odd seven-man fronts utilize three defensive linemen and two inside linebackers). Each front's name is given a three-digit designation which is dependent upon the alignment of the three defensive linemen. The 10 fronts presented in this chapter are used in conjunction with four-deep secondaries. Joker is the designated adjuster for eight of the 10 fronts and Rover is the adjuster for the remaining two defenses, which are: 505 and BA5. Coaches wishing to switch from eight-man odd fronts to seven-man odd fronts will usually do so by substituting an additional defensive back, dollar, for Mike.

Defensive Alignment: 505

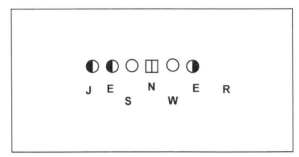

Diagram 9-1

Joker: Plays a 9 technique versus 20, 21, 22, 11, 12, 30, 31, and 32 personnel. *Keys:* (1) tight end, (2) near back, (3) pulling linemen. *Responsibilities:* Secures the D gap versus strongside run. Versus weakside run, defender will sink and check for throwback, bootleg, counter, and reverse before pursuing the ball from an inside-out position.

Left Strongside End: Plays a 5 technique. *Keys:* (1) tackle, (2) tight end, (3) ball. *Responsibilities:* Secures the C gap versus strongside run. Versus weakside run, defender will trail the play along the heel line checking for bootleg, counter, reverse, and cutback.

Sam: Plays a B-A technique. *Keys:* Backfield flow through the offensive line. *Responsibilities:* Secures the strongside B gap versus strongside run, and checks the strongside A gap before pursuing weakside runs from an inside-out position.

Nose: Plays a 0 technique. *Keys:* (1) center, (2) both guards, (3) ball. *Responsibilities:* Crushes the center, and secures the playside A gap versus both strongside and weakside runs.

Will: Plays a B-A technique. *Keys:* Backfield flow through the offensive line. Secures the weakside B gap versus weakside run, and checks the weakside A gap before pursuing strongside runs from an inside-out position.

Right Weakside End: Plays a 5 technique. *Keys:* (1) tackle, (2) tight end, (3) ball. *Responsibilities:* Secures the C gap versus weakside run. Trails strongside run along the heel line, checking for bootleg, counter, reverse, and cutback.

Rover: Plays a 9 technique versus 20, 21, 22, 12, 30, 31, and 32 personnel. *Keys:* (1) tight end, (2) near back, (3) pulling linemen. *Responsibilities:* Secures the D gap versus strongside run. Sinks versus weakside run, and checks for throwback, bootleg, counter, reverse, and cutback. Adjusts according to coverage versus 10 and 11 personnel.

Defensive Alignment: 5 Plus 3

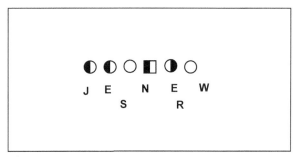

Diagram 9-2

Joker: Plays a 9 technique versus 20, 21, 22, 11, 12, 30, 31, and 32 personnel. *Keys:* (1) tight end, (2) near back, (3) pulling linemen. *Responsibilities:* Secures the D gap versus strongside run. Versus weakside run, defender will sink and check for throwback, bootleg, counter, and reverse before pursuing the ball from an inside-out position. Adjusts according to coverage versus 10 personnel.

Left Strongside End: Plays a 5 technique. *Keys:* (1) tackle, (2) tight end, (3) ball. *Responsibilities:* Secures the C gap versus strongside run. Versus weakside run, defender will trail the play along the heel line, checking for bootleg, counter, reverse, and cutback.

Sam: Plays a B-1 technique. *Keys:* Backfield flow through the offensive line. *Responsibilities:* Secures the strongside B gap versus strongside run and the weakside A gap versus weakside run.

Nose: Plays a plus technique. *Keys:* (1) center, (2) strongside guard, (3) ball. *Responsibilities:* Secures the strongside A gap versus both strongside run and pursues weakside run from an inside-out position.

Will: Plays a ghost 7 technique versus 10, 20, 30, 21, and 11 personnel. *Keys:* (1) tackle, (2) running back, (3) pulling linemen. *Responsibilities:* Contains weakside run and trails strongside runs along the heel line looking for bootleg, reverse, counter, or cutback. Adjusts to a 9 technique versus 12, 22, and 32 personnel.

Right Weakside End: Plays a 3 technique. *Keys:* (1) guard, (2) ball, (3) tackle, (4) pulling linemen. *Responsibilities:* Secures the B gap versus strongside run and squeezes the A gap as he pursues the ball from an inside-out position versus weakside run.

Rover: Plays a C-A technique versus 20, 21, 22, 11, 12, 30, 31, and 32 personnel. *Keys:* Backfield flow through the offensive line. *Responsibilities:* Secures the C gap versus weakside run and checks the weakside A gap before pursuing strongside run from an inside-out position.

Defensive Alignment: 303

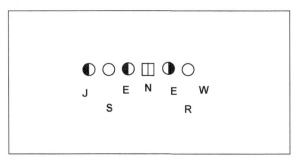

Diagram 9-3

Joker: Plays a 9 technique versus 20, 21, 22, 11, 12, 30, 31, and 32 personnel. *Keys:* (1) tight end, (2) near back, (3) pulling linemen. *Responsibilities:* Secures the D gap versus strongside run. Trails weakside run along the heel line, checking for bootleg, counter, reverse, and cutback. Adjusts to coverage if necessary versus 10 personnel.

Left Strongside End: Plays a 3 technique. *Keys:* (1) guard, (2) ball, (3) tackle, (4) pulling linemen. *Responsibilities:* Secures the B gap versus strongside run, and squeezes the A gap as he pursues weakside run from an inside-out position.

Sam: Plays a C-A technique. *Keys:* Backfield flow through the offensive line. Secures the strongside C gap versus strongside run and the strongside A gap versus weakside run. Adjusts to a ghost 7 technique versus 10 personnel.

Nose: Plays a 0 technique. *Keys:* (1) center, (2) both guards, (3) ball. *Responsibilities:* Crushes the center, and secures the playside A gap versus both strongside and weakside runs.

Will: Plays a ghost 7 technique versus 10, 20, 30, 21, and 11 personnel. *Keys:* (1) tackle, (2) running back, (3) pulling linemen. *Responsibilities:* Contains weakside run and trails strongside runs along the heel line, looking for bootleg, reverse, counter, or cutback. Adjusts to a 9 technique versus 12, 22, and 32 personnel.

Right Weakside End: Plays a 3 technique. *Keys:* (1) guard, (2) ball, (3) tackle, (4) pulling linemen. *Responsibilities:* Secures the B gap versus weakside run, and squeezes the A gap as he pursues the ball from an inside-out position versus strongside run.

Rover: Plays a C-A technique versus 20, 21, 22, 11, 12, 30, 31, and 32 personnel. *Keys:* Backfield flow through the offensive line. *Responsibilities:* Secures the C gap versus weakside run, and checks the weakside A gap before pursuing strongside run from an inside-out position.

Defensive Alignment: 5AB

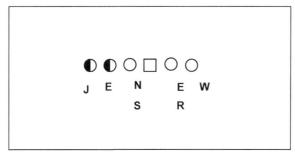

Diagram 9-4

Joker: Plays a 9 technique versus 20, 21, 22, 11, 12, 30, 31, and 32 personnel. *Keys:* (1) tight end, (2) near back, (3) pulling linemen. *Responsibilities:* Secures the D gap versus strongside run. Versus weakside run, defender will sink and check for throwback, bootleg, counter, and reverse before pursuing the ball from an inside-out position. Adjusts according to coverage versus 10 personnel.

Left Strongside End: Plays a 5 technique. *Keys:* (1) tackle, (2) tight end, (3) ball. *Responsibilities:* Secures the C gap versus strongside run. Versus weakside run, defender will trail the play along the heel line, checking for bootleg, counter, reverse, and cutback.

Sam: Plays a B-1 technique. *Keys:* Backfield flow through the offensive line. *Responsibilities:* Secures the strongside B gap versus strongside run and the weakside A gap versus weakside run.

Nose: Plays an A technique. *Keys:* (1) guard, (2) center, and (ball). *Responsibilities:* Secures the A gap versus strongside runs, and pursues weakside runs from an inside-out position.

Will: Plays a ghost 7 technique versus 10, 20, 30, 21, and 11 personnel. *Keys:* (1) tackle, (2) running back, (3) pulling linemen. *Responsibilities:* Contains weakside run and trails strongside runs along the heel line, looking for bootleg, reverse, counter, or cutback. Adjusts to a 9 technique versus 12, 22, and 32 personnel.

Right Weakside End: Plays a B technique. *Keys:* (1) guard, (2) ball, (3) tackle, (4) pulling linemen. *Responsibilities:* Secures the B gap versus weakside run, and squeezes the A gap as he pursues the ball from an inside-out position versus strongside run.

Rover: Plays a C-A technique versus 20, 21, 22, 11, 12, 30, 31, and 32 personnel. *Keys:* Backfield flow through the offensive line. *Responsibilities:* Secures the C gap versus weakside run, and checks the weakside A gap before pursuing strongside run from an inside-out position.

Defensive Alignment: BA5

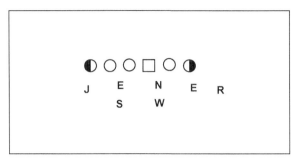

Diagram 9-5

Joker: Plays a 9 technique versus 20, 21, 22, 11, 12, 30, 31, and 32 personnel. *Keys:* (1) tight end, (2) near back, (3) pulling linemen. *Responsibilities:* Secures the D gap versus strongside run. Trails weakside run along the heel line, checking for bootleg, counter, reverse, and cutback.

Left Strongside End: Plays a B technique. *Keys:* (1) tackle, (2) guard, and (3) ball. *Responsibilities:* Secures the B gap versus strongside runs, and pursues weakside runs from an inside-out position.

Sam: Plays a C-A technique. *Keys:* Backfield flow through the offensive line. *Responsibilities:* Scrapes into and secures the strongside C gap versus strongside run and the strongside A gap versus weakside run.

Nose: Plays an A technique. *Keys:* (1) guard, (2) center, and (3) ball. *Responsibilities:* Secures the A gap versus weakside runs and pursues strongside runs from an inside-out position.

Will: Plays a B-1 technique. *Keys:* Backfield flow through the offensive line. *Responsibilities:* Secures the weakside B gap versus weakside run and the strongside A gap versus strongside run.

Right Weakside End: Plays a 5 technique. *Keys:* (1) tackle, (2) tight end, (3) ball. *Responsibilities:* Secures the C gap versus weakside run. Trails strongside run along the heel line, checking for bootleg, counter, reverse, and cutback.

Rover: Plays a 9 technique versus 20, 21, 22, 12, 30, 31, and 32 personnel. *Keys:* (1) tight end, (2) near back, (3) pulling linemen. *Responsibilities:* Secures the D gap versus strongside run. Sinks versus weakside run, and checks for throwback, bootleg, counter, reverse, and cutback. Adjusts according to coverage versus 10 and 11 personnel.

Defensive Alignment: S03

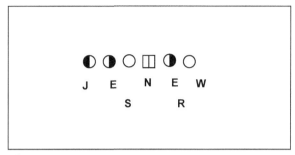

Diagram 9-6

Joker: Plays a 9 technique versus 20, 21, 22, 11, 12, 30, 31, and 32 personnel. *Keys:* (1) tight end, (2) near back, (3) pulling linemen. *Responsibilities:* Secures the D gap versus strongside run. Trails weakside run along the heel line, checking for bootleg, counter, reverse, and cutback. Adjusts to as necessary to coverage versus 10 personnel.

Left Strongside End: Plays an S technique. *Keys:* (1) tackle, (2) guard, (3) ball. *Responsibilities:* Secures the B gap versus strongside plays and pursues weakside plays from an inside-out position. Adjusts to a 5 technique versus 10 personnel.

Sam: Plays a C-A technique. *Keys:* Backfield flow through the offensive line. *Responsibilities:* Scrapes into and secures the strongside C gap versus strongside run and the strongside A gap versus weakside run.

Nose: Plays a 0 technique. *Keys:* (1) center, (2) both guards, (3) ball. *Responsibilities:* Crushes the center, and secures the playside A gap versus both strongside and weakside runs.

Will: Plays a ghost 7 technique versus 10, 20, 30, 21, and 11 personnel. *Keys:* (1) tackle, (2) running back, (3) pulling linemen. *Responsibilities:* Contains weakside run and trails strongside runs along the heel line, looking for bootleg, reverse, counter, or cutback. Adjusts to a 9 technique versus 12, 22, and 32 personnel.

Right Weakside End: Plays a 3 technique. *Keys:* (1) guard, (2) ball, (3) tackle, (4) pulling linemen. *Responsibilities:* Secures the B gap versus strongside run, and squeezes the A gap as he pursues the ball from an inside-out position versus weakside run.

Rover: Plays a C-A technique versus 20, 21, 22, 11, 12, 30, 31, and 32 personnel. *Keys:* Backfield flow through the offensive line. *Responsibilities:* Secures the C gap versus weakside run and checks the weakside A gap before pursuing strongside run from an inside-out position.

Defensive Alignment: 505 Stack

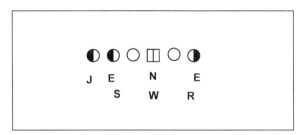

Diagram 9-7

Note: Weakside area of the front is vulnerable versus 22, 12, 30, 31, and 32 personnel. Coaches may compensate for this by rolling their secondary weak or checking to another defense. Also, this defense should be checked out of versus 10 and 11 personnel when coverage dictates that Rover must adjust.

Joker: Plays a 9 technique versus 20, 21, 22, 11, 12, 30, 31, and 32 personnel. *Keys:* (1) tight end, (2) near back, (3) pulling linemen. *Responsibilities:* Secures the D gap versus strongside run. Trails weakside run along the heel line, checking for bootleg, counter, reverse, and cutback. Adjusts to as necessary to coverage versus 10 personnel.

Left Strongside End: Plays a 5 technique. *Keys:* (1) tackle, (2) ball. *Responsibilities:* Bobtails strongside runs with Sam. If blocked by the tackle, the end will secure the C gap. If the tackle attempts to block Sam, the end will squeeze inside and secure the B gap. Chases weakside runs along the heel line, checking for counter, reverse, and bootleg.

Sam: Plays a bobtail-A technique. *Keys:* (1) tackle, (2) ball. *Responsibilities:* Bobtails strongside runs with the left end. Reacts to the movement of the offensive tackle. If the tackle blocks the defensive end, Sam will secure the B gap. If the tackle attempts to block Sam, will scrape outside and secure the C gap. Secures the A gap versus weakside run.

Nose: Plays a 0 technique. *Keys:* (1) center, (2) both guards, (3) ball. *Responsibilities:* Crushes the center, and secures the playside A gap versus both strongside and weakside runs.

Will: Plays an A-A technique. *Keys:* Backfield flow through the offensive line. *Responsibilities:* Secures the playside A gap versus both strongside and weakside runs.

Right Weakside End: Plays a 5 technique. *Keys:* (1) tackle, (2) ball. *Responsibilities:* Bobtails weakside runs with Will. If blocked by the tackle, the end will secure the C gap. If the tackle attempts to block Rover, the end will squeeze inside and secure the B gap. Chases strongside runs along the heel line, checking for counter, reverse, and bootleg.

Rover: Plays a bobtail-A technique. *Keys:* (1) tackle, (2) ball. *Responsibilities:* Bobtails weakside runs with the right end. Reacts to the movement of the offensive tackle. If the tackle blocks the defensive end, Rover will secure the B gap. If the tackle attempts to block Rover, Rover will scrape outside and secure the C gap. Secures the A gap versus strongside run.

Defensive Alignment: 523

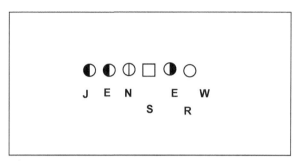

Diagram 9-8

Joker: Plays a 9 technique versus 20, 21, 22, 11, 12, 30, 31, and 32 personnel. *Keys:* (1) tight end, (2) near back, (3) pulling linemen. *Responsibilities:* Secures the D gap versus strongside run. Versus weakside run, defender will sink and check for throwback, bootleg, counter, and reverse before pursuing the ball from an inside-out position. Adjusts according to coverage versus 10 personnel.

Left Strongside End: Plays a 5 technique. *Keys:* (1) tackle, (2) tight end, (3) ball. *Responsibilities:* Secures the C gap versus strongside run. Versus weakside run, defender will trail the play along the heel line, checking for bootleg, counter, reverse, and cutback.

Sam: Plays an A-A technique. *Keys:* Backfield flow through the offensive line. *Responsibilities:* Secures the playside A gap versus both strongside and weakside runs.

Nose: Plays a 2 technique. Defender is a two-gap player. *Keys:* (1) guard, (2) ball, (3) center, (4) tackle. *Responsibilities:* Secures the B gap versus strongside run and the A gap versus weakside run.

Will: Plays a ghost 7 technique versus 10, 20, 30, 21, and 11 personnel. *Keys:* (1) tackle, (2) running back, (3) pulling linemen. *Responsibilities:* Contains weakside run and trails strongside runs along the heel line, looking for bootleg, reverse, counter, or cutback. Adjusts to a 9 technique versus 12, 22, and 32 personnel.

Right Weakside End: Plays a 3 technique. *Keys:* (1) guard, (2) ball, (3) tackle, (4) pulling linemen. *Responsibilities:* Secures the B gap versus strongside run, and squeezes the A gap as he pursues the ball from an inside-out position versus weakside run.

Rover: Plays a C-A technique versus 20, 21, 22, 11, 12, 30, 31, and 32 personnel. *Keys:* Backfield flow through the offensive line. *Responsibilities:* Secures the C gap versus weakside run, and checks the weakside A gap before pursuing strongside run from an inside-out position.

Defensive Alignment: 533

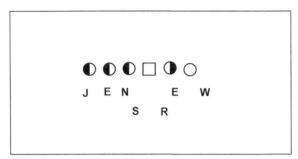

Diagram 9-9

Note: Weakside area of the front is vulnerable versus 22, 12, 30, 31, and 32 personnel. Coaches may compensate for this by rolling their secondary weak or checking to another defense.

Joker: Plays a 9 technique versus 20, 21, 22, 11, 12, 30, 31, and 32 personnel. *Keys:* (1) tight end, (2) near back, (3) pulling linemen. *Responsibilities:* Secures the D gap versus strongside run. Versus weakside run, defender will sink and check for throwback, bootleg, counter, and reverse before pursuing the ball from an inside-out position. Adjusts according to coverage versus 10 personnel.

Left Strongside End: Plays a 5 technique. *Keys:* (1) tackle, (2) tight end, (3) ball. *Responsibilities:* Secures the C gap versus strongside run. Versus weakside run, defender will trail the play along the heel line, checking for bootleg, counter, reverse, and cutback.

Sam: Plays a 0-1 technique. *Keys:* Backfield flow through the offensive line. *Responsibilities:* Pursues strongside run from an inside-out position, and secures the weakside A gap versus weakside run.

Nose: Plays a 3 technique. *Keys:* (1) guard, (2) ball, (3) tackle, (4) pulling linemen. *Responsibilities:* Secures the B gap versus strongside run, and squeezes the A gap as he pursues weakside run from an inside-out position.

Will: Plays a ghost 7 technique versus 10, 20, 30, 21, and 11 personnel. Adjusts to a 7 technique versus 12, 22, and 32 personnel. *Keys:* (1) tackle, (2) running back, (3) pulling linemen. *Responsibilities:* Secures the C gap versus weakside run, and trails strongside runs along the heel line, looking for reverse, counter, or cutback.

Right Weakside End: Plays a 3 technique. *Keys:* (1) guard, (2) ball, (3) tackle, (4) pulling linemen. *Responsibilities:* Secures the B gap versus weakside run, and squeezes the A gap as he pursues the ball from an inside-out position versus strongside run.

Rover: Plays a 0-1 technique versus 21 and 31 personnel. *Keys:* Backfield flow through the offensive line. *Responsibilities:* Pursues weakside run from an inside-out position, and secures the strongside A gap versus strongside run. Adjusts as dictated by the check versus 22, 11, 12, 30, 32, and 10 personnel.

Defensive Alignment: 513

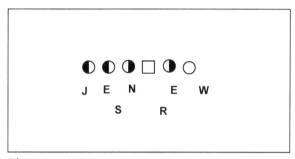

Diagram 9-10

Joker: Plays a 9 technique versus 20, 21, 22, 11, 12, 30, 31, and 32 personnel. *Keys:* (1) tight end, (2) near back, (3) pulling linemen. *Responsibilities:* Secures the D gap versus strongside run. Versus weakside run, defender will sink and check for throwback, bootleg, counter, and reverse before pursuing the ball from an inside-out position. Adjusts according to coverage versus 10 personnel.

Left Strongside End: Plays a 5 technique. *Keys:* (1) tackle, (2) tight end, (3) ball. *Responsibilities:* Secures the C gap versus strongside run. Versus weakside run, defender will trail the play along the heel line, checking for bootleg, counter, reverse, and cutback.

Sam: Plays a B-1 technique. *Keys:* Backfield flow through the offensive line. Secures the B gap versus strongside run and the weakside A gap versus weakside run.

Nose: Plays a 1 technique. *Keys:* (1) guard, (2) center. *Responsibilities:* Secures the A gap versus strongside runs, and pursues weakside runs from an inside-out position.

Will: Plays a ghost 7 technique versus 10, 20, 30, 21, and 11 personnel. *Keys:* (1) tackle, (2) running back, (3) pulling linemen. *Responsibilities:* Contains weakside run and trails strongside runs along the heel line, looking for bootleg, reverse, counter, or cutback. Adjusts to a 7 technique versus 12, 22, and 32 personnel.

Right Weakside End: Plays a 3 technique. *Keys:* (1) guard, (2) ball, (3) tackle, (4) pulling linemen. *Responsibilities:* Secures the B gap versus strongside run, and squeezes the A gap as he pursues the ball from an inside-out position versus weakside run.

Rover: Plays a C-A technique versus 20, 21, 22, 11, 12, 30, 31, and 32 personnel. *Keys:* Backfield flow through the offensive line. *Responsibilities:* Secures the C gap versus weakside run, and checks the weakside A gap before pursuing strongside run from an inside-out position.

CHAPTER 10
Establishing Run Responsibilities for the Defensive Secondary

Chapters 6 through 9 established basic gap responsibilities for 40 different seven- and eight-man defensive fronts. Chapter 11 will present strategies for stopping today's most explosive running plays. Before these strategies can be presented, however, it is first necessary to overview the basic run responsibilities of the defensive secondary. Two things will dictate these responsibilities: the offensive formation, and the specific pass coverage being employed.

Run Responsibilities for Man-to-Man Coverage

Obviously, if the coverage is some variation of man-to-man, the defenders responsible for covering receivers must maintain coverage on their assigned receiver until the ball crosses the line of scrimmage. The only exception to this applies to a defender assigned to cover a tightly aligned receiver such as tight end or wingback. This defender may move cautiously toward the line if his assigned receiver blocks and backfield flow indicates run. But (and this is a very big but) the defender must be able to react and cover delay routes if they should develop.

    A defender playing a loose technique versus a wide receiver will take a three-step shuffle when the ball is snapped. As he shuffles, the defender will focus his attention on the quarterback and backfield flow as he sees his assigned receiver through his periphery. If the quarterback and backfield flow indicates run, some defenders may possess the athleticism to throttle down, jam their assigned receiver in space, and maintain coverage until the ball cross the line of scrimmage. Not all defenders will have the ability to do so. These defenders must go into their backpedal, cover the receiver, and react to run only when the ball crosses the line. Defenders playing a man-to-man jam technique on a wide receiver at the line of must focus all of their attention on their coverage assignment and not concern themselves with run responsibilities.

The common high hat/low hat indicator used by many coaches has purposely been omitted because offensive line low-hat techniques are often used with play-action passes as a ploy to fool defenders. Furthermore, many coaches teach their offensive linemen low-hat pass protection techniques for their quick passing game.

Run Responsibilities for the Three-Deep Zone Secondary

Most coaches who adhere to an eight-man defensive front philosophy have replaced their 5-3 and 4-4 outside linebackers with defensive back/linebacker hybrids. As a result, they refer to their defense as a 3-3-5, or 4-2-5. No matter what label is given to the defense, whenever a zone coverage is employed, an eight-man front will play a three-deep, four-underneath zone coverage.

In describing the run responsibilities for the three-deep zone, we will use the letters established in previous chapters for an even eight-man front. Because run responsibilities vary depending upon the offensive formation, we will begin with the run responsibilities versus 12 personnel (Diagram 10-1):

Joker and Rover: *Run toward:* Primary containment. *Run away:* Sink and check for throwback, counter, and reverse before pursuing the ball.

Sam and Will: Play their assigned gap responsibility versus run toward and run away.

Free Safety: Alley player. Begins with a controlled backpedal. Reacts to the run from an inside-out position. Checks for a delayed route by the tight end as he approaches the line.

Cornerbacks: Begin with a three-step shuffle. Secure and maintain coverage of their zone until the ball crosses the line. Support run toward from an outside-in position, and take a deep pursuit angle for run away.

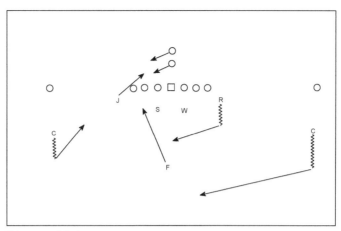

Diagram 10-1

Secondary run responsibilities change versus 10 personnel. If the Joker or Rover were to contain run toward their side, they would leave their respective cornerbacks in a 2-on-1 situation, which could prove to be devastating. It is, therefore, necessary to assign one of the inside linebackers the responsibility of primary containment. The run responsibilities versus 10 personnel are as follows (Diagram 10-2A):

Joker and Rover: *Run toward:* Jam the slot receiver, and maintain control of the curl zone. Assist with containment when the ball nears the line. *Run away:* Jam the slot receiver, and maintain control of the curl zone. Sink and check for throwback, counter, and reverse before pursuing the ball.

Sam and Will: *Run toward:* Primary containment. *Run away:* Secure their assigned gap, and pursue the ball from an inside-out position.

Free Safety: Alley player. Begins with a controlled backpedal. Reacts to the run from an inside-out position.

Cornerbacks: Begin with a three-step shuffle. Secure and maintain coverage of their zone until the ball crosses the line. Support run toward from an outside-in position, and take a deep pursuit angle for run away.

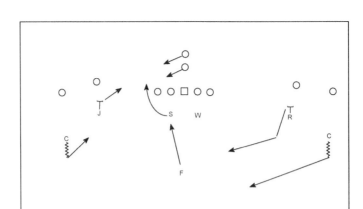

Diagram 10-2A

Obviously, the inside linebacker assigned primary containment versus 10 personnel cannot simply scrape outside and vacate his playside gap responsibility every time he is confronted by an outside run. Probably the best solution for the linebacker is to employ a bobtail technique with the defensive end (Diagrams 10-2B and 10-2C).

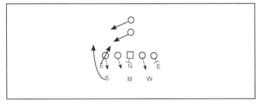
Diagram 10-2B

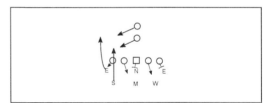
Diagram 10-2C

When employing a bobtail technique, both the Sam and the defensive end will key and react to the block of the offensive tackle. In Diagram 10-2B, the defensive tackle attempts to block Sam. Versus this scheme, Sam will avoid the tackle's block, immediately scrape outside, and contain the play. The defensive end will momentarily jam the tackle, close inside, and secure the B gap. In Diagram 10-2C, the tackle attempts to block the defensive end. Versus this scheme, the end will rip through the tackle's block and contain the play, and Sam will immediately secure the B gap.

Diagrams 10-3A and 10-3B illustrate run responsibilities versus 11 personnel. In Diagram 10-3A, the run is directed toward the tight end. Versus this scheme, Joker will contain the play. Rover will jam the slot receiver and sink as he checks for throwback, counter, and reverse before pursuing the ball. Will and Sam will secure their assigned gap responsibility The free safety will fill the alley from an inside-out position and checks for a delayed route by the tight end as he approaches the line, and the cornerbacks will secure and maintains coverage of their zone until the ball crosses the line.

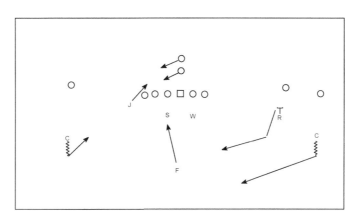

Diagram 10-3A

In Diagram 10-3B, the run is directed toward the slot receiver side. Versus this scheme, Will becomes the primary contain player, and Sam maintains his backside gap responsibility. Joker sinks as he checks for throwback, counter, and reverse before pursuing the ball. The free safety fills the alley from an inside-out position, and the cornerbacks secure and maintains coverage of their zone until the ball crosses the line.

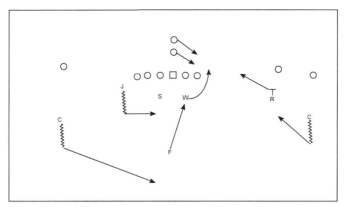

Diagram 10-3B

Diagram 10-4 illustrates run responsibilities versus 20 personnel. Some eight-man front coaches adjust Joker to the slot and leave Sam and Will in their normal eight-man front positions. Others will adjust the two inside linebackers into a position that will enable Sam to secure immediate containment of runs toward his side of the ball (as diagramed). The following are the run responsibilities versus 20 personnel:

Joker: *Run toward:* Jams the slot receiver and maintains control of the curl zone. Assists with containment when the ball nears the line. *Run away:* Jams the slot receiver, and maintains control of the curl zone. Sinks and checks for throwback, counter, and reverse before pursuing the ball.

Sam and Rover: *Run toward:* Primary containment. *Run away:* Sink and check for throwback, counter, and reverse before pursuing the ball.

Will: Maintains his playside and backside gap responsibilities.

Free Safety: Alley player. Begins with a controlled backpedal. Reacts to the run from an inside-out position.

Cornerbacks: Begin with a three-step shuffle. Secure and maintain coverage of their zone until the ball crosses the line. Support run toward from an outside-in position, and take a deep pursuit angle for run away.

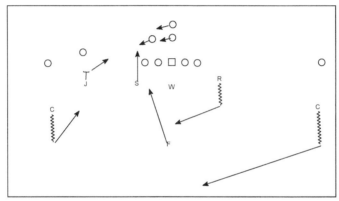

Diagram 10-4

Diagram 10-5 illustrates run responsibilities versus 21 personnel. The following are the run responsibilities versus 21 personnel:

Joker and Rover: *Run toward:* Primary containment. Run away: Sink and check for throwback, counter, and reverse before pursuing the ball.

Sam and Will: Play their assigned gap responsibility versus run toward and run away.

Free Safety: Alley player. Begins with a controlled backpedal. Reacts to run from an inside-out position. Checks for a delayed route by the tight end when securing runs toward the tight end side of the formation.

Cornerbacks: Begin with a three-step shuffle. Secure and maintain coverage of their zone until the ball crosses the line. Support run toward from an outside-in position, and takes a deep pursuit angle for run away.

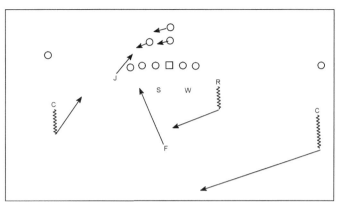

Diagram 10-5

Diagram 10-6 illustrates run responsibilities versus 30 personnel. The following are the run responsibilities versus 30 personnel:

Joker and Rover: *Run toward:* Primary containment. *Run away:* Sink and check for throwback, counter, and reverse before pursuing the ball.

Sam and Will: Play their assigned gap responsibility versus run toward and run away.

Free Safety: Alley player. Begins with a controlled backpedal. Reacts to the run from an inside-out position.

Cornerbacks: Begin with a three-step shuffle. Secure and maintain coverage of their zone until the ball crosses the line.

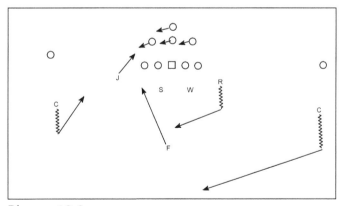

Diagram 10-6

Run Responsibilities for the Four-Deep Zone Secondary

Run support from a three-deep shell is probably simpler than it is with a four-deep shell because only one basic zone coverage (with a few variations) is used in conjunction with the three-deep shell. The four-deep shell provides the defense with a number of zone variations, and each variation has three different possible run support schemes at its disposal:

- Cloud containment: The cornerback is responsible for primary containment.
- Sky containment: The safety is responsible for primary containment.
- EMOL containment: The end or outside linebacker (whichever player is positioned at the end of the line of scrimmage) is responsible for primary containment.

Because a four-deep shell features two safeties, each safety is usually (depending upon each coach's preference) responsible for communicating which type of containment will be used versus run toward his side of the formation. Because one side of the formation may be completely different than the other side, the two calls may be different. For example, one safety may give a sky call, and the other safety may give a cloud call.

Diagram 10-7 illustrates EMOL containment versus 10 personnel. If the ball is positioned in the middle of the field, both safeties would give an EMOL because both sides of the formation are identical. If the ball were positioned on the hash, the safety positioned into the boundary might give a different call depending upon the distance of the two receivers to his side from the sideline. The following are EMOL run responsibilities versus 10 personnel:

Joker and Rover: *Run toward:* Primary containment. *Run away:* Sink, wall off the slot receiver, and check for throwback, counter, and reverse before pursuing the ball.

Mike: Plays his assigned gap responsibility.

Dollar Player and Free Safety: *Run toward:* Alley player. Begin with a controlled backpedal. React to the run from an inside-out position. *Run away:* Rotate to midfield, make certain that the play is a run, and then provide support from an inside-out position.

Cornerbacks: Begin with a three-step shuffle. Secure and maintain coverage of their zone until the ball crosses the line. Support run toward from an outside-in position, and take a deep pursuit angle for run away.

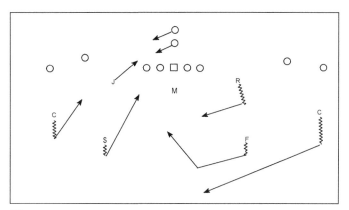

Diagram 10-7

Diagrams 10-8A and 10-8B illustrate a situation in which the two safeties have given different containment calls. Diagram 10-8A illustrates EMOL run support responsibilities versus a trips formation featuring 11 personnel when run is directed toward the three-receiver side. EMOL run responsibilities in this situation are as follows:

Rover: Primary containment.

Joker: Sinks and checks for throwback, counter, and reverse before pursuing the ball.

Mike: Plays his assigned gap responsibility.

Dollar Player: Cautiously makes certain the play is a run before providing outside-in support.

Free Safety: Alley player. Begins with a controlled backpedal. Reacts to the run from an inside-out position.

Left Cornerback: Begins with a three-step shuffle. Secures and maintains coverage of his zone until the ball crosses the line. Supports run toward from an outside-in position.

Right Cornerback: Takes a three-step shuffle, checking the tight end's release. Maintains coverage until the ball crosses the line, and then takes a deep pursuit angle.

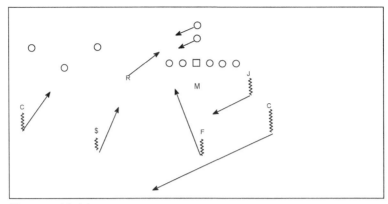

Diagram 10-8A

Diagram 10-8B illustrates cloud run responsibilities when run is directed to the other side of the formation. Cloud support responsibilities in this situation are as follows:

Rover: Sinks and walls off the inside receiver as he checks for throwback, counter, and reverse before pursuing the ball.

Joker: Reacts to the tight end's block.

Mike: Plays his assigned gap responsibility.

Dollar Player: Cautiously makes certain the play is a run before rotating to the deep middle and providing inside-out run support.

Free Safety: Alley player. Begins with a controlled backpedal. Reacts to the run from an inside-out position.

Left Cornerback: Takes a three-step shuffle, checking the tight end's release. Maintains coverage until the ball crosses the line and then takes a deep pursuit angle.

Right Cornerback: Keys the tight end's block and provides primary containment.

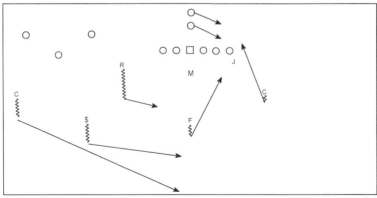

Diagram 10-8B

The ball is positioned on the right hash in Diagrams 10-9A and 10-9B, and run support is illustrated toward both the wideside and the shortside of the field versus 12 personnel. Diagram 10-9A illustrates wideside run support featuring a sky call. Responsibilities in this situation are as follows:

Rover: Sinks and walls off the #1 receiver to his side as he checks for throwback, counter, and reverse before pursuing the ball.

Joker: Reacts to the tight end's block.

Mike: Plays his assigned gap responsibility.

Dollar Player: Provides primary run support.

Free Safety: Alley player. Begins with a controlled backpedal, and keys the tight end's block. Supports run from an inside-out position.

Left Cornerback: Takes a three-step shuffle and maintains coverage until the ball crosses the line and then supports run from an inside-out position.

Right Cornerback: Takes a three-step shuffle, maintains coverage of the deep third until the ball crosses the line, and then takes a deep pursuit angle.

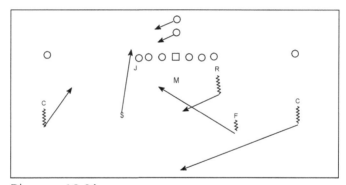

Diagrams 10-9A

EMOL run support is illustrated in Diagram 10-9B versus run into the boundary. The assignments in this situation are as follows:

Rover: Provides primary containment.

Joker: Keys the tight end's release, and sinks as he checks for throwback, counter, and reverse before pursuing the ball.

Mike: Plays his assigned gap responsibility.

Dollar Player: Cautiously makes certain the play is a run before rotating to the deep middle and providing inside-out run support.

Free Safety: Alley player. Begins with a controlled backpedal. Reacts to the run from an inside-out position.

Left Cornerbacks: Takes a three-step shuffle, maintains coverage of the deep third until the ball crosses the line, and then takes a deep pursuit angle to the ball.

Right Cornerbacks: Takes a three-step shuffle, maintains coverage of the deep third until the ball crosses the line, and then provides outside-in run support.

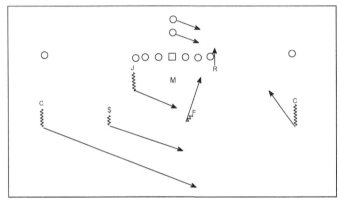

Diagrams 10-9B

Diagrams 10-10A and 10-10B illustrate run support versus 21 personnel. Diagram 10-10A illustrates EMOL run support versus run toward the two-receiver side of the formation. Run responsibilities in this situation are as follows:

Rover: Primary containment.

Joker: Sinks and checks for throwback, counter, and reverse before pursuing the ball.

Mike: Plays his assigned gap responsibility.

Dollar Player: Cautiously makes certain the play is a run before providing outside-in support.

Free Safety: Alley player. Begins with a controlled backpedal. Reacts to the run from an inside-out position.

Left Cornerback: Begins with a three-step shuffle. Secures and maintains coverage of the outside third zone until the ball crosses the line. Supports run toward from an outside-in position.

Right Cornerback: Takes a three-step shuffle, checking the tight end's release. Maintains coverage until the ball crosses the line, and then takes a deep pursuit angle.

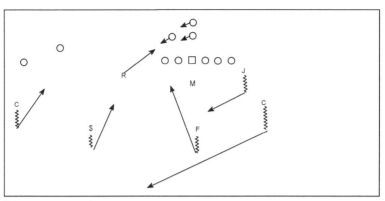

Diagram 10-10A

Diagram 10-10B illustrates cloud run support when the run is directed toward the tight end side of the formation. Run responsibilities are as follows:

Rover: Sinks and walls off the #2 receiver as he checks for throwback, counter, and reverse before pursuing the ball.

Joker: Reacts to the tight end's block.

Mike: Plays his assigned gap responsibility.

Dollar Player: Cautiously makes certain the play is a run before rotating to the deep middle and providing inside-out run support.

Free Safety: Alley player. Begins with a controlled backpedal. Reacts to the run from an inside-out position.

Left Cornerbacks: Takes a three-step shuffle, maintains coverage of the deep third until the ball crosses the line, and then takes a deep pursuit angle.

Right Cornerbacks: Keys the tight end's block, and provides primary containment.

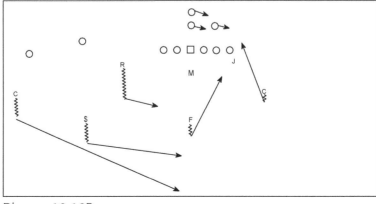

Diagram 10-10B

Diagram 10-11 illustrates EMOL run support versus 30 personnel. Both safeties would give the same call versus this personnel grouping because both sides of the formation are identical. Run responsibilities are as follows:

Joker and Rover: *Run toward:* Primary containment. *Run away:* Sink and check for throwback, counter, and reverse before pursuing the ball.

Mike: Plays his assigned gap responsibility.

Dollar Player and Free Safety: *Run toward:* Alley player. Begin with a controlled backpedal. React to run from an inside-out position. *Run away:* Rotate to midfield, make certain that the play is a run, and then provide support from an inside-out position.

Cornerbacks: Begin with a three-step shuffle. Secure and maintain coverage of their zone until the ball crosses the line. Support run toward from an outside-in position, and take a deep pursuit angle for run away.

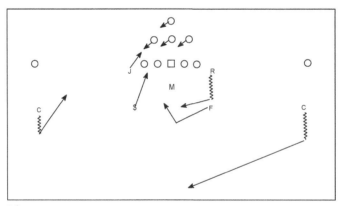

Diagram 10-11

CHAPTER 11
Defending the Contemporary Run Game

The contemporary run game is in a constant state of evolution; consequently, modern defenses must also be in a constant state of evolution to keep pace. This chapter will present the most potent running plays that are plaguing modern defenses and then provide suggestions as to how they can be successfully defended. Obviously, it is impossible to analyze each play versus every defense in football; consequently, a number of different defenses are illustrated.

The Speed Option

This play necessitates that the defense must stop both the pitch and the quarterback keep. As mentioned in previous chapters, the bobtail technique is an effective method of securing both the B and C gaps without requiring a defensive back to provide primary run support. Diagrams 11-1A and 11-1B illustrate how the 3-3-5 would react to the playside tackle's block and stop the option with the bobtail technique versus 10 personnel. The advantage of the bobtail is that it enables an eight-man front to employ either a man or zone secondary coverage.

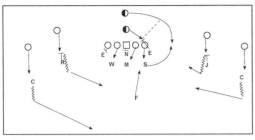 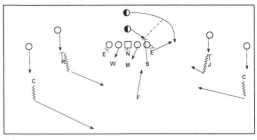

Diagram 11-1A   Diagram 11-1B

The speed option can also be successfully defended without employing a bobtail technique. Diagram 11-2 illustrates how a 3-4 stunts can be used with success. In this diagram, the Joker is coming off the edge and immediately attacking the quarterback. The playside defensive end is slanting into the B gap, which enables Sam to scrape outside and tackle the pitchback.

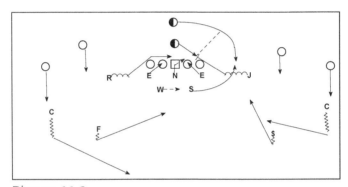

Diagram 11-2

Diagram 11-3 illustrates how the 4-3 can be used to successfully stop the speed option. In this diagram, Joker is attacking the pitchback. Because the playside defensive tackle is aligned in a 3 technique, the offensive tackle is forced to block inside and either double-team the 3 technique or chip to the next level and block Mike. This approach enables the defensive end to attack the quarterback. When attacking the quarterback, the end should attack the shoulder of the quarterback's pitch arm.

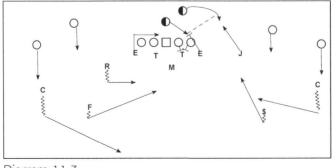

Diagram 11-3

Although some coaches may favor feathering (soft playing) the quarterback rather than attacking him, it is far more advantageous for the defense to get the ball out of the quarterback's hands as quickly as possible and turn the play into a sweep. Furthermore, the offensive risk of subjecting the quarterback to being tackled and possibly injured or intimidated by an extremely aggressive defensive end weigh heavily in favor of the defense.

The Veer

The veer, which is the true triple option, requires the offense to stop: the dive, the quarterback keep, the pitch, and all of the eligible pass receivers that release downfield. Most veer teams prefer to run the veer versus a 5 technique. Although some teams execute the veer from the gun, it is most effectively implemented with the quarterback positioned under center. Diagram 11-4A illustrates the veer versus the 3-4 defense from a double slot formation.

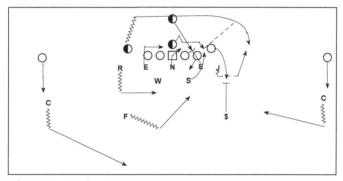

Diagram 11-4A

The most effective deterrent in stopping the veer is the bobtail technique. When executing this technique, the playside defensive end will make a "down-down" call and jam the tackle as he simultaneously closes inside and attacks the fullback as close to the mesh point as possible. As Sam hears the "down-down" call, he will avoid the tackle's block, scrape outside, and tackle the quarterback. Joker is employing a feather technique to contain the pitch. Dollar will cover the releasing slotback until he is absolutely positive that the play is a run. The free safety will provide alley support, and the remainder of the defense will execute their run responsibilities as required.

Diagram 11-4B illustrates the veer versus the 3-3-5. In this diagram, the offense is employing a different blocking scheme. Instead of closing inside in an attempt to block Sam, the playside offensive tackle is blocking whichever defender (Sam or end) that is responsible for tackling the quarterback in the C gap. When employing a bobtail technique versus this scheme, Sam will attack the B gap and tackle the diveback. The defensive end's assignment to tackle the quarterback has becomes more difficult because he is being blocked; consequently, Joker will hold his ground if he is aligned off the ball and sink if he is aligned on the line of scrimmage. If the end is able to attack the quarterback,

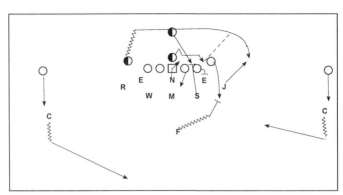

Diagram 11-4B

Joker will immediately react to the pitch. If the quarterback enters the perimeter with the ball, Joker will employ a feather technique, string the play laterally for as long as possible, and attack quarterback if the quarterback turns upfield. If the quarterback eventually pitches the ball, Joker will react by taking a 45-degree pursuit angle to the pitchback.

The Midline Option

Most option teams prefer to run the midline toward a 3 technique. The midline can be run effectively from either a pistol or a quarterback-under-center formation. Diagram 11-5A illustrates the most popular variation of midline in which the quarterback reads the reactions of the playside 3 technique and either gives the ball to the aceback or keeps it. In defending this play, Sam and the playside 3 technique will bobtail. The 3 technique will jam the offensive guard and tackle the aceback as close to the mesh point as possible. Sam will scrape into the C gap, defeat the block of the slotback, and tackle the quarterback. The free safety is Sam's backup; he will slide playside as he sees motion and be prepared to cover the slotback's release. Since the slotback blocks inside rather than releasing, the free safety is immediately led to a position that will enable him to assist Sam. Joker is responsible for the pitch, and all other defenders will secure their run responsibilities.

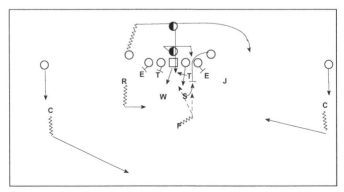

Diagram 11-5A

Although most midline teams employ the previous play as their staple, they may occasionally execute the midline triple, which is illustrated in Diagram 11-5B. This play is somewhat easier to defend. The bobtail reactions of Sam and the playside 3 technique are identical to the previous play. The distinguishing factor in this play is that the offensive tackle attempts to block Sam. Upon seeing this, the defensive end will close inside and attack the quarterback. Joker is responsible for the pitch, and the free safety will cover the slotback's release. All other defenders will secure their run responsibilities.

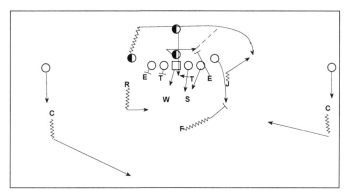

Diagram 11-5B

The Counter Trey

The four requirements for stopping the counter trey are as follows:
- All defenders must read their keys and react correctly.
- The playside defensive end must close inside and cut block the pulling guard. This technique will close the hole, create a pile, and prevent the offensive tackle from leading the ballcarrier through the hole. Coaches seem to disagree as to which arm the defensive end should attack the pulling guard with. In reality, there is no correct answer except this one: *Knock the guard off his feet, and create a pile that prevents the tackle from continuing down the line*.
- There must be a defender outside of the playside defensive end that is in position to tackle the ballcarrier when he tries to bounce the play outside.
- There must be a backside defender that attacks the quarterback to make certain that the quarterback has not kept the ball.

Diagrams 11-6A and 11-6B illustrate both an aceback and quarterback counter trey versus a bear 46 defensive front. In Diagram 11-6A, the left defensive end closes the hole, attacks the pulling guard, and forces the aceback to bounce the play outside. Mike reads his keys properly, scrapes outside, and tackles the aceback. The right defensive end attacks the quarterback and makes certain that the quarterback has not kept the ball. He does not simply check the quarterback to make certain the quarterback does not have the ball—by attacking the quarterback, the defensive end dispels the possibility of uncertainty. Furthermore, if the defensive end repeatedly attacks the quarterback in an extremely aggressive manner, the quarterback's fakes will eventually become nonexistent; he may even raise his hands after the handoff in an attempt to let the end know that he doesn't have the ball.

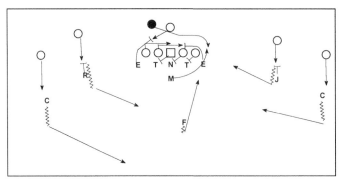

Diagram 11-6A

A similar scenario exists in the quarterback counter trey, which is illustrated in Diagram 11-6B. In this diagram, the right defensive end, closes the hole and cuts the pulling guard. Mike scrapes outside and tackles the quarterback as he tries to bounce the play outside, and the left defensive end tackles the aceback.

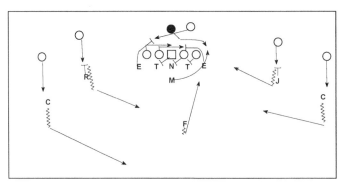

Diagram 11-6B

The Jet Sweep

The jet sweep, as an isolated play, is not a great football play. What makes the jet sweep a great football play is the combination of defensive adjustments that are made to stop it along with the supplementary packaged plays that exploit faulty defensive adjustments when the sweep is faked. Diagram 11-7 illustrates an example of a sound adjustment that might be made by a 4-3 defense (tackles aligned in an 11 front) versus the jet sweep. In this diagram, the defenders assume their base front and a

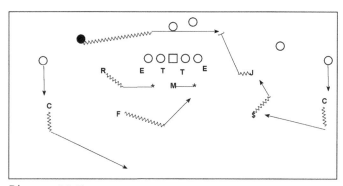

Diagram 11-7

four-deep secondary prior to motion. Once the motion commences, the free safety will begin rotating into the middle. If the jest sweep is faked, this will put him in an ideal position to provide alley support versus run and cover the deep middle versus pass. Both Rover and Mike will slide to B gap alignments. This alignment will ensure that all gaps are secured and allow both linebackers to bobtail if necessary. Joker will slide back inside and immediately tackle the motioned player as the ball is snapped. Dollar will begin spiraling down to a position that will enable him to cover the flats versus pass or to assist in supporting outside run. Both cornerbacks will begin their three-step shuffle as the ball is snapped and react to run or pass appropriately.

Zone and Stretch

The keys to stopping the zone and the stretch are as follows:
- Creating a wall along the line of scrimmage and aggressively securing all gaps.
- Having an alley defender that pursues the ball from an inside-out position and tackles the ballcarrier if the wall breaks down and the ballcarrier cuts back.
- Having a backside defender that attacks the quarterback immediately after the fake or handoff.

Diagram 11-8 illustrates how an eight-man front would defend the zone or stretch versus 10 personnel. In this diagram, the tackles are securing the A gaps, and the playside end is securing the C gap. The backside end is attacking the quarterback. The Sam is aggressively securing the B gap. The Will linebacker will first secure his B gap and then pursue the ball from an inside-out position. Joker is hanging tough in the flats, analyzing his pass/run keys and reacting appropriately. Rover is walling off the #2 receiver and then taking his proper pursuit angle. The free safety is providing alley support, and the cornerbacks are making certain that the play is a run before taking their proper pursuit angles to the ball.

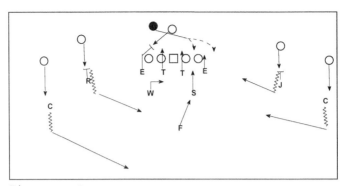

Diagram 11-8

Zone Read

Diagrams 11-9A and 11-9B illustrate the two ways in which offensive teams execute the zone read when the aceback is aligned in an offset position. In Diagram 11-9A, the quarterback is reading the reaction of the defensive end. As previously mentioned, when discussing the zone and stretch plays, it is the responsibility of the backside end not only to check the quarterback, but to aggressively attack him.

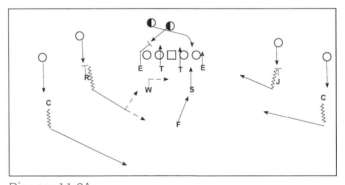

Diagram 11-9A

Diagram 11-9B illustrates a variation of the zone read that evolved as defenses learned how defend the original version. The new variation requires the offensive tackle to block the defensive end and the quarterback to read Will. Will's key to stopping this play is the offensive tackle's block. As soon as Will sees the tackle block the end, he should shoot the B gap and immediately tackle the quarterback. It is also important that the defensive end maintains containment in the event that the quarterback is able to elude Will and scramble to the perimeter.

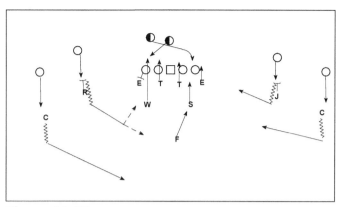

Diagram 11-9B

Diagram 11-10 illustrates the zone read from a pistol formation that employs 20 personnel. This play can also be run from 21, 10 or 11 personnel. When defensing the play from one of these personnel groupings, the same coaching points for defensing the zone read versus 20 personnel are applicable. When 20 or 21 personnel is used for the implementation of the zone read, the offense gains the advantage of having an additional blocker (the offset running back) to either block the defensive end or to block the primary contain player. On the other hand, 20 and 21 personnel create the offensive disadvantage of adding extra defender to the box. Diagram 11-10 illustrates how the double eagle-double flex defenses the zone read. In this diagram, the defensive end is responsible for the quarterback. It is important to note the free safety's angle of run support. Since the aceback's landmark is the A gap, it is vital that the free safety begin his angle of alley support toward the offensive center and maintain an inside-out position on the aceback until the tackle is made. It is also vital that Will squeezes the backside B gap remains alert for cutback.

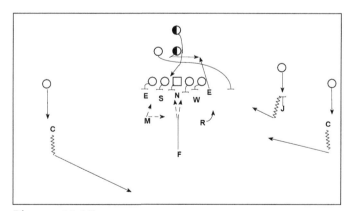

Diagram 11-10

One of the best tactics versus any type of option is to confuse the quarterback's read keys, and to also to confuse offensive blocking assignments. Diagrams 11-11A through 11-11 E illustrate five weakside double eagle-double flex twists and stunts that can be used for this purpose versus the zone read or any other option.

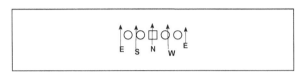

Diagram 11-11A

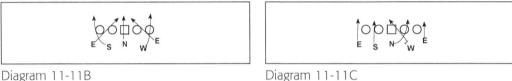

Diagram 11-11B

Diagram 11-11C

Diagram 11-11D

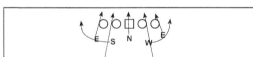

Diagram 11-11E

Triple Zone Read

Diagram 11-12 illustrates the triple zone read employed from 20 personnel. The play can be run with almost any personnel grouping. Teams frequently run it from 10, 11, and 12 personnel by sending a wide receiver in motion to serve as the pitchback, or by using a stationary wide receiver as the pitchback.

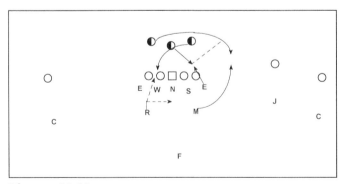

Diagram 11-12

The play is illustrated versus the double eagle-double flex defense. Versus this defense, the offense will begin by executing a zone read. The quarterback will read the right defensive end. If the right end trails the zone play, the quarterback will pull the ball and option Rover. If Rover attacks the quarterback, the quarterback will pitch the ball. If Rover plays the pitch, the quarterback will keep the ball. In defending this play, it is imperative that the right end attacks the quarterback, and Rover scrapes downhill to the pitch. It is also imperative that the remaining defenders in the box build a wall and stop the zone play. The free safety has the most difficult task. He must hold his ground until he is certain which side of the line is being attacked and then provide alley support to the appropriate side. The Joker and cornerbacks must also attain certitude before reacting.

It may be helpful for the reader to note the mathematically balanced alignment of double eagle-double flex defenders in Diagram 11-12 versus 20 personnel. Many eight-man fronts adjust to 20 personnel in the manner illustrated in Diagram 11-13. This type of unbalanced adjustment gives the offense a numbers advantage toward the slot receiver and is, therefore, not mathematically sound.

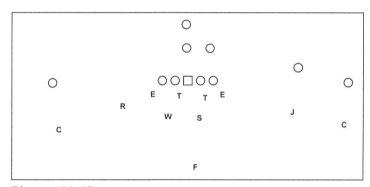

Diagram 11-13

Lead Read

Diagrams 11-14 illustrates the lead read versus an eight-man front in which both defensive tackles are aligned in 1 techniques. The quarterback is assigned to give or keep the ball based upon the reaction of the left defensive end. Versus this scheme, the defensive end will attack the quarterback. The backside guard is pulling and isolating Sam, who is aligned in the B gap. Versus this variation, Sam must read the block of the offensive guard and tackle, fill the B gap, and attack the pulling guard as close to the line of scrimmage as possible. The right defensive end must squeeze the B gap, maintain outside leverage, and force the play inside. Both defensive tackles must secure their respective A gaps versus cutback. It is important that Will does not pursue the play too quickly. Will must first make certain that the quarterback is tackled and then pursue the aceback slowly while maintaining an inside-out position on the ball.

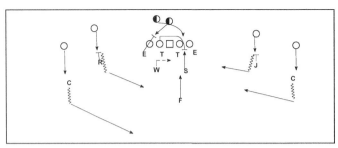

Diagrams 11-14

G and T Trap Reads

Diagram 11-15A illustrates the G trap read in which the offensive guard traps the defensive end. Diagram 11-15B illustrates the T trap read in which the offensive tackle pulls and traps the defensive end. Both plays assign the quarterback to give or pull the ball based upon the reactions of the defensive left end. Versus both plays, the defensive end attacks the quarterback. The right defensive end who is being trapped must close inside and violently attack the trapper. Sam must move outside, avoid the offensive tackle's block, work downhill, and expect the ballcarrier to bounce the play outside. Both defensive tackles must secure their respective A gaps versus cutback, and Mike must pursue the ball slowly while maintaining an inside-out position on the ballcarrier.

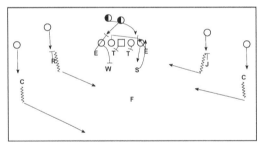

Diagram 11-15A

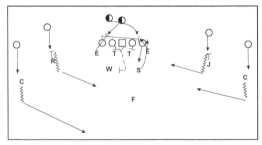

Diagram 11-15B

Iso Read

Diagram 11-16 illustrates the iso read versus an 11 defense front in which the offense is employing 21 personnel. Like the previous read plays, the quarterback is basing his give/keep read upon the reactions of the defensive end, who will attack the quarterback. Sam must read the block of the offensive tackle, fill the B gap, and attack the lead blocker as close to the line of scrimmage as possible. The playside defensive end must squeeze the B gap, maintain outside leverage, and force the play inside. The playside tackle must secure the playside A gap and not get driven back. Will must attack the offensive tackle, secure the B gap, and pursue the ball from an inside-out position.

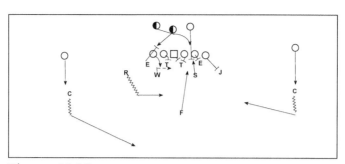

Diagram 11-16

Joker's reaction is based upon the movement of the tight end (block or release) and the specific coverage being employed. The free safety will provide alley support from an inside-out position.

Off-Tackle Read

The final read play is illustrated from 21 personnel versus the 3-4 defense in Diagram 11-17. The right defensive end is being blocked, and the quarterback is reading Will. Will must read the blocking scheme and immediately penetrate the B gap and attack the quarterback. Joker must jam the tight end, close inside as tight to the double-team as possible, and attack the near back with his inside forearm, It is important that Joker maintains outside leverage on the near back's block. Dollar must provide primary run support, and the free safety must provide alley support. The remainder of the defense must secure their gap responsibilities and pursue the football.

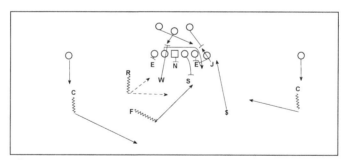

Diagram 11-17

Dart

Dart is a predetermined cutback play. Diagrams 11-18A through 11-18C illustrate three blocking schemes that a defense may encounter versus dart. Diagram 11-18A illustrates dart with a zone blocking scheme. Diagram 11-18B illustrates dart with a lead blocking scheme, and Diagram 11-18C illustrates dart with a trap blocking scheme. The same coaching points that have been previously explained for dealing with these three blocking schemes are applicable for these plays.

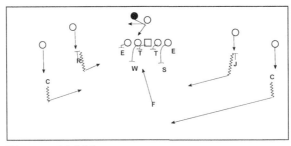

Diagram 11-18A

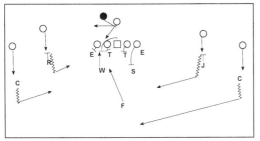

Diagram 11-18B   Diagram 11-18C

Quarterback Keep

This play requires the quarterback to fake to the aceback and keep the ball. Diagrams 11-19A through 11-19C illustrate three blocking schemes that a defense may encounter versus the quarterback keep. Diagram 11-19A illustrates the quarterback keep with a zone blocking scheme. Diagram 11-19B illustrates the quarterback keep with a lead blocking scheme, and Diagram 11-19C illustrates the keeper with a trap blocking scheme. The same coaching points that have been previously explained for dealing with these three blocking schemes are applicable for these plays.

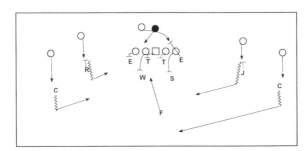

Diagram 11-19A

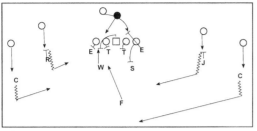
Diagram 11-19B

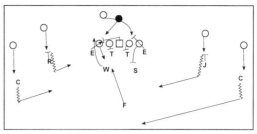
Diagram 11-19C

Quarterback Iso

There is nothing subtle about this play. The quarterback simply receives the ball and follows the aceback through the hole (Diagram 11-20). The same coaching points that were previously discussed in dealing with an iso blocking scheme are also applicable versus this play.

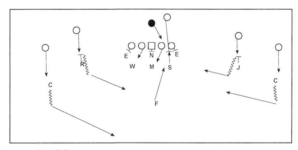
Diagram 11-20

Quarterback Sweep

Diagram 11-21 illustrates the quarterback sweep utilizing 10 personnel versus an even seven-man front. Although the diagramed play is a predetermined run, a similar version can be employed that gives the quarterback the option to run or pass. With both versions, the quarterback will usually hold the ball in a passing position as he initially sprints to the perimeter, which forces the defense to be sound versus both pass and run. Joker and the playside defensive end are key players in successfully defending this play. The defensive end must defeat the block of the lead back, and Joker must immediately provide primary run support. Dollar must first make absolutely certain that the play is a run before providing outside support. The free safety will rotate to deep middle and hopefully see that the playside offensive tackle has released downfield in an attempt to block Mike. If he sees this, the free safety should alert the defense that the play is in fact a run and then provide alley support. Rover will first wall of the #2 receiver to his side of the formation and eliminate any possibility of a pass before pursuing the ball. Defenders

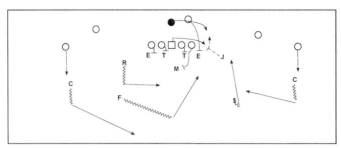

Diagram 11-21

in the box must secure their gap responsibilities and then pursue the ballcarrier from an inside-out position. The cornerbacks will analyze the play as they execute their three-step shuffle and then react when they are positive that the play is a run.

Toss

This play is particularly effective versus an eight-man front that is employing a cover 1 pass coverage (Diagram 11-22). The key players in stopping this play are the playside defensive end and Joker. The defensive end's pursuit angle is critical. If he penetrates upfield, the play has a good chance of gaining yardage, but if he pursues flat down the line and maintains an inside-out position on the ballcarrier, the play is usually stopped at the line. Joker's responsibility is to jam the #2 receiver, defeat the #2 receiver's block, and contain the play. The remaining player will react as they did on the quarterback sweep.

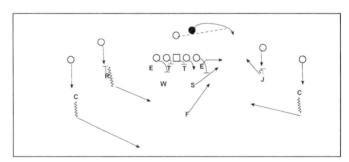

Diagram 11-22

CHAPTER 12
Man-to-Man Pass Coverage Techniques

Loose Man Techniques for Defensive Backs

Defensive backs playing loose man assume a stance and alignment that enable them to use their peripheral vision to see both the quarterback and the receiver that they are assigned to cover. When employing loose man, defenders should adhere to the following guidelines:

- They must concentrate on covering their assigned receiver and not concern themselves with run support unless they are absolutely certain that the ball has crossed the line of scrimmage.
- Cornerbacks should align one yard inside of #1 and seven to eight yards deep. Safeties should align one yard outside of a tight end and seven to eight yards deep.
- Defensive backs should keep their outside foot up (toe-to-heel relationship) with their weight on their front foot. They keep a narrow base with their feet close together and let their arms hang loosely. They also drop their hips and round their backs slightly so that their nose is in front of their toes. A free safety keeps his feet parallel with his weight evenly distributed. He has a slight bend at his knees and waist.
- Defensive backs should anticipate potential routes that a receiver may run prior to the snap, based upon the receiver's split. If a receiver has a wide split, the defender anticipates an inside route. If the receiver's alignment is tight, the defender should expect an outside route.

- As the ball is snapped, the defender pushes off his front foot and takes three quick shuffle steps. As he shuffles, he reads the drop of the quarterback, which enables him to react to and defend the patterns that are ascribed to a three-step drop. Although the defender sees his assigned receiver out of his periphery, his main focus is on the quarterback during this initial three-step shuffle.
- Once the quarterback continues to drop past three steps, the defender commences backpedaling and focuses his attention on the receiver.
- As he backpedals, the cornerback defending a wide receiver must maintain inside leverage on the receiver and never allow the receivers to get head-up with himself. Safeties playing a tight end will maintain outside leverage.
- The defensive back must keep a good forward lean as he backpedals and keep his weight on the balls of his feet.
- The defensive back must keep his feet close to the ground and take small to medium steps. It is a serious mistake to overstride or to lift his feet high off the ground.
- The defensive back keeps his arms relaxed and bent at a 90-degree angle. His arms should pump comfortably as he backpedals.
- The defensive back should maintain a cushion of approximately three to four yards from the receiver. It is important that he keeps his shoulders parallel to the line and not turn them unless his cushion is broken.
- The defensive back should turn his hips to the receiver and mirror the receiver's movements.
- Controlling speed during the backpedal is vital. When the receiver makes his break, the defender must be under control and able to gather and break quickly in the direction of the receiver's break.
- The defensive back must concentrate on the base of a receiver's numbers until the receiver makes his final break. The defender should not look at the receiver's head.
- The defensive back should anticipate the receiver's break by looking for the receiver to change his forward lean, begin to chop his feet, or widen his base.
- The defensive back must turn and run with the receiver, keeping his body between the ball and the receiver whenever the receiver gets within two yards.
- When the receiver makes his final break, the defensive back drops his shoulders in the direction of the receiver's break and explodes in that direction. The defender quickly closes the cushion between himself and the receiver, and breaks to the interception point. The defender must maintain concentration on the receiver and not look for the ball until he's closed the cushion and he sees the receiver look for the ball.
- The defensive back should play the ball, not the receiver, when the ball is inside and the receiver is outside of himself. When the receiver is between the defender and the ball, the defender should play the ball through the receiver's upfield shoulder.
- It is important that the defensive back understands which hand is the receiver's catch hand, which is the hand with which the receiver can make a one-handed catch. It is important that the defender concentrate on this hand and attack it when trying to break up a pass.

- The defensive back should never cut in front of a receiver to make an interception unless he is absolutely sure that he can get two hands on the ball.
- The defensive back should try to catch the ball or break up a pass with two hands, not one, and knock the ball toward the ground, never up in the air.
- If the receiver catches the ball, the defender should try to strip the ball out of the receiver's hands.
- When attempting to intercept a pass, the defender should attack the ball at its highest point.
- If an interception is made, the defender should yell "Oskie" and head toward the nearest sideline.

Defending Football's Most Common Pass Routes With Loose Man

Note: When mentioning the length of quarterback's drop (three-, five-, or seven-step) in this section, it is assumed that the quarterback is receiving the snap from a position under center. The length of the quarterback's drop for the same routes when he is positioned in the gun will vary. A general, and not always accurate, formula for gun drops is as follows:
- A three-step drop under center equals a one-step gun drop
- A five-step drop under center equals a three-step gun drop
- A seven-step drop under center equals a five-step gun drop

The only way to ensure the accuracy of this formula is to study the films each individual opponent because variations may exist.

Slant Route (Diagram 12-1)

The receiver most likely breaks inside at a 45-degree angle on his third or fourth step. He may try to stem the defender outside on his release. The quarterback should throw the ball as the receiver makes his break. The defender must maintain inside leverage and keep his shoulders parallel to the line of scrimmage as he makes his three-step shuffle. He must use his peripheral vision to not only see the receiver, but to also recognize the quarterback's drop. The defender's three-step shuffle read alerts him that a quick pass is in progress (the quarterback's shortened second step and/or low front shoulder are the defender's key indicators). Once the slant is recognized, the defender should plant and drive to the interception point, which is a point approximately four to six yards in front of the receiver. Some contact may happen as the ball is thrown. If the receiver catches the ball, the defender must ensure the tackle and rip the ball out of the receiver's possession.

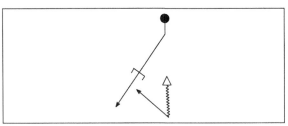

Diagram 12-1

Five- to Six-Yard Out Route (Diagram 12-2)

The quarterback should throw the ball as the receiver makes his break. The receiver should see the ball before the defender does. The defender's three-step shuffle read alerts him that a quick pass is in progress. Once the out route is recognized, the defender plants, drives, and breaks to the receiver's upfield shoulder. The defender must attack the receiver's catch hand with his own upfield hand. The defender should never undercut the ball unless he has read the route and is in perfect position.

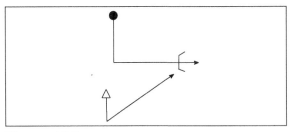

Diagram 12-2

Five- to Six-Yard Hitch Route (Diagram 12-3)

The quarterback should throw the ball as the receiver makes his break. The receiver should see the ball before the defender does. The defender's three-step shuffle read alerts him that a quick pass is in progress. Once the hitch is recognized, the defender should plant and drive to the outside shoulder of the receiver. The defender must ensure the tackle with his outside arm over the outside shoulder pad of the receiver and rip the arm or punch the ball with his inside hand.

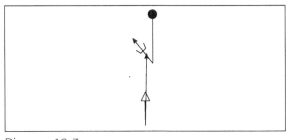

Diagram 12-3

Hitch and Go Route (Diagram 12-4)

Once the hitch is recognized, the defender should plant and drive to the outside shoulder of the receiver. When the quarterback pumps the ball, the receiver turns and runs the go route. If the defender is in good position, he collisions the receiver as he runs his go route. The route should be eliminated at this point. If the receiver gets by the defender, he must run with him, trying to cut off the route.

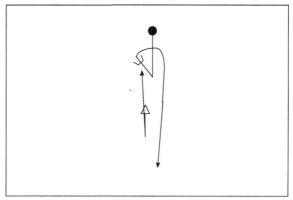

Diagram 12-4

Curl Route (Diagram 12-5)

The defender must maintain inside leverage and keep his shoulders parallel to the line of scrimmage as he backpedals. The defender should be able to sense the receiver's break by the quarterback's drop. The receiver breaks his pattern at about 12 yards if the quarterback takes a five-step drop and about 16 yards if the quarterback takes a seven-step drop. When the receiver begins to chop his feet or raises his pad level, the defender should begin to plant his feet. As the receiver breaks his route toward the quarterback, the defender drives to the interception point. He ensures the tackle with his outside arm over the outside shoulder pad and rips or punches with his inside hand.

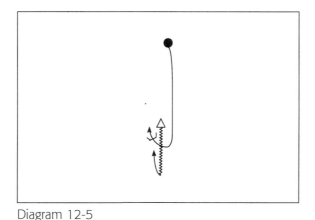

Diagram 12-5

In Route (Diagram 12-6)

The defender must maintain inside leverage and keep his shoulders parallel to the line of scrimmage as he backpedals. He should be able to sense the receiver's break by the quarterback's drop. The receiver breaks his pattern at about 12 yards if the quarterback takes a five-step drop and about 16 yards if the quarterback takes a seven-step drop. When the receiver breaks inside and begins running down the line, the defender must plant and drive to the upfield shoulder of the receiver. More than likely, the defender will be right behind the receiver. When the ball is thrown, the defender attacks the receiver's catch hand and tries to strip the ball out.

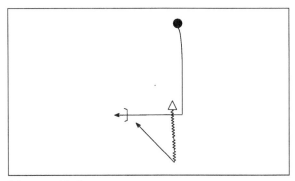

Diagram 12-6

Post Route (Diagram 12-7)

The defender must maintain inside leverage and keep his shoulders parallel to the line of scrimmage as he backpedals. He should be able to sense the receiver's break by the quarterback's drop. When the receiver breaks to the post, the defender must turn his hips to the inside and drive to a point in front of the receiver, allowing no more than one yard of separation. The defender will be right behind he receiver, on his hip pocket. When the ball is thrown, the defender attacks the receiver's catch hand.

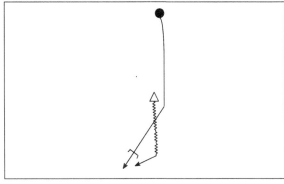

Diagram 12-7

Post-Corner Route (Diagram 12-8)

Initially, the defender uses the same rules as covering the post pattern. When the receiver breaks to the corner, the defender uses a speed turn and tracts the receiver's break. When employing the speed turn, the defender must plant with his inside foot, whip his head around, and drive hard to the corner.

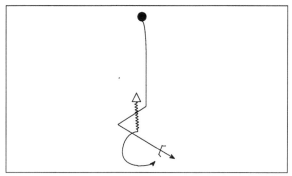

Diagram 12-8

Fade Route (Diagram 12-9)

The defender's three-step shuffle read alerts him that a quick pass is in progress. He should be able to recognize the fade route immediately. He must keep a three-yard cushion between himself and the receiver. If he cushion is broken, the defender must turn his hips to the receiver and begin to run to cut off the fade route, which is done by leaning his outside shoulder pad into the receiver. He may only look back at the quarterback if he is maintaining contact with the receiver. As the ball nears the receiver, he rips up through the receiver's catch hand and strips the ball out of the receiver's hands.

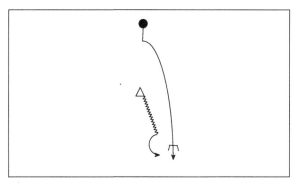

Diagram 12-9

Comeback Route (Diagram 12-10)

The defender must maintain inside leverage and keep his shoulders parallel to the line of scrimmage as he backpedals. He rules out a fade pattern because of the quarterback's drop. After the receiver clears 12 yards, the defender expects the pattern to break at about 16 yards. When the receiver makes his break, the defender must plant his outside leg and drive to the receiver's upfield shoulder. The defender will probably get there as the ball is thrown. He attacks the receiver's catch hand with his upfield arm.

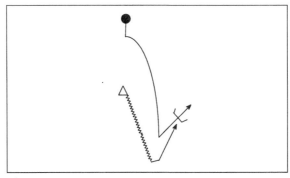

Diagram 12-10

Dig Route (Diagram 12-11)

This pattern is one of the most difficult to cover in football. Initially, the defender uses the same rules for covering the post. As the receiver begins his second break parallel to the line of scrimmage, the defender must plant with his outside leg and drive to the receiver. The defender will probably trail the receiver, but must be in a position to make the tackle, break up the pass, or strip the ball.

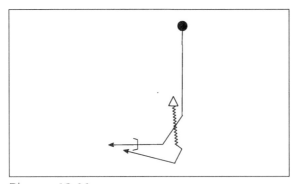

Diagram 12-11

Flag Route (Diagram 12-12)

Initially, this route is covered just like a post route. When the receiver breaks to the corner, the defender must turn his hips to the outside and drive to a point in front of the receiver, allowing no more than one yard separation. The defender is on the receiver's hip pocket. When the ball is thrown, he attacks the receiver's catch hand.

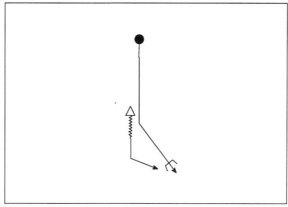

Diagram 12-12

Inside Bump Man Techniques

The purpose of the inside bump man technique is to jam all inside releases and force the receiver to release outside away from the quarterback. The primary advantages of the technique are that it limits the offense's pass route selection and disrupts the timing between the quarterback and the receivers. It also often gives the pass rushers additional time to get to the quarterback because it delays a receiver's ability to get free. Normally, this technique is used by cornerbacks for cover 2 man, but anytime a coach feels that a defender can adequately cover his designated receiver with an inside bump technique, he may consider its use. When employing this technique, the defender will do the following:

- Lines up on the inside eye of the receiver. The normal depth is crowding the line of scrimmage to one to two yards deep.
- Keeps his feet shoulder-width apart and parallel.
- Evenly distributes his weight on the balls of his feet.
- Keeps his eyes focused on the receiver's midsection.
- Does not move until the receiver moves. He will instantly react to and jam all inside releases, but react slowly to outside releases. When the receiver releases, the defender simultaneously punches with his inside arm and shuffles in the direction of

the receiver's release. He attempts to keep his hips parallel to the line of scrimmage as he immediately jams all inside releases. It is important that the defender does not overstride while shuffling. He also shuffles and punches versus outside releases, but he is careful not to open his hips until the route has been established.

- Punches the receiver's sternum with his palm out as he punches with his inside arm. He must be careful not to overextend when punching and lose his balance.
- Does not get faked or juked by the receiver. He must be aware that if the receiver makes a hard outside move, he is likely to come back and run an inside route. On the other hand, if the receiver makes a hard inside move, he is likely to run an outside route.
- Trails the receiver's back hip if the receiver releases outside, keeping his outside hand on the receiver's inside hip. The defender should pressure the receiver's hip and push it farther away from the quarterback.
- Trails the receiver's inside hip, which enables him to stay between the quarterback and the receiver. It also prevents the receiver from getting back inside. In the event that the receiver attempts to work back inside, the defender is in an excellent position jam him with his inside hand.
- Does not peek back at the quarterback; he finds the ball when the receiver looks for it.

Outside Bump Technique

An outside bump technique is only used when the defender is attempting to funnel the receiver inside and is insured of inside help. A cornerback aligned into the boundary, Joker and Rover are normally the only players who will use this as a man-to-man technique. The outside bump technique has similar advantages to the inside bump technique. As a general rule, the outside bump technique should only be used in passing situations, because if the free safety were to bite on a play-action pass, the bump defender would be confronted with the dilemma of defending the entire middle of the field from an outside leverage position. When employing this technique, the defender will do as follows:

- Lines up with his nose on the outside shoulder of the receiver.
- Keeps his outside foot up and tilts his butt slightly toward the sideline.
- Lines up two yards deep (however, this technique may vary from an alignment that crowds the line of scrimmage to one that is five yards deep).
- Positions his hands at his midsection in a ready position to jam the receiver.
- Focuses his eyes on the midsection of the receiver.
- Jams all inside releases with his outside arm and forces the receiver into the free safety.
- Shuffles his feet parallel to the line of scrimmage as he jams the receiver.
- Denies the receiver outside releases.
- Pushes the receiver as far inside as he can and does not allow any separation after the initial bump.

Linebackers Assigned to Cover a Running Back Man-to-Man

Covering a defensive back man-to-man is an extremely difficult assignment for any linebacker because of the running back's obvious speed advantage. A linebacker should only be assigned to cover a running back when he is provided with help from another defender and/or a defensive scheme that puts extreme pressure on the quarterback is being employed. When given this assignment, the linebacker must follow all of the sound coverage principles that have already been mentioned. Additionally, he should do the following:

- Closes the gap between himself and the running back when the back runs a pattern behind the line of scrimmage. It is important for the linebacker to reduce as much space between himself and the running back as possible. Allowing the running back to operate in space usually ends up being a major disadvantage for the defender.
- Jams and walls off all vertical and crossing routes. Maintains a position between the quarterback and the receiver.
- Jumps all out routes from an inside-out position and attempts to rip through the receiver's catch hand.
- Continues coverage on the running back that initially blocks. The back may end up running a screen or delayed route.
- Tries to penetrate the wall as a screen pass begins to develop. Once the wall is formed, the defender is at a big disadvantage.

Techniques of a Single Free Safety

Stance and Alignment

- Lines up 8 to 18 yards deep (depending upon down-and-distance and offensive tendency).
- Lines up directly in front of the center when the ball is in the middle of the field.
- Lines up on the outside shoulder of the offensive tackle (toward the wideside of the field) in a passing situation when the ball is on the hash or when the offense splits two or more receivers toward one side of the field.
- Assumes a parallel stance (a slight stagger is permissible if the defender feels more comfortable in this position).
- Distributes his weight on the balls of his feet with his heels slightly raised off the ground.
- Bends his knees slightly and lowers his hips.
- Bends his waist slightly, which causes his back to appear slightly rounded.
- Relaxes his hands and arms and allows them to hang loosely.
- Keys the ball through an uncovered lineman.

Techniques and Responsibilities vs. the Pass

The defender's first three steps are extremely important because they will enable him to read the play and to begin moving toward the best possible position to make a great play. He must keep his eyes on all of the receivers being funneled inside because it is his responsibility to provide deep help in covering these receivers. As he reads pass, the free safety will do the following:

- Sprints to a position that places him inside of the receivers who are being funneled into him.
- Continues to gain depth by backpedaling or sprinting until the quarterback has finished setting up.
- Stays deeper than any of the receivers who are being funneled into him.

Techniques and Responsibilities vs. the Run

The free safety is responsible for providing alley support to all running plays. When providing alley support, the defender will do the following:

- Goes directly to the ball inside of the primary force player.
- Approaches the ballcarrier from an inside-out position and expects that the ballcarrier will cut back.
- Protects his legs and prevents blockers from getting into his body. The defender should try to avoid blockers if at all possible (without taking himself out of the play). When avoiding blockers becomes impossible, he should become the hammer, not the nail, and punish the blocker.
- Reacts to crack blocks. The defender assigned to cover a receiver who is crack blocking gives the free safety a "crack-crack" call. The free safety then attacks and/or covers the cracking receiver, and the other defender replaces the free safety and supports the run.

Sky, Cloud, and Star Calls

The single free safety should alert any defender that he is able to assist in pass coverage with help over the top. If he is able to assist the boundary corner, he alerts this defender with a "cloud" call. He alerts Joker or Rover with a "sky" call when he is able to assist either defender. When he is able to assist two defenders (the boundary corner and either Joker or Rover), he alerts both defenders with a "star" call. The free safety can almost always assist one or two defenders with help over the top when the ball is on one of the hash marks, because approximately 80 percent of the plays in high school and college football originate from the hash. The following guidelines can assist the free safety to understand when it is mathematically possible for him to give help over the top:

- The free safety can assist a defender with any deep route if his depth equals the depth of the receiver's split. In other words, if the free safety is aligned in front of the center, he must be 15 yards deep if the receiver is 15 yards from the center.
- The free safety doesn't have to be as deep to assist a defender with inside routes, such as the post or curl, but he won't be able to assist on deep outside routes, such as the flag or fade.
- A bump technique by the primary cover defender usually enables the free safety to shorten his depth by as much as five yards.
- When assisting two defenders, it is advantageous for the free safety to split the distance between the two defenders.

Techniques and Responsibilities of Dual Free Safeties

When man coverage is employed, the two free safeties are each responsible for defending one half of the field. Both safeties will line up 12 yards deep with their inside foot back. Although their alignment will vary depending upon the offensive formation and the position of the ball on the field, a general rule for each safety is to line up on the hash mark when playing on a high school field and slightly outside of the hash mark when playing on a college field. As the ball is snapped, each safety will take a three-step read shuffle. Versus run, the playside safety will provide primary run support, and the backside safety will provide alley support. Versus pass, with two receivers positioned toward his side of the formation, each safety must do the following:

- Gains depth; he must cover half of the field and keep all receivers in front of himself.
- Reads the release of the #1 and #2 receivers to his side of the field. He will work toward and maintain an adequate cushion on the deepest receiver.
- If both receivers go deep, the safety moves outside of #2 so that he will be able to break to #1. Gaining depth is vital. The defender should favor the shortest throw for the quarterback, but stay deep enough to react to both receivers.
- If #2 releases into the flats, the defender gains width and depth and puts himself in a position to react to the route being run by #1.
- If #2 releases inside, the defender gains width and looks first to #1 and then to a deep crossing route.
- Versus a trips or quads formation, the safety must take into consideration the release of the extra receiver(s). Versus these formations, the safety aligned toward the strength of the formation will widen slightly, and the safety away from strength will cheat slightly toward strength so that he may assist his counterpart if necessary.

CHAPTER 13
Man-to-Man Pass Coverages

This chapter will present the most common man-to-man pass coverages that can be implemented from both three-deep and four-deep shells. A three-deep shell is used in conjunction with an eight-man defensive front, and a four-deep shell is used in conjunction with a seven-man front. The symbols for an even defense will be used for both seven- and eight-man defensive fronts in the presentation of these coverages.

Three-Deep Man-to-Man Pass Coverages

Cover 1

Cover 1 is probably the most commonly used man-to-man pass coverage from a three-deep shell. Its major advantage is that it provides the defense with an extra defender (the free safety) to deliver alley support versus the run and act as backup versus the pass. It also enables the defense to employ a five-man pass rush, or to rush four and drop a fifth defender into the intermediary middle to rob crossing routes (robber coverage). Diagrams 13-1A through 13-1J illustrate cover 1 versus 10 of the most commonly used contemporary personnel groupings. Coaching points for each are as follows:

- Versus 21 personnel (Diagram 13-1A), any one of the three undesignated linebackers (Sam, Will or Rover) can be used to blitz or to drop into the middle and rob crossing routes.
- Versus 20 personnel (Diagram 13-1B), any one of the three undesignated linebackers (Sam, Will, or Rover) can be used to blitz or to drop into the middle and rob crossing routes.
- Versus 21 twin personnel (Diagram 13-1C), the corner over alignment enables Joker to remain in the box and cover the tight end, and assigns coverage responsibilities of the two wide receivers to the best two cover players. Any one of the three undesignated linebackers (Sam, Will, or Rover) can be used to blitz or to drop into the middle and rob crossing routes.
- Versus 11 doubles personnel (Diagram 13-1D), either Sam or Will is assigned to cover the aceback, and the remaining linebacker can be used to blitz or to drop into the middle and rob crossing routes.
- Versus 12 doubles personnel (Diagram 13-1E), either Sam or Will is assigned to cover the aceback, and the remaining linebacker can be used to blitz or to drop into the middle and rob crossing routes.

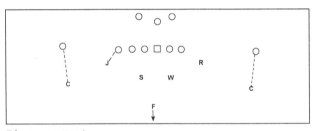

Diagram 13-1A

Diagram 13-1B

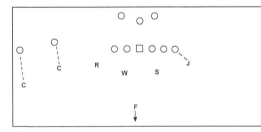

Diagram 13-1C

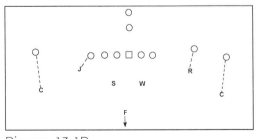

Diagram 13-1D

Diagram 13-1E

- Versus 10 doubles personnel (Diagram 13-1F), either Sam or Will is assigned to cover the aceback, and the remaining linebacker can be used to blitz or to drop into the middle and rob crossing routes.
- Versus 11 trips personnel (Diagram 13-1G), either Sam or Will is assigned to cover the aceback, and the remaining linebacker can be used to blitz or to drop into the middle and rob crossing routes.
- Versus 12 trips personnel (Diagram 13-1H), the corner over alignment enables Joker to remain in the box and cover the tight end, and assigns coverage responsibilities of the two wide receivers to the best two cover players. Either Sam or Will is assigned to cover the aceback, and the remaining linebacker can be used to blitz or to drop into the middle and rob crossing routes.
- Versus 10 trips personnel (Diagram 13-1I), either Sam or Will is assigned to cover the aceback, and the remaining linebacker can be used to blitz or to drop into the middle and rob crossing routes.
- Versus 30 personnel (Diagram 13-1J), three of the four linebackers aligned in the box (Joker, Sam, Will, or Rover) will be assigned to cover the three running backs, and the extra linebacker can be used to blitz or to drop into the middle and rob crossing routes.

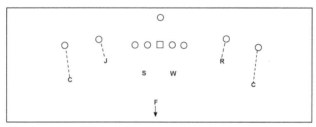

Diagram 13-1F

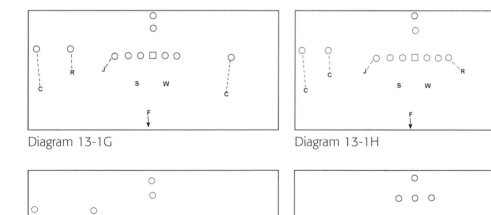

Diagram 13-1G

Diagram 13-1H

Diagram 13-1I

Diagram 13-1J

Zero Coverage

Zero coverage enables the defense to rush six defenders. Its major disadvantage is that no free safety is available to provide alley support versus run or to back up the defenders assigned coverage versus pass. An additional disadvantage is that it is not always possible for the free safety to disguise his coverage assignment versus all formations. Diagrams 13-2A through 13-2J illustrates zero coverage versus 10 of the most commonly used contemporary personnel groupings. Coaching points for each are as follows:

- Versus 21 personnel (Diagram 13-2A), two of the four undesignated linebackers in the box (Joker, Sam, Will, and Rover) must be assigned to cover the two running backs, and the remaining two linebackers are free to blitz. It is easy for the free safety to disguise his coverage of the tight end versus this formation.
- Versus 20 personnel (Diagram 13-2B), two of the four undesignated linebackers in the box (Joker, Sam, Will, and Rover) must be assigned to cover the two running backs, and the remaining two linebackers are free to blitz. It is impossible for the free safety to disguise his coverage of the tight end versus this formation.
- Versus 21 twin personnel (Diagram 13-2C), two of the four undesignated linebackers in the box (Joker, Sam, Will, and Rover) must be assigned to cover the two running backs, and the remaining two linebackers are free to blitz. The corner over alignment places the two best cover players on the two wide receivers and makes it easy for the free safety to disguise his coverage of the tight end versus this formation.
- Versus 11 doubles personnel (Diagram 13-2D), two of the three linebackers aligned in the box (Joker, Sam, and Will) are free to blitz, but one of them must be assigned to cover the aceback. It is easy for the free safety to disguise his coverage of the tight end versus this formation.

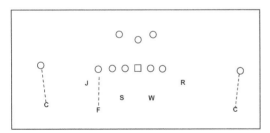

Diagram 13-2A

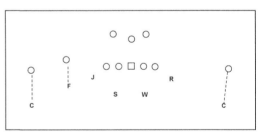

Diagram 13-2B

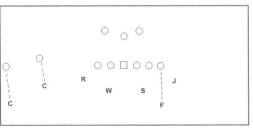

Diagram 13-2C

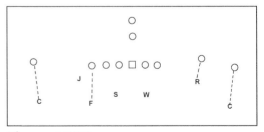

Diagram 13-2D

- Versus 12 doubles personnel (Diagram 13-2E), two of the three linebackers aligned in the box (Joker, Sam, and Will) are free to blitz, but one of them must be assigned to cover the aceback. It is easy for the free safety to disguise his coverage of the tight end versus this formation.
- Versus 10 doubles personnel (Diagram 13-2F), two of the three linebackers aligned in the box (Joker, Sam, and Will) are free to blitz, but one of them must be assigned to cover the aceback. It is impossible for the free safety to disguise his coverage of the tight end versus this formation.
- Versus 11 trips personnel (Diagram 13-2G), two of the three linebackers aligned in the box (Joker, Sam, and Will) are free to blitz, but one of them must be assigned to cover the aceback. It is easy for the free safety to disguise his coverage of the tight end versus this formation.
- Versus 12 trips personnel (Diagram 13-2H), two of the three linebackers aligned in the box (Joker, Sam, and Will) are free to blitz, but one of them must be assigned to cover the aceback. It is easy for the free safety to disguise his coverage of the tight end versus this formation.
- Versus 10 trips personnel (Diagram 13-2I), two of the three linebackers aligned in the box (Joker, Sam, and Will) are free to blitz, but one of them must be assigned to cover the aceback. It is impossible for the free safety to disguise his coverage of the tight end versus this formation.

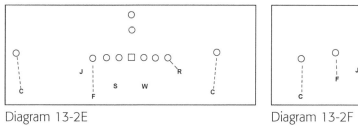

Diagram 13-2E

Diagram 13-2F

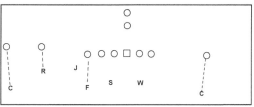

Diagram 13-2G

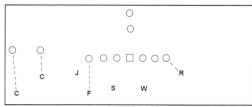

Diagram 13-2H

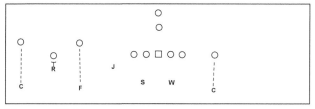

Diagram 13-2I

- Versus 30 personnel (Diagram 13-2J), two of the four linebackers aligned in the box (Joker, Sam, Will, and Rover) are free to blitz, and two of them must be assigned to cover the two remaining running backs. It is very easy for the free safety to disguise his pass coverage assignment versus this formation.

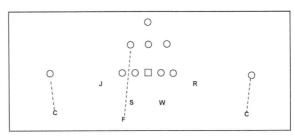

Diagram 13-2J

Cover 5

Cover 5 is a variation of zero coverage that assigns the free safety to cover the strongside running back versus two-back formations and the aceback versus single-back formations. Akin to zero coverage, cover 5 enables the defense to rush six defenders. It also enables the free safety to always disguise his coverage responsibility. Furthermore, the free safety's alignment enables him to provide run support, which he was unable to do in zero coverage. Versus every personnel grouping, Sam is assigned to blitz. Versus 20 and both 21 personnel groupings, either Will or Rover must cover the weakside running back, and the other is free to blitz. Versus 30 personnel both Sam and Joker are free to blitz, and Will and Rover will be assigned coverage of two remaining running backs. Versus all other aceback personnel groupings, both Sam and Will are free to blitz. Diagrams 13-3A through 13-3J illustrate the assignments for cover 5.

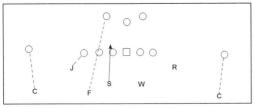

Diagram 13-3A

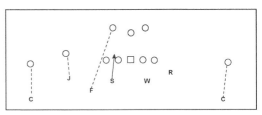

Diagram 13-3B

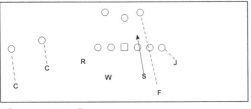

Diagram 13-3C

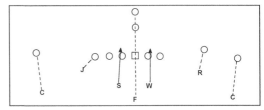

Diagram 13-3D

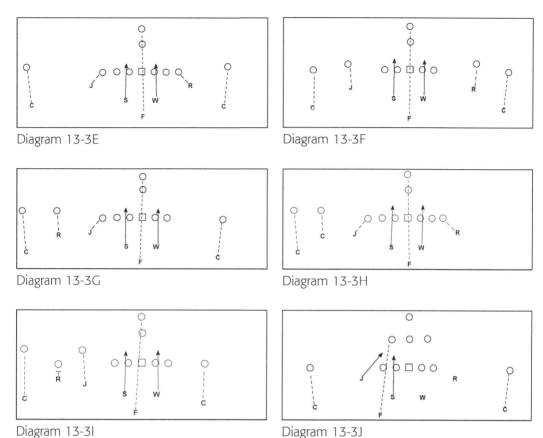

Diagram 13-3E
Diagram 13-3F
Diagram 13-3G
Diagram 13-3H
Diagram 13-3I
Diagram 13-3J

Four-Deep Man-to-Man Pass Coverages

Cover 1

Versus most offensive formations, coverage disguises are usually more subtle with a four-deep secondary than they are with three-deep secondary. When employing cover 1 from a four-deep secondary, dollar will cover the #2 receiver toward the strength of the formation, and the free safety will drop to the middle versus pass. The free safety will serve as the primary force player versus runs toward himself and the alley support player versus runs away from himself. Joker will provide primary run support against runs toward himself versus all formations except the three trips formations. Versus trips formations, Rover will provide primary run support against running plays directed at himself. Diagrams 13-4A through 13-4J illustrate cover 1 versus 10 of the most commonly used contemporary personnel groupings. Coaching points for each are as follows:

- Versus 21 personnel (Diagram 13-4A), Joker will blitz from the edge and serve as the primary run support player versus runs toward himself. Mike and Rover must be assigned coverage the two running backs.

- Versus 20 personnel (Diagram 13-4B), Joker will blitz from the edge and serve as the primary run support player versus runs toward himself. Mike and Rover must be assigned coverage the two running backs.
- Versus 21 twin personnel (Diagram 13-4C), Joker will blitz from the edge and serve as the primary run support player versus runs toward himself. Mike and Rover must be assigned coverage the two running backs.
- Versus 11 doubles personnel (Diagram 13-4D), Joker will blitz from the edge and serve as the primary run support player versus runs toward himself. Mike must be assigned coverage the aceback.
- Versus 12 doubles personnel (Diagram 13-4E), Joker will blitz from the edge and serve as the primary run support player versus runs toward himself. Mike must be assigned coverage the aceback.
- Versus 10 doubles personnel (Diagram 13-4F), Joker will blitz from the edge and serve as the primary run support player versus runs toward himself. Mike must be assigned coverage the aceback.

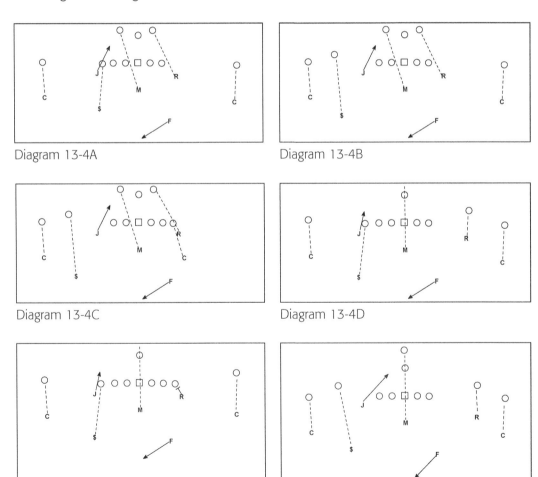

Diagram 13-4A

Diagram 13-4B

Diagram 13-4C

Diagram 13-4D

Diagram 13-4E

Diagram 13-4F

- Versus 11 trips personnel (Diagram 13-4G), Rover will blitz from the edge and serve as the primary run support player versus runs toward himself. Mike must be assigned coverage the aceback.
- Versus 12 trips personnel (Diagram 13-4H), Rover will blitz from the edge and serve as the primary run support player versus runs toward himself. Mike must be assigned coverage the aceback. *Note:* Versus this formation, some coaches may prefer to have the right corner cover the #2 receiver toward strength, have dollar cover the #3 receiver toward strength, blitz Joker from the edge, and have Rover cover #1 away from strength. Obviously, this variation would deviate from the basic coverage rules and necessitate considerable practice repetitions.
- Versus 10 trips personnel (Diagram 13-4I), Rover will blitz from the edge and serve as the primary run support player versus runs toward himself. Mike must be assigned coverage the aceback.
- Versus 30 personnel (Diagram 13-4J), dollar will cover the running back toward the designated strength of the formation. Joker will blitz from the edge and serve as the primary run support player versus runs toward himself. Mike and Rover must be assigned coverage of the remaining two remaining running backs.

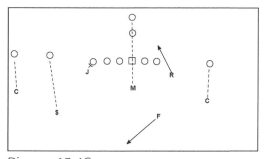

Diagram 13-4G

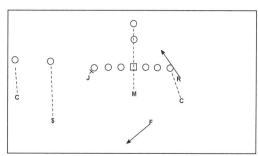

Diagram 13-4H

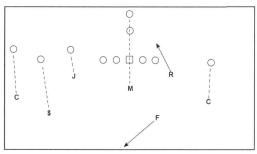

Diagram 13-4I

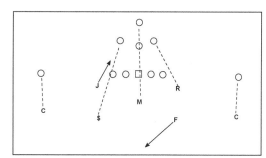

Diagram 13-4J

Zero Coverage

Zero coverage assigns both dollar and the free safety a coverage responsibility. This coverage enables the defense to rush six defenders. Its major disadvantage is that the secondary is unable to provide either alley or primary run support. Unlike zero coverage from a three-deep secondary, zero coverage from a four-deep secondary makes it easier for dollar and the free safety to disguise their coverage assignments. Diagrams 13-5A through 13-5J illustrate zero coverage versus 10 of the most commonly used contemporary personnel groupings. Coaching points for each are as follows:

- Versus 21 personnel (Diagram 13-5A), one of the three linebackers in the box (Joker, Mike, and Rover) must cover the running back not covered by the free safety. The remaining two linebackers are free to blitz.
- Versus 20 personnel (Diagram 13-5B), one of the three linebackers in the box (Joker, Mike, and Rover) must cover the running back not covered by the free safety. The remaining two linebackers are free to blitz.
- Versus 21 twin personnel (Diagram 13-5C), one of the three linebackers in the box (Joker, Mike, and Rover) must cover the running back not covered by the free safety. The remaining two linebackers are free to blitz.
- Versus 11 doubles personnel (Diagram 13-5D), one of the three linebackers in the box (Joker, Mike, and Rover) must cover the aceback. The remaining two linebackers are free to blitz.

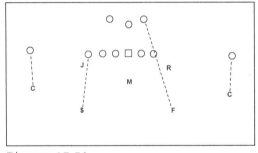

Diagram 13-5A

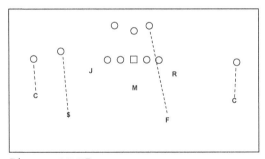

Diagram 13-5B

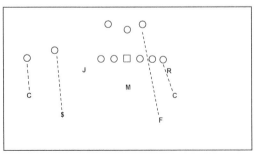

Diagram 13-5C

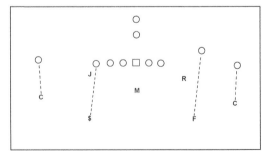

Diagram 13-5D

- Versus 12 doubles personnel (Diagram 13-5E), one of the three linebackers in the box (Joker, Mike, and Rover) must cover the aceback. The remaining two linebackers are free to blitz.
- Versus 10 doubles personnel (Diagram 13-5F), one of the three linebackers in the box (Joker, Mike, and Rover) must cover the aceback. The remaining two linebackers are free to blitz.
- Versus 11 trips personnel (Diagram 13-5G), one of the three linebackers in the box (Joker, Mike, and Rover) must cover the aceback. The remaining two linebackers are free to blitz.
- Versus 12 trips personnel (Diagram 13-5H), one of the three linebackers in the box (Joker, Mike, and Rover) must cover the aceback. The remaining two linebackers are free to blitz.
- Versus 10 trips personnel (Diagram 13-5I), the free safety is unable to disguise his coverage assignment versus this formation. One of the three linebackers in the box (Joker, Mike, and Rover) must cover the aceback. The remaining two linebackers are free to blitz.

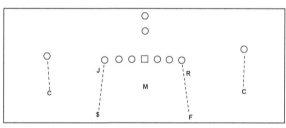
Diagram 13-5E

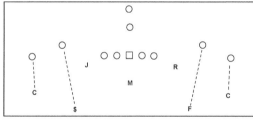
Diagram 13-5F

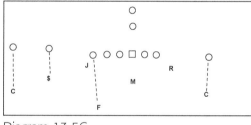
Diagram 13-5G

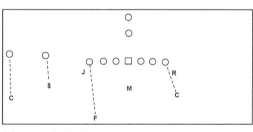
Diagram 13-5H

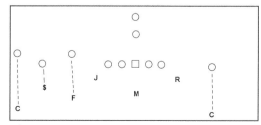
Diagram 13-5I

- Versus 30 personnel (Diagram 13-5J), one of the three linebackers in the box (Joker, Mike, and Rover) must cover the running back not covered by dollar or the free safety. The remaining two linebackers are free to blitz.

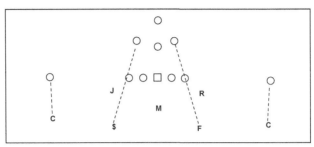

Diagram 13-5J

Cover 6

Cover 6 is a variation of cover 1. Versus all formations except trips, cover 6 gives the free safety a coverage assignment and assigns dollar to drop to deep middle versus pass. Versus trips, dollar is given a coverage assignment, and the free safety drops to the deep middle versus pass. With cover 6, dollar will serve as the primary force player versus runs toward himself and the alley support player versus runs away from himself. Rover will provide primary run support versus runs toward himself. Versus trips, cover 6 will revert back to cover 1 assignments. Diagrams 13-6A through 13-6J illustrates cover 6 assignments versus 10 personnel groupings. Coaching points for each are as follows:

- Versus 21 personnel (Diagram 13-6A), Rover blitzes from the edge and provides primary run support versus running plays toward himself. Joker covers #2 strong, Mike covers #3 strong, and the free safety covers #2 weak.
- Versus 20 personnel (Diagram 13-6B), Rover blitzes from the edge and provides primary run support versus running plays toward himself. Joker covers #2 strong, Mike covers #3 strong, and the free safety covers #2 weak.

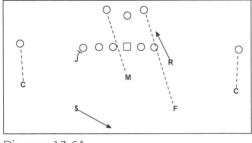

Diagram 13-6A

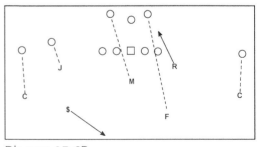

Diagram 13-6B

- Versus 21 twin personnel (Diagram 13-6C), Rover blitzes from the edge and provides primary run support versus running plays toward himself. Joker covers #2 strong, Mike covers #3 strong, and the free safety covers #2 weak.
- Versus 11 doubles personnel (Diagram 13-6D), Rover blitzes from the edge and provides primary run support versus running plays toward himself. Mike is assigned to cover the aceback.
- Versus 12 doubles personnel (Diagram 13-6E), Rover blitzes from the edge and provides primary run support versus running plays toward himself. Mike is assigned to cover the aceback.
- Versus 10 doubles personnel (Diagram 13-6F), Rover blitzes from the edge and provides primary run support versus running plays toward himself. Mike is assigned to cover the aceback.
- Versus 11 trips personnel (Diagram 13-6G), coverage checks to cover 1. Rover blitzes from the edge and provides primary run support versus running plays toward himself. Mike is assigned to cover the aceback.

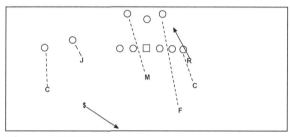

Diagram 13-6C

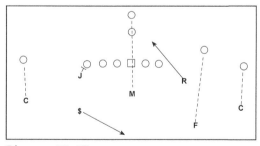

Diagram 13-6D

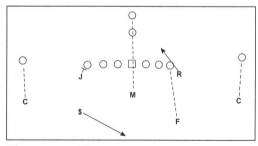

Diagram 13-6E

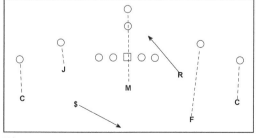

Diagram 13-6F

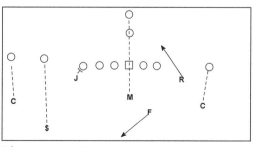

Diagram 13-6G

- Versus 12 trips personnel (Diagram 13-6H), coverage checks to cover 1. Rover blitzes from the edge and provides primary run support versus running plays toward himself. Mike is assigned to cover the aceback.
- Versus 10 trips personnel (Diagram 13-6I), coverage checks to cover 1. Rover blitzes from the edge and provides primary run support versus running plays toward himself. Mike is assigned to cover the aceback.
- Versus 30 personnel (Diagram 13-6J), Rover blitzes from the edge and provides primary run support versus running plays toward himself. Mike and Joker are assigned to cover the remaining two running backs.

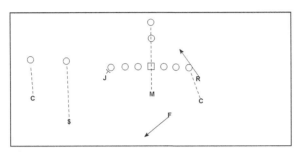

Diagram 13-6H

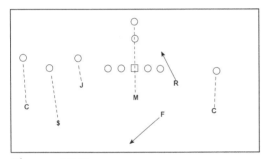

Diagram 13-6I

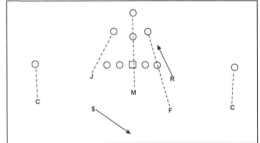

Diagram 13-6J

Cover 2 Man

Cover 2 man provides the defense with a four-man pass rush. Both the free safety and dollar will cover one half of the field each versus pass. Versus run, they will serve as the primary force player versus running plays toward themselves and alley support versus runs away from themselves. The advantage of the coverage is that it enables defenders assigned to cover wide receivers the freedom to employ jam techniques and disrupt the timing of pass routes. The assignments, which are very specific for this coverage, are illustrated in Diagrams 13-7A through 13-7J.

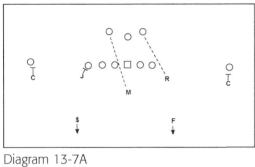
Diagram 13-7A

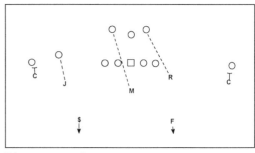
Diagram 13-7B

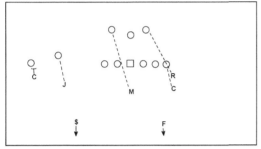
Diagram 13-7C

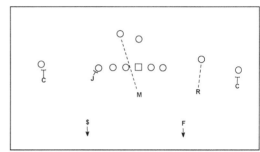
Diagram 13-7D

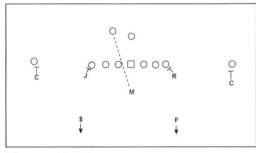
Diagram 13-7E

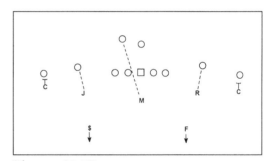
Diagram 13-7F

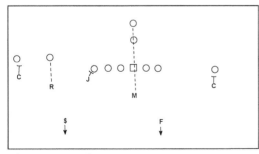
Diagram 13-7G

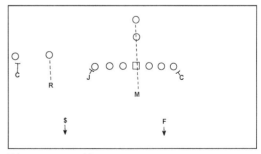
Diagram 13-7H

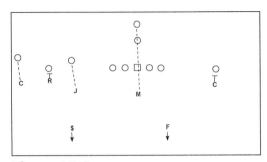 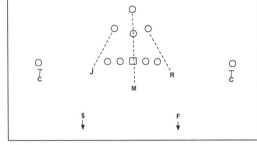

Diagram 13-7I　　　　　　　　　　Diagram 13-7J

CHAPTER 14
Zone and Combo Coverage Techniques and Assignments

Fire Zone Blitz Coverage

This coverage is a variation of cover 1 because it employs a free safety. Versus 20, 21, and 22 personnel, two receivers are covered man-to-man while the remaining three receivers are combo covered by defenders dropping into three zones, which are referred to in this text as Abel, Baker, and Charlie. Versus 10, 11, and 12 personnel, three receivers are covered man-to-man and the remaining two receivers are combo covered by defenders that drop into the Abel and Baker zones. The distinctive feature of this coverage is that linebackers are often assigned to blitz and defensive linemen are assigned to drop into some or all of the three zones. The advantage of this coverage is that it forces the offense to devise pass protection schemes that account for all of the defenders aligned in the box. The first things that need to be addressed when discussing this coverage are how receivers are numbered, how strength is designated, and the location of each zone. Diagrams 14-1A through 14-1I illustrate this system versus nine different personnel groupings. Also illustrated in these diagrams is the 3-3-5 defense and how it adjusts versus each personal grouping.

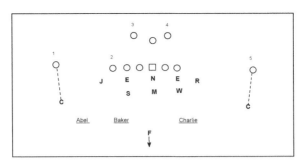

Diagram 14-1A

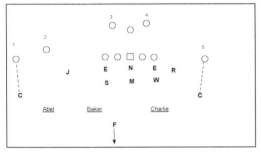

Diagram 14-1B

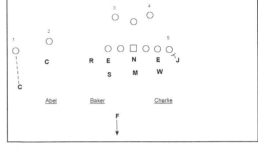

Diagram 14-1C

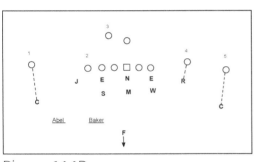

Diagram 14-1D

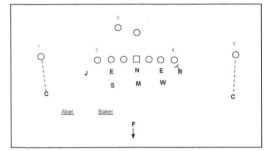

Diagram 14-1E

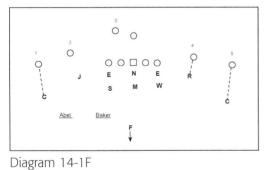

Diagram 14-1F

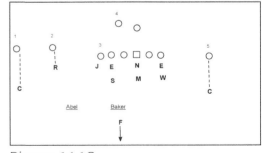

Diagram 14-1G

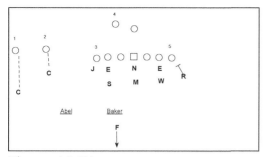
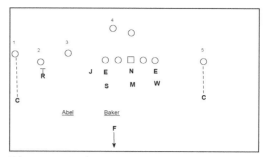

Diagram 14-1H   Diagram 14-1I

In all nine diagrams, the strength of the formation is toward the left of the defense because that is where the majority of the eligible pass receivers are located. After the strength of the formation is determined, defenders will simply number the five eligible receivers in the order in which they appear in the formation.

The next order of business is to discuss the specific responsibilities and techniques required of a defender dropping into each zone.

Assignments and Techniques for Abel's Drop

- Drops to a position that will enable him to attain outside leverage on #2.
- Keys #2 to #3.
- If #2 runs a quick out (six yards or less), immediately jumps his pattern, and establishes a three-yard cushion.
- If #2 runs a vertical route and #3 runs an out pattern of six yards or less, the defender gains depth and squeezes #2 inside. He should not be in a big hurry to jump #3's out pattern because #2 may turn his vertical route into a deep out. The defender relinquishes his cushion on #2 and tries to work to a depth of 8 to 10 yards. As #3 starts to cross his face, the defender begins to widen and establish a loose cushion on #3, but tries to stay in the throwing lane between the quarterback and #2 for as long as possible. Baker will help Abel by alerting him with an "out-out" call in the event that #2 does turn his vertical route into a deep out.
- If #2 runs a vertical route and #3 either blocks or runs a short inside route, Abel will lock on to #2, squeeze him inside, maintain outside leverage, and force him to run a collision course.
- If #2 runs a quick crossing pattern, the defender keys #3 to #4.

Assignments and Techniques for Baker's Drop

- Drops to a position that will enable him to establish inside leverage on #2, but keeps #3 in his periphery.
- Keys #2 to #3.

- If #2 runs a vertical route, the defender will gain depth and cover him from an inside-out position, keeping #3 in his periphery. If #3 blocks or runs a short out pattern, Baker will lock on to #2. If #3 runs a short in pattern, he will release his coverage of #2 and lock on to #3.
- If #2 runs a quick crossing pattern (six yards or less), Baker will immediately call "in-in," jam #2, wall him off, and force him to deepen his pattern. Baker will then lock on to #2 unless Charlie echoes Baker's "in-in" call. If Charlie echoes the call, it is because #2 and #4 are crossing. Versus a cross by #2 and #4, Baker will release his coverage of #2, gain depth, and lock on to #4.
- If #2 runs a quick out pattern, Baker will immediately redirect his attention to #3 and cover him. If #3 and #4 try to run short crossing patterns, Baker will follow the same rules he did when #2 and #4 ran short crossing patterns.

Assignments and Techniques for Charlie's Drop

- Opens up and drops to a position that will enable him to cover #4 from an inside-out position.
- Keys #4, but stays alert for an "in-in" call from Baker.
- If #4 runs a quick crossing pattern (six yards or less), Charlie will immediately jam #4, wall him off, and force him to deepen his pattern. He will lock on to #4 unless Baker has given him an "in-in" call (Baker will be the first one to give the call because #2 is aligned on the line of scrimmage, and #4 is in the backfield). If Baker calls "in-in," Charlie will echo his call, release his coverage of #4, gain depth, and lock on to #2 or #3.
- Charlie will cover #4 on all other routes.

Next the function of this coverage versus the each personnel groupings will be discussed:

- Versus 21 personnel (Diagram 14-1A), Joker will drop Abel because he is in the best position to squeeze #2 inside. Any two of the remaining seven defenders in the box will drop Baker and Charlie. The other five will blitz according to the designated scheme.
- Versus 20 personnel (Diagram 14-1B), Joker will drop Abel because he is in the best position to squeeze #2 inside. Any two of the remaining seven defenders in the box will drop Baker and Charlie. The other five will blitz according to the designated scheme.
- Versus 21 twin personnel (Diagram 14-1C), the cornerback will drop Abel because he is in the best position to squeeze #2 inside. Joker will cover #5 man-to-man. Any two of the remaining seven defenders in the box will drop Baker and Charlie. The other five will blitz according to the designated scheme.

- Versus 11 doubles personnel (Diagram 14-1D), Joker will drop Abel because he is in the best position to squeeze #2 inside. Any of the six defenders remaining in the box will drop Baker. Because #4 is detached from the formation, it is much simpler to have Rover cover this receiver man-to-man than it is to complicate coverage by creating a large space between Baker and Charlie.
- Versus 12 doubles personnel (Diagram 14-1E), Joker will drop Abel because he is in the best position to squeeze #2 inside. Any two of the remaining seven defenders in the box will drop Baker and Charlie. The other five will blitz according to the designated scheme.
- Versus 10 doubles personnel (Diagram 14-1F), Joker will drop Abel because he is in the best position to squeeze #2 inside. Any of the six defenders remaining in the box will drop Baker. Because #4 is detached from the formation, it is much simpler to have Rover cover this receiver man-to-man that it is to complicate coverage by creating a large space between Baker and Charlie.
- Versus 11 trips personnel (Diagram 14-1G), the simplest way to cover this formation is to have Rover cover #2 man-to-man, have Joker drop Abel, and assign one of the remaining six defenders aligned in the box to drop Baker. This approach enables the Abel/Baker drop defenders to combo cover the #3 and #4 receivers.
- Versus 12 trips personnel (Diagram 14-1H), the simplest way to cover this formation is to have the cornerback cover #2 man-to-man, have Rover cover #5 man-to-man, have Joker drop Abel, and assign one of the remaining six defenders aligned in the box to drop Baker. This approach enables the Abel/Baker drop defenders to combo cover the #3 and #4 receivers.
- Versus 10 trips personnel (Diagram 14-1I), the simplest way to cover this formation is to have Rover cover #2 man-to-man, have Joker drop Abel, and assign one of the remaining six defenders aligned in the box to drop Baker. This approach enables the Abel/Baker drop defenders to combo cover the #3 and #4 receivers.

Cover 3

Cover 3 is a three-deep, four-underneath zone coverage. It is one the most common coverages of both three- and four-deep secondaries. Like all coverages, it has its strengths and weaknesses.

Weaknesses of Cover 3 Zone

- Horizontal seams exist between each zone.
- Each zone can be high-lowed (vertically stretched) by putting one receiver at the bottom of the zone and another one at the top.
- Linebackers can be prevented from dropping to their assigned zone or momentarily frozen with run-action fakes.

- Cover 3 features a four-man pass rush, which is usually predictable, and frequently does not exert enough pressure on the quarterback.
- Most variations of cover 3 do not collision pass routes and disrupt the timing between the quarterback and his receivers.
- It is often easier for offensive coaches to create mismatches by motioning a receiver from one zone into another zone that is being guarded by a less skillful defender.

Strengths of Cover 3

- Because defensive backs are keying the quarterback (along with the receivers), they can break on the quarterback's throw, which often results in more interceptions.
- Defensive backs are seldom isolated on an island. Another defender is usually providing help.
- The defense is less likely to give up the big play while in a zone coverage.
- It is much more difficult for the offense to create rubs (a legal version of the old pick play).
- If the quarterback is accustomed to seeing mostly man coverage, it may surprise him; furthermore, it may disrupt his play calling.

Zone Drop Pattern Reads

It is important to not only have a defender drop to a spot on the field, but also to give him specific keys so that he can read and react to not only the quarterback, but also to his specific keys. The following pattern-read guidelines (versus a standard pro formation) will assist defenders who are dropping into one of the cover 3 zones.

Strong Hook-Curl Drop

The defender drops to a depth of 12 to 15 yards into the strong hook zone. He keys #2 (the tight end). If #2 runs a vertical route, he stays in the hook and collisions #2. If #2 releases into the flats, the defender sprints to the curl and looks for #1 (the flanker) to run a curl or a post. If #2 runs inside and across his face, the defender tries to collision #2, and then looks for another receiver to run a crossing route into his zone.

Weak Hook-Curl Drop

The defender opens up and drops to a depth of 12 to 15 yards into the weak hook zone. He keys #2 (the weakside halfback). If #2 runs a vertical route, the defender stays in the hook and collisions #2. If #2 releases into the flats, the defender sprints to the curl and looks for #1 (the split end) to run a curl or a post. If #2 runs inside and across his face, the defender tries to collision #2 and then looks for another receiver to run a crossing route into his zone.

Strong Curl-Out Drop

The defender opens up and drops to a depth of 10 to 12 yards. His aiming point is three yards inside of where #1 (the flanker) lined up. He keys #1. If #1 runs an out, the defender tries to get into the throwing lane and get a piece of the ball. If #1 runs a curl or a post, the defender stays inside of #1's pattern and checks #2 (the tight end). If #2 runs an out, the defender must release from #1's curl or post when #2 crosses his face. If #1 runs a vertical route, the defender sinks and checks #2 and #3.

Weak Curl-Out Drop

The defender opens up and drops to a depth of 10 to 12 yards. His aiming point is three yards inside of where #1 (the split end) lined up. He keys #1. If #1 runs an out, the defender tries to get into the throwing lane and get a piece of the ball. If #1 runs a curl or a post, the defender stays inside of his pattern and checks #2 (the weakside halfback). If #2 runs an out, the defender must release from #1's curl or post when #2 crosses his face. If #1 runs a vertical route, the defender sinks and checks #2.

Deep Outside-Third Drop

The defenders covering these two areas must see both #1 and #2 as they backpedal. They must be deeper than any receiver in their zone. If #1 runs a short or intermediate route, the defender looks for #2 to run a deep pattern in his zone. He must communicate with the underneath defenders on the type of route #1 is running. For example, if #1 runs an out, the deep-third defender should be yelling "Out, out" to the underneath defender and then looking back at #2 to threaten him deep. If #2 runs a short or intermediate route, the deep-third defender must control the speed of his backpedal in order to break on the ball. If #1 runs a vertical route, the defender maintains a cushion of three to four yards. If #1 runs a post, the defender stays on the receiver's outside hip and maintains a sufficient cushion.

Deep Middle-Third Drop

The defender responsible for this area (Rover or the free safety) must never allow any receiver in his zone to beat him deep. He must be ready to break on any routes in his zone. He will key #2's release. If it is vertical, the defender must be in a position to cover it. If #2 goes flat, the free safety looks for #1 on either side to run a post. It is vital that the free safety communicates with the underneath defenders.

Most coaches prefer to have their defenders pattern read by keying receivers and adjusting their drops as they drop into their zones, but some coaches prefer to have their defenders spot drop (drop to a specific area of the field and read the quarterback). Having experienced both the pattern read and spot drop systems for more than 45 years, it is the opinion of this author that the pattern read system is superior, and that's why it was presented in this section. It should be noted, however, that the pattern read system has one flaw: five eligible pass receivers are in every offensive formation. By having four defenders drop into the four-underneath zones and key a specific receiver, one receiver has not been accounted for. Versus a standard 21 personal pro formation, that receiver is #3, the strongside running back. It is, therefore, important that the linebacker dropping hook-to-curl strongside keeps the #3 receiver in his periphery and maintains the ability to react to a hook pattern by #3 if he is drawn out of the hook zone into the curl zone by his primary key, the #2 receiver.

Adjusting Zone Drops to Spread Formations

Diagrams 14-2A through 14-2J illustrate cover 3 drops, implemented from a three-deep shell, versus 10 different personnel groupings.

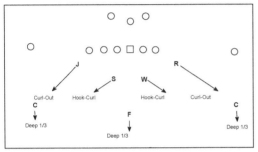

Diagram 14-2A

Diagram 14-2B

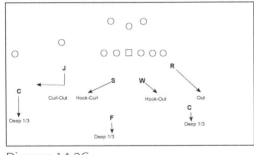

Diagram 14-2C

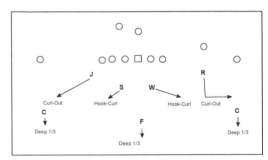

Diagram 14-2D

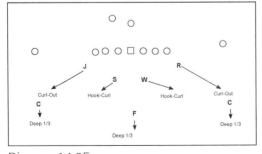

Diagram 14-2E

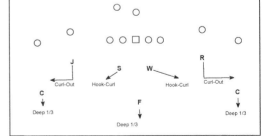

Diagram 14-2F

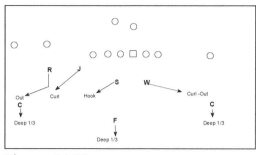
Diagram 14-2G

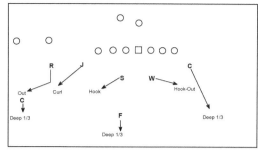
Diagram 14-2H

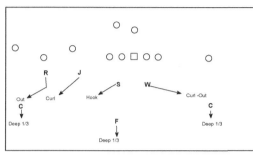
Diagram 14-2I

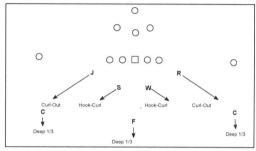
Diagram 14-2J

In these diagrams, it becomes apparent that the four-underneath zones change somewhat according to the offensive formation. In Diagram 14-2, for example, Joker is assigned to drop curl-to-out and Sam is assigned to drop hook-to-curl. Versus this formation, Joker will not immediately drop to the #1 receiver; he will first jam the #2 receiver and remain in the curl zone versus a vertical release by #2. This will provide Sam with extra time to get to the curl. After jamming #2, Joker will then release to #1. Sam will release directly to the curl zone because no receiver can provide an immediate threat to the curl. As previously noted, however, Sam must keep #3 the strongside halfback in his periphery as he drops.

It should also be noted that versus all of the trips formations (Diagrams 14-2G through 14-2I) that the Rover, Joker, and Sam are providing flood coverage to the out, curl, and hook zones. If they did not, the offense would gain an instant numbers advantage and easily exploit the underneath coverage.

Cover 3 From a Four-Deep Secondary

Two basic variations of cover 3 can be run from a four-deep secondary: cover 3 sky and cover 3 cloud. Sky and cloud designate which receiver is responsible for the strongside deep third and which defender is responsible for the strongside curl-out zone. Cover 3 sky assigns dollar to the strongside curl-out zone and the cornerback to the deep third. Cover 3 cloud assigns the cornerback to the strongside curl-out zone and dollar to the deep third. By mixing the two variations, the defense attempts to confuse the quarterback's reads and to also provide the defense with optimal field position run support from the secondary, Diagrams 14-3A through 14-3J illustrate 3 sky drops. No illustration of cover 3 cloud drops is provided because it only involves two defenders.

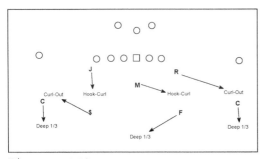

Diagram 14-3A

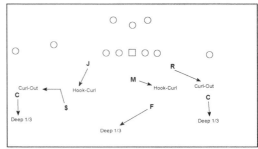

Diagram 14-3B

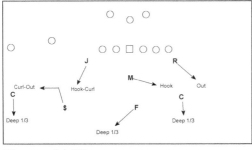

Diagram 14-3C

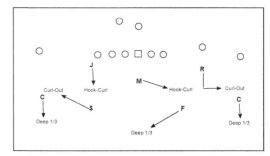

Diagram 14-3D

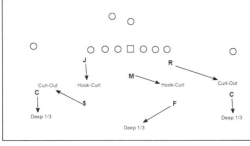

Diagram 14-3E

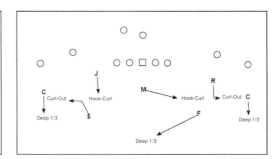

Diagram 14-3F

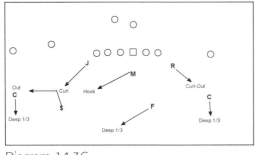

Diagram 14-3G

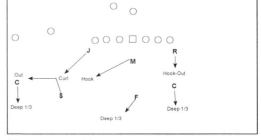

Diagram 14-3H

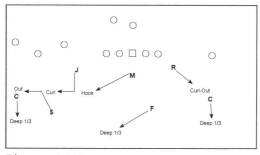

Diagram 14-3I   Diagram 14-3J

Cover 2 Zone

Cover 2 zone employs a five-under two-deep coverage with a four-man pass rush. The strength of this coverage is that it enables defenders to jam receivers at the line of scrimmage and thus redirect pass routes and disrupt the timing between the quarterback and the receivers. Its weakness, if not played properly, is four-vertical pass routes. Diagrams 14-4A through 14-4J illustrate 2 zone versus 10 personnel groupings.

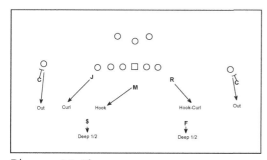

Diagram 14-4A   Diagram 14-4B

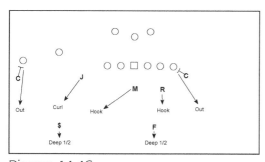   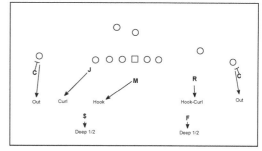

Diagram 14-4C   Diagram 14-4D

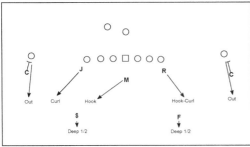

Diagram 14-4E

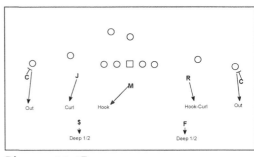

Diagram 14-4F

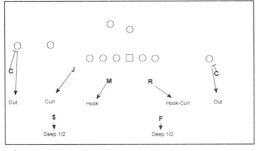

Diagram 14-4G

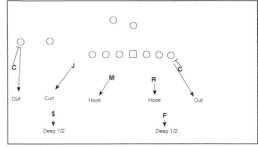

Diagram 14-4H

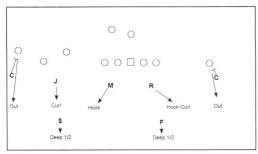

Diagram 14-4I

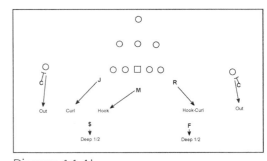

Diagram 14-4J

The linebackers dropping into the underneath zones will employ the same pattern reads and techniques as they did in cover 3. The only players who need to alter their technique are the defenders responsible for the deep half of the field and the cornerbacks who are assigned to jam and funnel the wide receivers inside and then cover the out zones. The following are the techniques and responsibilities of those defenders.

Deep-Half Coverage

- The defender gains depth as the ball is snapped; he must cover half of the field and keep all receivers in front of himself.
- He must communicate routes to defenders dropping into the underneath zones.

- He reads #1 and #2. He will work toward and maintain an adequate cushion on the deepest receiver. If both receivers go deep, defender moves outside of #2 so that he will be able to break to #1. Gaining depth is vital. The defender should favor the shortest throw for the quarterback, but stay deep enough to react to both receivers.
- If #2 releases into the flats, the defender gains width and depth and put himself in a position to react to the route being run by #1.
- If #2 releases inside, the defender gains width and looks first to #1 and then to a deep crossing route.

Cornerback Jam Techniques

- The defender jams #1, stays on the receiver's outside shoulder, and funnels him inside. The defender must not allow #1 an outside release.
- If #1 runs a vertical route, the defender continues to funnel the receiver's pattern inside. The defender should also continue to gain depth as long as no immediate threat is present in the flats.
- As he funnels #1 inside, the defender must see the release of #2.
- If #2 releases short into the flat, the defender will not react to his pattern until #2 crosses his face.
- If #2 runs the wheel route, the defender will collision and run with #2.
- If #2 runs a vertical or crossing route, the defender stays with #1 unless threatened by #3. If #3 releases into the flats, he must be in a position to rally up.

Quarter-Half Coverage

This very popular and effective coverage enables dollar to rob post and curl patterns, and also to load the box with eight or nine defenders. Many variations of this coverage can be found. The variation presented in this text features quarter coverage toward the strength of the formation and cover 2 man toward the weakside of the formation. Diagrams 14-5A through 14-5I illustrate this coverage versus nine personnel groupings.

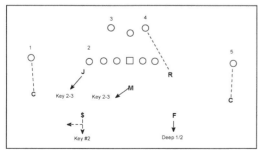

Diagram 14-5A

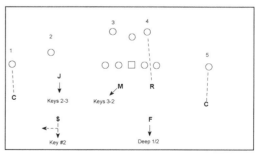

Diagram 14-5B

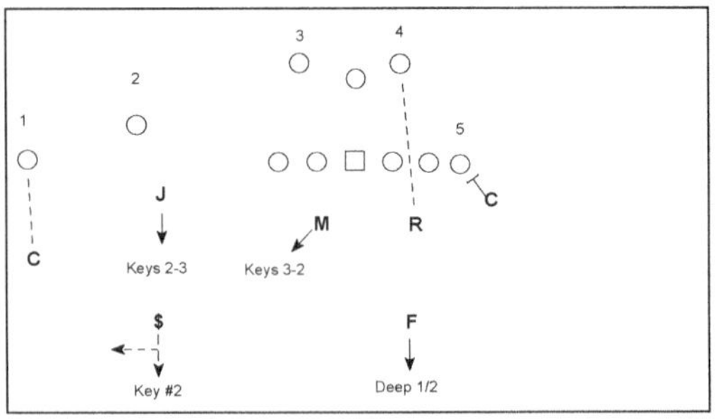

Diagram 14-5C

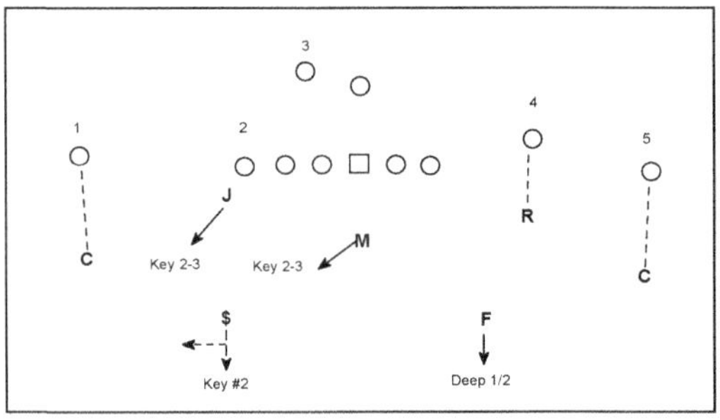

Diagram 14-5D

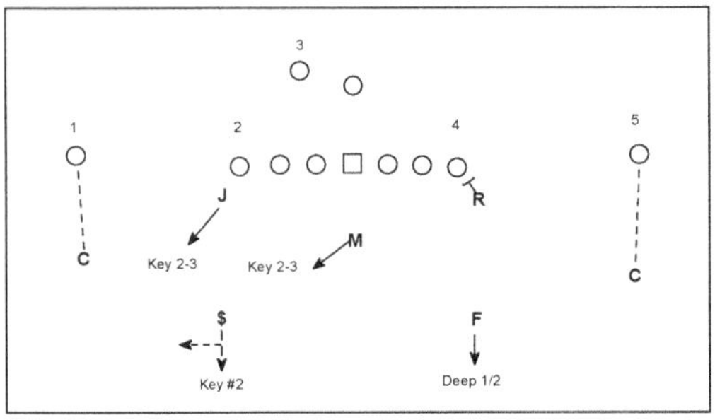

Diagram 14-5E

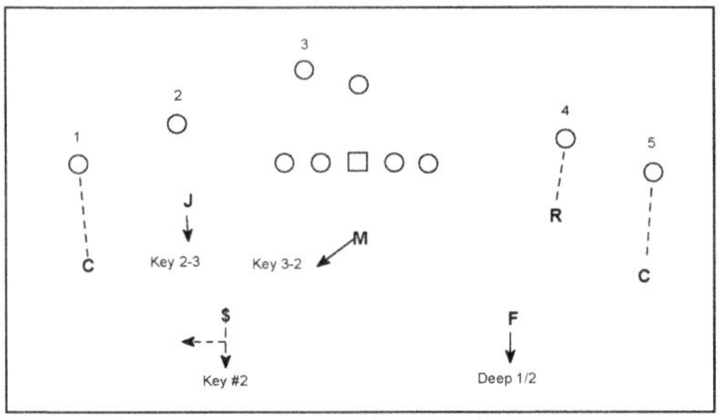

Diagram 14-5F

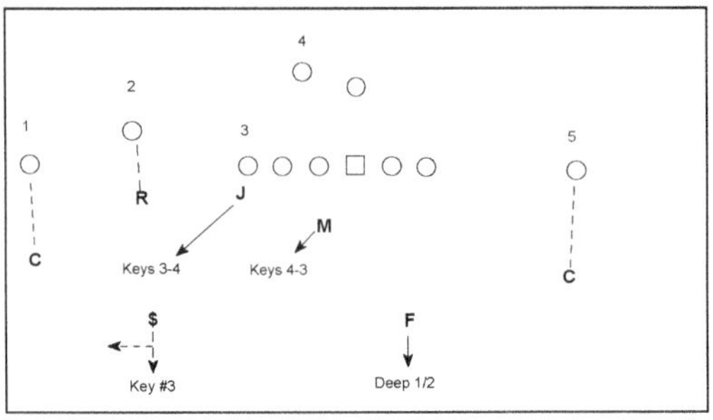

Diagram 14-5G

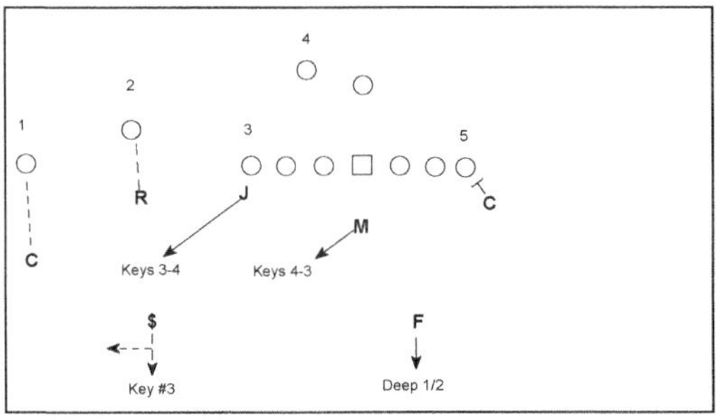

Diagram 14-5H

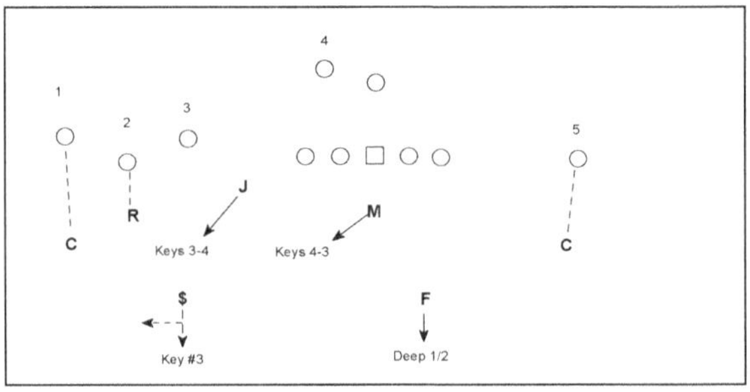

Diagram 14-5I

The following guidelines should be followed when employing this coverage:
- The secondary will remain four deep versus all personnel groupings.
- Dollar and the free safety will provide primary force to runs toward themselves and alley support to runs away from themselves.
- Dollar will key the #2 receiver to his side of the formation versus all personnel groupings, except those involving trips. Versus trips he will key #3. If his key runs a vertical route, dollar will cover him. If his key blocks or runs a short route, dollar will sprint to the #1 receiver to his side of the formation and help the cornerback cover the post and curl.
- The cornerbacks will maintain inside leverage on their assigned receivers because one of the ways that coaches try to attack cover 4 is to force dollar to cover a vertical route by his key and then having #1 run a post or curl. The cornerbacks must be made to realize that they may have to cover the post and curl with no help from dollar.
- Joker and Mike will combo coverage #2 and #3 versus all personnel groupings, except those involving trips. Versus trips, they will combo #3 and #4. The two defenders assigned combo coverage will follow the same basic rules of Abel and Baker that are used for fire zone blitz coverage with one exception: Baker must continue to cover any crossing routes into his area because Charlie doesn't exist in this coverage.
- Rover will cover #4 versus all personnel groupings except trips. Versus trips, he will cover #2.

Defending Empty Formations

Many different philosophies have been developed as to how empty sets should be covered. Diagrams 14-6A through 14-6C illustrate three ways in which the 3-3-5 could be used to cover empty. Diagram 14-6A illustrates cover 1, Diagram 14-6B illustrates cover 3, and Diagram 14-6C illustrates zero coverage. In deciding which coverage to choose, a coach should consider the mobility of the quarterback and the athleticism of his defense compared to that of the offense.

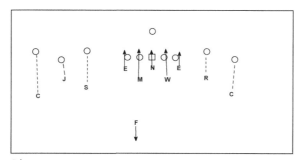

Diagram 14-6A

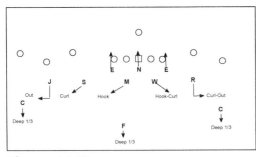
Diagram 14-6B

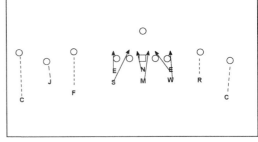
Diagram 14-6C

CHAPTER 15
Stunt Strategies and Techniques

12 Stunt Strategies That Win Games

Note: With the exception of hybrid fire zone blitz, two diagrams are used to illustrate each blitzing strategy. The first diagram is versus 21 personnel, and the second is versus 10 personnel. Different fronts and coverages have been selected when illustrating each strategy for the purpose of providing the reader with a comprehensive view of how different fronts and coverages function versus different personnel groupings.

Illusion Blitzes

The term *blitz* refers to a stunt that employs a six-man pass rush. An *illusion blitz* is a specific type of blitz that gives the offense the illusion that the defense is "sending the house." When an illusion blitz is employed, seven or eight defenders will attack the line of scrimmage at the snap. Versus run, these seven or eight defenders will attempt to penetrate the gaps, control the line of scrimmage, force the ballcarrier out of his intended course, and ultimately stop the play in the backfield. Versus pass, six of these defenders will continue to rush the quarterback and the remaining one or two fake pass rushers will spy the running back(s). Versus pass, illusion blitzes hold the offense accountable for blocking all seven or eight defenders aligned in the box and thereby limit the number of receivers an offense can put into pass pattern and safely protect its quarterback. Furthermore, illusion blitzes make pass protection a chaotic guessing game. Because the spy defenders are often defensive linemen, illusion blitzes not only cause offensive linemen to end up blocking air, they eliminate many protection schemes that require offensive linemen to double read defensive alignments. Illusion blitzes are employed from zero coverage.

Diagrams 15-1A and 15-1B illustrate two illusion blitzes. Diagram 15-1A shows an illusion blitz in which eight 3-3-5 defenders are attacking the line of scrimmage at the snap versus 21 personnel. As these defenders recognize pass, Joker and Rover will spy the two running backs. If the running backs block instead of releasing for a pattern, the two spy defenders will continue as fake rushers. It is vital that fake pass rushers understand that spying the running backs takes precedence over pretending to rush the quarterback. Otherwise, these defenders may become vulnerable to delay pass routes or screen patterns. Diagram 15-1B illustrates an illusion blitz from a 3-4 defense versus 10 personnel. In this diagram, Joker is spying the aceback.

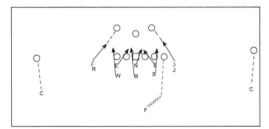

Diagram 15-1A   Diagram 15-1B

Blitzes

Illusion blitzes are usually called when the offense is expected to pass. Blitzes, on the other hand, are usually called in run situations. Most coaches use blitzes to pressure the offense from the edge and free up one or two inside linebackers so that they can pursue the ballcarrier from an inside-out position, but they can also be used to stop inside runs or pressure the quarterback in passing situations. Like illusion blitzes, blitzes are used with zero coverages. Diagram 15-2A illustrates an even eight-man front in which Sam and Will are blitzing, and Joker and Rover are covering the two running backs. Diagram 15-2B illustrates an even seven-man front in which Mike and Will are blitzing and Joker is covering the aceback. Both examples would most likely be used versus the pass or to stop inside runs.

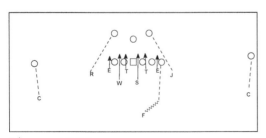 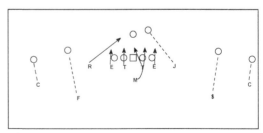

Diagram 15-2A   Diagram 15-2B

Illusion Dogs

The term dog refers to a stunt that employs a five-man pass rush. Illusion dogs are almost identical to illusion blitzes. The differences between these two tactics are as follows:
- Illusion dogs employ five-man pass rushes, and illusion blitzes employ six-man pass rushes.
- Cover 1 is usually used with illusion dogs. Although illusion dogs put less pressure on a quarterback than illusion blitzes, many coaches feel more secure using them because their defense is afforded the luxury of a free safety who is backing up the defenders in the box, providing alley support versus run and playing centerfield versus pass.

Diagram 15-3A illustrates an example of an even eight-man front in which Sam and Will are blitzing, Rover and the strongside tackle are spying the quarterback, and Joker is covering the tight end. Diagram 15-3B illustrates an illusion dog being executed from an odd seven-man front in which Joker and Will are blitzing and Sam is spying the quarterback.

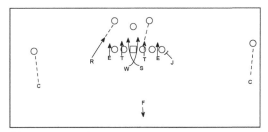
Diagram 15-3A

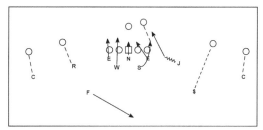
Diagram 15-3B

Dogs

Dogs and blitzes are similar and different in the same manner as illusion dogs and illusion blitzes are. Diagram 15-4A illustrates an example of dog being employed from an odd eight-man front in which Mike and Rover cover the two running backs, and Joker covers the tight end. Diagram 15-4B illustrates a dog from an even eight-man front in which Will is blitzing and Sam is covering the aceback. Both examples would be particularly effective versus both run and pass.

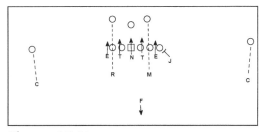
Diagram 15-4A

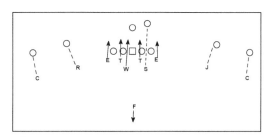
Diagram 15-4B

Fire Zone Blitzes

It should be noted that fire zone blitzes are not really blitzes; they're dogs because they involve five-man pass rushes, and they're used with cover 1. However, since fire zone blitz has become the universal term used to describe this tactic, it will also be used that way in this text. A fire zone blitz is a variation of an illusion dog. Unlike illusion dogs, however, fire zone blitzes have three defenders drop off into the under coverage and combo cover the tight end and two running backs versus 21 personnel and combo cover the tight end and aceback versus 10 personnel. In addition to the all of the advantages gained by illusion blitzes and dogs, fire zone blitzes often cause the quarterback to quickly dump the ball off to a hot receiver in a long passing situation, which frequently results in an offensive failure to gain a first down. Diagram 15-5A illustrates an odd seven-man front fire zone blitz versus 21 personnel, and Diagram 15-5B illustrates an even eight-man front fire zone blitz versus 10 personnel. Chapter 14 explains the essential information about the pass coverage techniques of fire blitz coverage.

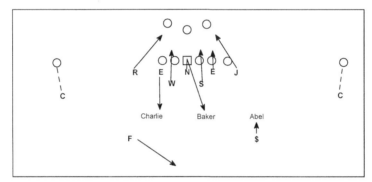

Diagram 15-5A

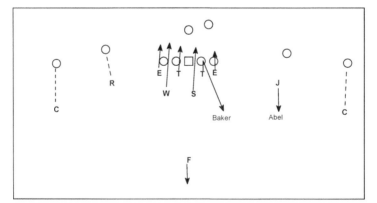

Diagram 15-5B

Hybrid Fire Zone Blitzes

This tactic is only used versus two back formations; it combines a strongside fire zone concept with a weakside illusion. Diagram 15-6 illustrates an odd seven-man front in which Joker and nose are dropping into Abel and Baker, and the weakside tackle is spying the running back.

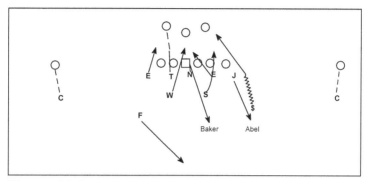

Diagram 15-6

Old-School Zone Blitzes

When Tom Bass was coaching in the NFL, he frequently blitzed linebackers and dropped defensive linemen into coverage. Unlike today's fire zone blitz, the pass coverage Tom employed this tactic with a two- or three-deep zone. Diagram 15-7A illustrates an example of an old-school blitz in which nose drops into a cover 2 hook zone, and Diagram 15-7B illustrates the strongside tackle dropping hook-curl in cover 3.

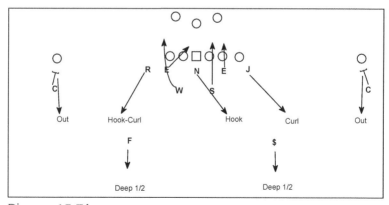

Diagram 15-7A

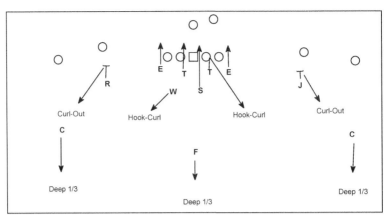

Diagram 15-7B

Overloads

Overloads attempt to get more pass rushers on one side of the ball than available pass blockers. Diagrams 15-8A and 15-8B illustrate two examples of overloads being employed from odd defensive fronts. Both examples put the offense in the dilemma of trying to block four strongside pass rushers.

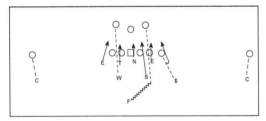

Diagram 15-8A

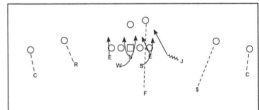

Diagram 15-8B

Line Twists

Line twists have always been an effective weapon versus both pass and run. Line twists can occur as the ball is being snapped, or they can be implemented as delayed reactions to the pass. Diagram 15-9A illustrates a cover 1 double twist involving the strongside tackle and nose, and the weakside tackle and end. Diagram 15-9B illustrates cover 2 man double twist involving both the strongside and weakside tackles and ends.

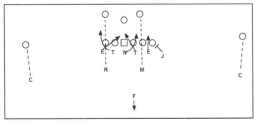

Diagram 15-9A

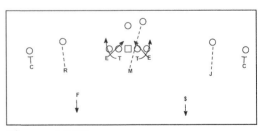

Diagram 15-9B

Secondary Blitzes

Secondary blitzes and fake secondary blitzes are powerful multifaceted weapons that can easily be incorporated into a multitude of blitz and illusion-blitz schemes. Diagram 15-10A illustrates a free safety blitz being executed with a seven-man front, and Diagram 15-10B illustrates a free safety blitz being executed with an eight-man front.

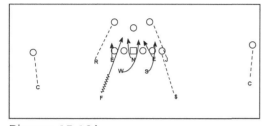

Diagram 15-10A   Diagram 15-10B

Twin Stunts

Whenever two players stunt through the same gap, it is referred to as a *twin stunt*. Twin stunts are delayed reactions to pass that are called in passing situations. The two players involved in the stunt will first employ run responsibility techniques, but as they read pass, they will then execute the stunt. Defensive backs, linebackers, or linemen can be used to create twin stunts. This is an unusual tactic, and because few offensive teams ever see this type of stunt, it is often very effective. Diagram 15-11A illustrates a twin stunt in which nose is following the strongside end into the B gap, and Diagram 15-11B illustrates a twin stunt in which the weakside end is following nose into the weakside A gap. Both examples being employed with cover 1.

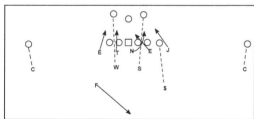

Diagram 15-11A   Diagram 15-11B

Delayed Stunts

Twin stints are one example of a delayed stunt. Defenders can also be called upon to play their base responsibility versus run and then stunt into a designated gap once they read pass. Diagrams 15-12A illustrates an example in which the strongside end, nose, and Will are delayed stunting once they read pass. Diagrams 15-12B illustrates a cover 2 zone example of nose and Will executing a delayed stunt.

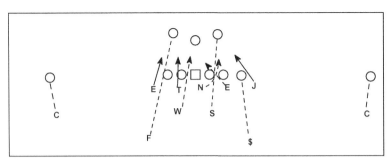

Diagram 15-12A

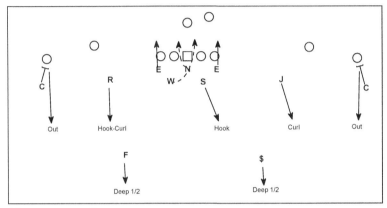

Diagram 15-12B

Basic Principles and Techniques of Stunting

- If a stunt is used as an element of surprise and it is done infrequently, it is important that the intent is disguised.
- If stunts are frequently employed, disguising your intention may not be as important because defenders may want to occasionally give the offense a false key by showing blitz, but then playing straight at the snap of the ball. Whatever is decided, it is important that a pattern is not established which becomes a key that can be exploited.
- A player's eyes are one of his most important tools when stunting. To be an effective stunter, a player must be able to see (on the run) the keys that will lead him to the ball. Seeing these keys is the first step in being able to read and react to them.
- Unless the stunt is a delayed reaction to a pass, it is critical that the stunt occurs as the ball is snapped. The stunter(s) should be moving, attacking, and penetrating the line of scrimmage immediately at the snap.
- Stunters must keep their feet moving at all times. This movement is especially important when they become engaged with a blocker.
- Stunters must use their quickness in an attempt to avoid blockers.

- If the play is a pass, and the stunter becomes engaged with a blocker, he must keep his hands inside of the blocker's hands and try to maintain separation from the blocker. He should not look at the passer too soon and lose sight of the blocker. He must first defeat the blocker before he can sack the quarterback. The stunter should have a predetermined pass-rush move in mind before the snap but be ready to change his move according to the circumstance. A stunter must take what the blocker gives him and make his move at the appropriate time. It is important for a stunter to remember that if he makes his pass-rush move too soon, the blocker will have time to recover. On the other hand, if he makes his move too late, he will probably be too close to the blocker, and the blocker will be able to get into his body and nullify his charge. If possible, a stunter should try to get the blocker turned one way and then make his move in the opposite direction. He should also use his forward momentum to manipulate the blocker's momentum. If the blocker's momentum is back, he should attack the blocker with a power move and knock him backward. If his momentum is forward, he should use a move that pulls the blocker forward and destroys his balance. Lastly, a stunter should never leave his feet to bat a ball down. He should get his hands up as the quarterback begins his throwing motion, but keep charging toward the quarterback. Too often when a stunter jumps up to bat a pass down, the quarterback will duck under, elude the defender, and scramble out of the pocket.
- If the play is a run, the stunter should react to his keys and the pressure of blocks as he would if he was employing a base read technique. Since he has forward momentum to his advantage, the stunter should use his hands rather than his forearm when attacking a blocker. A stunter must maintain separation from the blockers and not let them get into his legs. If possible, he should make the blockers miss him.
- A stunter should keep his body under control at all times and try to maintain a low center of gravity. Providing a small target for blockers is a big advantage.
- A stunter must study his opponent's game films carefully. He must know how potential blockers react and what techniques they favor. He must also know their strengths and weaknesses.
- A stunter must study his opponents' eyes as they're getting set at the line of scrimmage. Their eyes will often tell him where they're going. He should also study the pressure that they put on their down hands when they get into their stances. He can frequently find a player who will give him a pass/run or a directional key by the pressure he puts on his down hand.
- A stunter must study the scouting report. He must know his opponent's formation, down-and-distance, and field-position tendency. He should use this information to anticipate, but never to guess.
- All defenders should gang tackle, and if possible try to strip the ball out of the ballcarrier's arm. No defender should ever take for granted that a running back or a quarterback has been downed. If he arrives at a pile late, he must be on the alert for a loose ball.

- All defenders must maintain total intensity from the time the ball is snapped until the whistle is blown.
- Before the snap, a stunter must anticipate potential blockers and be prepared to react to these blockers as he penetrates the line.
- On plays directed toward his side of the line, every defender should make the tackle. On plays directed away from him, every defender should take the proper angle of pursuit and be in on the tackle. Relentless pursuit is vital. Every defender must remember that if he is not within five yards of the ball when the whistle blows that he is probably loafing.
- If the backfield action does not indicate flow, every defender should secure his gap until he finds the ball. He must never guess.
- If a defender's assigned to spy (cover a back) when he's stunting, he must expect that the back will first block and then run a delayed route. He must never be fooled. He must cover the back until the whistle blows, no matter what he does.
- The ball is every defender's trigger. When the ball is snapped, he must immediately go. A defender must not listen to an opponent's cadence; the quarterback is not talking to the defense.
- No defender should rely upon the lines that are marked on the field. The ball—not lines—establishes the line of scrimmage.

CHAPTER 16
Enhancing Fronts and Coverages With Stunts and Twists

Using Phonics to Create Complex Stunt Maneuvers

Because so many teams are now employing no-huddle offenses, defensive huddles should be stored on the same shelf as leather helmets. Defensive calls should be conveyed to players from the sideline via wristbands. Also, excessive verbiage should be minimized from the call.

Many coaches avoid implementing complex stunt maneuvers or comprehensive stunt packages because they are unable to express the information required to achieve their objective in a concise, precise manner. Combining sounds into words enables any coach to formulate a sophisticated system of conveying complex stunt maneuvers. Following are examples of how this system is accomplished.

Sounds for Linebacker and Secondary Blitzes

- Joker Stunt Maneuvers (Diagram 16-1)
    - ✓ Joe = Joker stunts outside.
    - ✓ Ji = Joker stunts inside.
- Sam Stunt Maneuvers (Diagram 16-2)
    - ✓ So = Sam stunts outside.
    - ✓ Sock = Sam stunts through the strongside C gap.

- ✓ Sob = Sam stunts through the strongside B gap.
- ✓ Say = Sam stunts through the strongside A gap.
- ✓ Sax = Sam stunts through the weakside A gap.
- ✓ Sex = Sam stunts through the weakside B gap.
• Mike Stunt Maneuvers (Diagram 16-3)
  - ✓ Mack = Mike stunts through the strongside C gap.
  - ✓ Mob = Mike stunts through the strongside B gap.
  - ✓ May = Mike stunts through the strongside A gap.
  - ✓ Max = Mike stunts through the weakside A gap.
  - ✓ Mex = Mike stunts through the weakside B gap.
• Will Stunt Maneuvers (Diagram 16-4)
  - ✓ Wex = Will stunts through the strongside B gap.
  - ✓ Wax = Will stunts through the strongside A gap.
  - ✓ Way = Will stunts through the weakside A gap.
  - ✓ Web = Will stunts through the weakside B gap.
  - ✓ Wack = Will stunts through the weakside C gap.
• Rover Stunt Maneuvers (Diagram 16-5)
  - ✓ Roe = Rover stunts outside.
  - ✓ Ri = Rover stunts inside.
  - ✓ Ray = Rover stunts through the A gap.
• Free Safety Stunt Maneuvers (Diagram 16-6)
  - ✓ X Fire = Free safety stunts through the strongside A gap.
  - ✓ A Fire = Free safety stunts through the weakside A gap.
  - ✓ B Fire = Free safety stunts through the weakside B gap.
• Cornerback Stunt Maneuvers (Diagram 16-7)
  - ✓ Crash = Strongside cornerback blitzes from the edge.
  - ✓ Crunch = Weakside cornerback blitzes from the edge.

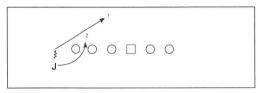

Diagram 16-1

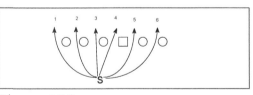

Diagram 16-2

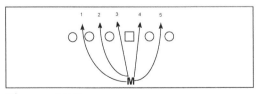

Diagram 16-3

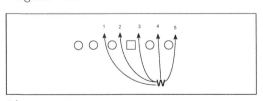

Diagram 16-4

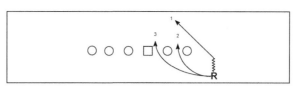

Diagram 16-5

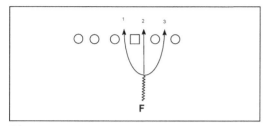

Diagram 16-6

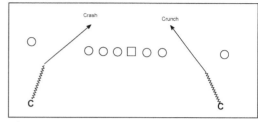

Diagram 16-7

Sounds for Defensive Line Twists and Slants

- Tim = Tackles penetrate inside through the A gaps (Diagram 16-8).
- Tom = Tackles penetrate outside through the B gaps (Diagram 16-9).
- Texas = Tackles twist strongside (Diagram 16-10).
- Tex = Tackles twist weakside (Diagram 16-11).
- Tyz = Tackles slant strongside (Diagram 16-12).
- Ty = Tackles slant weakside (Diagram 16-13).

Diagram 16-8

Diagram 16-9

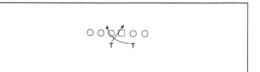

Diagram 16-10

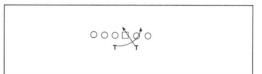

Diagram 16-11

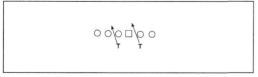

Diagram 16-12

Diagram 16-13

- Teez = Strongside tackle and end twist (Diagram 16-14).
- Tee = Weakside tackle and end twist (Diagram 16-15).
- Notz = Strongside tackle and nose twist (Diagram 16-16).
- Not = Weakside tackle and nose twist (Diagram 16-17).
- Truckz = Both tackles and nose twist strongside (Diagram 16-18).
- Truck = Both tackles and nose twist weakside (Diagram 16-19).

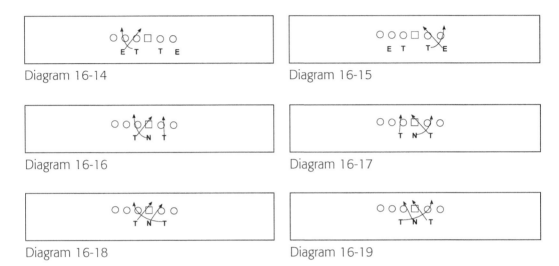

10 Examples of How the System Works

The following 10 examples are illustrate versus both 21 and 10 personnel for the purpose of demonstrating how the same stunt call functions versus both two-back and aceback formations. The first two or three numbers designate the defensive front. Next, the stunt is stated, and lastly, the coverage. It should be noted that there is no need to convey the defensive alignment if it is the team's base alignment.

505—Web Sob—1

This stunt is illustrated from a variation of the 3-3-5 defense. 505 designates the alignment of both ends and the nose. Web Sob assigns Sam and Will to blitz the B gaps. The secondary coverage is cover 1.

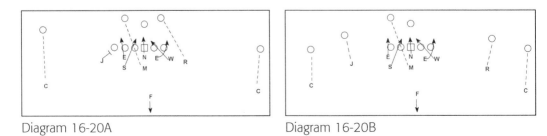

Diagram 16-20A   Diagram 16-20B

Minus 3—Say Wex Tee—5

This stunt is executed from a variation of the 4-2 defense. Minus 3 denotes the alignment of both tackles. Say Wex is Sam and Will's stunt assignment, telling Sam to blitz through the strongside A gap and Will to blitz through the strongside B gap. Tee tells the right tackle and end to twist. The secondary coverage is cover 5.

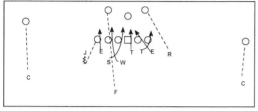

Diagram 16-21A   Diagram 16-21B

03—Tex—2 Man

This stunt is employed from a variation of the 4-3 defense. Zero 3 designates the alignment of the two tackles. Tex assigns the tackles to twist, and the secondary coverage is 2 man.

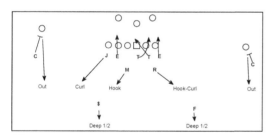 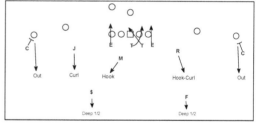

Diagram 16-22A   Diagram 16-22B

303—Tee Notz—1

This stunt is implemented from a variation of the bear 46 defense. Tee assigns the right tackle and end to twist. Notz assigns the left tackle and nose to twist. The secondary coverage is cover 1.

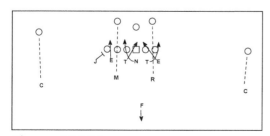 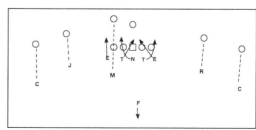

Diagram 16-23A   Diagram 16-23B

31 Mob—Tim—B Fire—0

This stunt is executed from a 4-3 defense. 31 denotes the alignment of the two tackles. Mob tells Mike to blitz through the strongside B gap, and Tim tells both tackles to penetrate the A gaps. B Fire tells the free safety to blitz through the weakside B gap. The secondary coverage is 0.

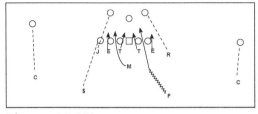

Diagram 16-24A   Diagram 16-24B

13—Tee Way—1

This stunt is employed from a variation of the 4-2 defense. 13 designates the alignment of the two tackles. Tee assigns the right end and tackle to twist. Way tells Will to blitz the weakside A gap. The secondary coverage is cover 1.

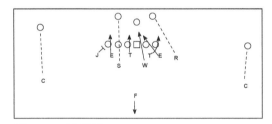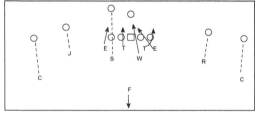

Diagram 16-25A   Diagram 16-25B

Five Plus 3—Joe Wack—1 Fire

This stunt is illustrated from the weak eagle defense. 5 Plus 3 designates the alignment of the two ends and the nose. Joe assigns Joker to blitz off the edge, and Wack assigns Whip to blitz the C gap. The secondary coverage is cover 1 fire.

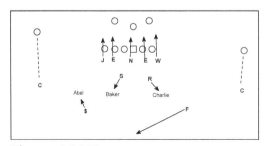

Diagram 16-26A   Diagram 16-26B

505—Joe Roe Wax—0

This stunt is demonstrated from the 3-4 defense. 505 denotes the alignments of the two ends and nose. Joe Roe assigns Joker and Rover to blitz from the edge, and Wax assigns Whip to blitz the strongside A gap. The secondary coverage is 0.

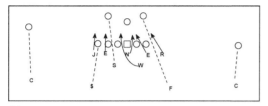

Diagram 16-27A   Diagram 16-27B

22—Tee Teez—3 Cloud

This stunt is illustrated from a variation of the 4-3 defense. 22 denotes the alignment of the two tackles. Tee and Teez assigns both the strongside and weakside tackles to twist, and the secondary coverage is 3 cloud.

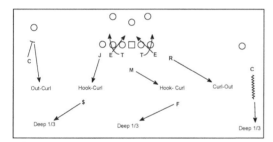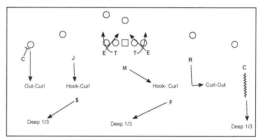

Diagram 16-28A   Diagram 16-28B

303—Mob Tuck—5

This stunt is illustrated from a variation of the bear 46. 303 designates the alignment of the nose and two tackles. Mob assigns Mike to blitz through the strongside B gap, and Truck denotes the line twist of the nose and two tackles. The secondary coverages is cover 5.

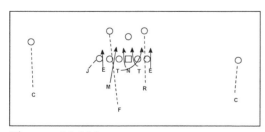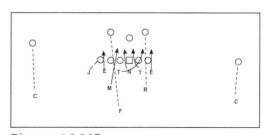

Diagram 16-29A   Diagram 16-29B

Sample Menus for Standard Contemporary Defenses

This section will present many of the appropriate stunts and twists that can be called in conjunction with the most common coverages associated with the base alignment of each defense. It should be noted some of these stunts and twists may not be applicable for the many variations of each defense's base alignment.

The 3-3-5 Defense (Diagram 16-30)

- Cover 3:
  - ✓ May 3
  - ✓ Max 3
  - ✓ Sock 3
  - ✓ Sob 3
  - ✓ Web 3
  - ✓ Wack 3
- Cover 1:
  - ✓ Sock Web 1
  - ✓ Sock Wack 1
  - ✓ Sob Web 1
  - ✓ Sob Wack 1
  - ✓ May Web 1
  - ✓ Mack Wack 1
  - ✓ Max Web 1
  - ✓ Max Wack 1
  - ✓ Mex Way 1
- Cover 0:
  - ✓ Joe Sock Web 0
  - ✓ Joe Sock Wack 0
  - ✓ Joe Sob Web 0
  - ✓ Joe Sob Wack 0
  - ✓ Joe May Web 0
  - ✓ Joe Mack Wack 0
  - ✓ Joe Mex Web 0
  - ✓ Joe Max Wack 0
  - ✓ Joe Mex Way 0
  - ✓ Sock May Web 0
  - ✓ Sob Max Wack 0
  - ✓ Say Mob Web 0
  - ✓ Say Mob Wack 0
  - ✓ Mex Way Sock 0
  - ✓ Mex Way Sob 0
- Cover 5:
  - ✓ Sock May Web 5
  - ✓ Sock Mob Web 5
  - ✓ Sob May Web 5
  - ✓ Sob Mob Web 5
  - ✓ Sob May Wack 5
  - ✓ Say Mob Web 5
  - ✓ Say Mob Wack 5
  - ✓ Sock Mex Way 5
  - ✓ Sob Mex Way 5

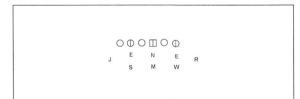

Diagram 16-30

The 4-2-5 Defense (Diagram 16-31)

Note: Coaches who employ this defense use variations of their base alignment to generate sophisticated stunt packages; however, the stunt possibilities from their base alignment are somewhat limited.

- Cover 3:
  ✓ Tim 3
  ✓ Tex 3
  ✓ Tyz 3
- Cover 1:
  ✓ Web 1
  ✓ Wack 1
  ✓ Tim Wack 1
  ✓ Tyz Web 1
- Cover 0:
  ✓ Say Web 0
  ✓ Say Wack 0
  ✓ Say Tim Wack 0
  ✓ Sob Web 0
  ✓ Sob Wack 0
- Cover 5:
  ✓ Say Web 5
  ✓ Say Wack 5
  ✓ Sob Web 5
  ✓ Sob Wack 5

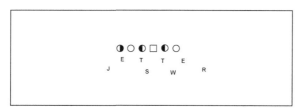

Diagram 16-31

The Bear 46 Defense (Diagram 16-32)

- Cover 3:
  ✓ Tee 3
  ✓ Notz 3
  ✓ Notz Tee 3
  ✓ Not 3
  ✓ Truckz 3
  ✓ Truck 3
- Cover 1:
  ✓ So Tee 1
  ✓ So Notz 1
  ✓ So Notz Tee 1
  ✓ So Not 1
  ✓ So Truckz 1
  ✓ So Truck 1
  ✓ Mack Tee 1
  ✓ Mack Not 1
  ✓ Mack Truckz 1
  ✓ May Tee 1
  ✓ May Not 1
  ✓ May Truck 1
  ✓ Max Tee 1
  ✓ Max Not 1

- Cover 0:
  - ✓ So Jim Tee 0
  - ✓ So Jim Notz 0
  - ✓ So Jim Notz Tee 0
  - ✓ So Jim Not 0
  - ✓ So Jim Truckz 0
  - ✓ So Jim Truck 0
  - ✓ So Mack Tee 0
  - ✓ So Mack Not 0
  - ✓ So Mack Truckz 0
  - ✓ So May Tee 0
  - ✓ So May Not 0
  - ✓ So May Truck 0
  - ✓ So Max Tee 0
  - ✓ So Max Not 0
  - ✓ Jim Mack Tee 0
  - ✓ Jim Mack Not 0
  - ✓ Jim Mack Truckz 0
  - ✓ Jim May Tee 0
  - ✓ Jim May Not 0
  - ✓ Jim May Truck 0
  - ✓ Jim Max Tee 0
  - ✓ Jim Max Not 0
- Cover 5:
  - ✓ So Mack Tee 5
  - ✓ So Mack Not 5
  - ✓ So Mack Truckz 5
  - ✓ So May Tee 5
  - ✓ So May Not 5
  - ✓ So May Truck 5
  - ✓ So Max Tee 5
  - ✓ So Max Not 5

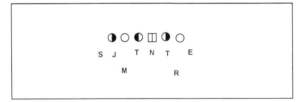

Diagram 16-32

The 3-4 Defense (Diagram 16-33)

- Cover 3 (sky or cloud):
  - ✓ Joe 3
  - ✓ Sob 3
  - ✓ Sock 3
- Cover 1:
  - ✓ Joe Web 1
  - ✓ Joe Wack 1
  - ✓ Web Sock 1
  - ✓ Web Sob 1
  - ✓ Wack Sock 1
  - ✓ Wack Sob 1
- Cover 0:
  - ✓ Joe Roe Web 0
  - ✓ Joe Roe Wack 0
  - ✓ Sock Roe Web 0
  - ✓ Sock Ri Wax 0
  - ✓ Sock Ri Wex 0
  - ✓ Sob Ri Waa 0
  - ✓ Sob Ri Wex 0
  - ✓ Sob Wax Fire B 0
  - ✓ Sock Wax Fire B 0

- Cover 6:
  - ✓ Roe Way 6
  - ✓ Roe Wack 6
  - ✓ Ri Wax 6
- Cover 2 man and cover 2 zone:
  - ✓ Web 2
  - ✓ Wack 2

Diagram 16-33

The 4-3 Defense (Diagram 16-34)

- Cover 3 (sky or cloud):
  - ✓ Tim 3
  - ✓ Texas 3
  - ✓ Tex 3
  - ✓ Tyz 3
- Cover 1:
  - ✓ Ji Tim 1
  - ✓ Ji Tex 1
  - ✓ Ji Ty 1
  - ✓ Tim Mob 1
  - ✓ Tex Mob 1
  - ✓ Ty Mob 1
- Cover 0:
  - ✓ May Ray Tom 0
  - ✓ Mob Ray Ty 0
  - ✓ Mob Ri Tim 0
  - ✓ May Ri Tyz 0
  - ✓ Tim Mob Fire B 0
- Cover 6:
  - ✓ Tim Ri 6
  - ✓ Texas Ri 6
  - ✓ Tyz Ri 6
- Cover 2 man and cover 2 zone:
  - ✓ Tim 2
  - ✓ Texas 2
  - ✓ Tex 2
  - ✓ Ty 2
  - ✓ Tyz 2

Diagram 16-34

The Weak Eagle Defense (Diagram 16-35)

- Cover 3 (sky or cloud):
  - ✓ Tee 3
  - ✓ Tim 3
- Cover 1:
  - ✓ Joe Tee 1
  - ✓ Joe Tim 1
  - ✓ Mob Tee 1
  - ✓ Mack Tee 1
- Cover 0:
  - ✓ Joe Ray 0
  - ✓ Mob Ray 0
  - ✓ Mack Ray 0
- ✓ Mack Tim Ri 0
- ✓ Mob Tim Ri 0
- ✓ Sob Tim Fire B 0
- ✓ Sack Tim Fire B 0
- ✓ Joe Tim Fire B 0
- Cover 6:
  - ✓ Tim Ri 6
  - ✓ Ray 6
- Cover 2 man and cover 2 zone:
  - ✓ Tee 2
  - ✓ Tim 2

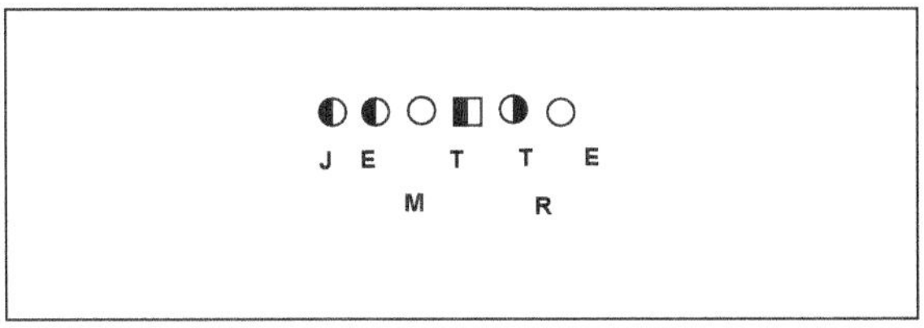

Diagram 16-35

CHAPTER 17
Preparing to Win

Practice Planning and Organization

Note: The following guidelines have assisted me in my career. Like everything in football, none of these guidelines is written in concrete. It is suggested that the reader select those guidelines that best fit his personality and situation.

- Develop a playbook that incorporates the philosophy, strategy, and techniques that you and the head coach have agreed best suits your particular situation. Depending upon the maturity and experience of your staff you may or may not want them involved in this process. Once developed, introduce the playbook to your staff, and explain that you welcome any suggestion that may improve the defense, but make it clear that if anyone is totally dissatisfied with the plan that he should be careful to not let the door hit his behind as he leaves.
- Make certain that your staff has a complete grasp of the techniques that they are responsible for teaching. Test them by having them demonstrate to the staff how these techniques are to be taught.
- Get rid of the word drills. Skills are taught through sequentially well-defined "teaching progressions."
- Develop a comprehensive yearly plan that thoroughly prepares your defense for all potential contingencies that they will face before they play their first game. Create a list of the skills that each position will need to be successful and make sure that everything is covered in the off-season and pre-season practices.

- Each day, have specific goals that need to be accomplished, and focus all activities on accomplishing these goals. Never give your associate coaches the blanket assignment of "working on individual skills" without defining exactly which skills should be worked on. For example, on a specific day, the defensive backfield coach should be assigned the goal of teaching the techniques necessary to defend the curl pattern, and the defensive line coach assigned the goal of defending the counter trey. This is especially important during spring football and two-a-days.
- Practices should be conducted in a businesslike fashion. Time should not be wasted, coaches should be taught to coach on the run, using key words in their correction and complementary comments.
- No coach should bring a cell phone to practice or to a meeting unless his wife expecting a baby or one of his family members is in critical condition in the hospital.
- Make copies of all practice plans. Make certain that all staff members receive a copy before practice. Do not deviate from the times allocated for each activity unless absolutely necessary.
- Keep staff meetings focused. State specific practice goals that need to be accomplished. Solicit and welcome feedback from associate coaches, but don't allow a meeting to deteriorate into lengthy discussions about a trivial matter that can be resolved by simply delegating the matter to a specific coach.
- Some staff members may need considerable assistance and supervision, but don't make the mistake of micromanaging competent coaches. Stand back, and let competent coaches do their job.
- Develop an aura of positivity among the staff and the team.

Practice Plan Examples

The two types of practice plans are those in which the entire practice is devoted to defense, and those in which only a portion of practice is devoted to defense. Diagram 17-1 is an example of a two-a-day practice plan in which the entire practice (2 hours and 15 minutes) is devoted to defense. It is a plan that I used when employing the double eagle-double flex defense in Texas. The same terminology that was used at that time is included in the plan. Explanatory notes will be provided at the end of the plan whenever necessary.

Segment #1—10 Minutes:	Team stretch	
Segment #2—15 Minutes:	Team tackling and cut block techniques	
Segment #3—15 Minutes:		
Front 5	*Stud, Whip, Rover, and Free Safety*	*Cornerbacks*
Stance starts, punch, and get-off	Reads vs. two-back sets	Shuffle, pedal, ball

Diagram 17-1

Segment #4—15 Minutes:

Front 5	*Stud, Whip, Rover, and Free Safety*	*Cornerbacks*
Zone/counter trey	Counter trey/option vs. ace	Jam technique

Segment #5—15 Minutes:

Front 5	*Defensive Backs and Backers*
Pass rush techniques	1-on-1 vs. out, out-and-up, hitch, hitch-and-go, and fade

Segment #6—15 Minutes:

Front 5	*Defensive Backs and Backers*
Moe, Toe, Me, Tee, Nat, Nam	7-on-7 vs. out, out-and-up, hitch, hitch-and-go, and fade

Segment #7—15 Minutes:

Front 5, Backers, Free Safety	*Cornerbacks*
Read drill vs. zone and CT	Shed 7 run support techniques

Segment #8—15 Minutes:

Team Adjustment Period: vs. ace and two-back sets
Coverage: Cover 1
Front 5: Moe, Toe, Me, Tee, Nat, Nam

Segment #9—10 Minutes:

Team Pursuit

Segment #9—10 Minutes:

Team Agility Period: Step-overs and ladders

Notes:

Segment 2: This is how we started every practice. We divided the team into 10 lines because we had 10 coaches. Each coach coached one line. The entire team worked every day on both tackling and dealing with the cut block. Texas high schools play by NCAA rules. Cut blocking is, therefore, legal. All 10 lines responded to the whistle. The first player in line was the one being tackled and after the tackle, the tackler would become the player to be tackled. There was very little time between whistles. Players were required to get up quickly and get ready for the next whistle. Coaches coached on the run, using key words. The first few days of implementing this activity, we worked slowly, making certain that safe and proper techniques and were adhered to.

Segment 4: The coach responsible for the front five used index cards that illustrated the two blocking scheme of the day. This afforded the front more reps.

Segments 5 and 6: Defensive backs and backers were exposed to the pass patterns that they have worked on thus far in 7-on-7 and 1-on-1.

Segment 6: The front five executed their twists versus the barrels. This was a rapid movement period.

Diagram 17-1 (cont.)

> **Notes:** (cont.)
>
> *Segment 7:* There was no ball or backfield present. Players had to react to the blocking scheme. I would simulate backfield flow by pretending to be the quarterback. This gave me an opportunity to evaluate whether the players had grasped the reads and techniques that they had been taught. As time went on, more blocking schemes were added until the players had been exposed to all of the blocking schemes that they might encounter.
>
> *Segment 8:* One coach would have the various formation diagramed on index card. He would rapidly huddle six players who would quickly break the huddle and line up on five barrels. The defense would immediately adjust to the formation and on a command the front five would execute their twist.

Diagram 17-1 (cont.)

Diagram 17-2 is a sample practice plan in which the defense is only afforded 65 minutes of practice time.

Segment #1—10 Minutes: Team tackling and cut block techniques

Segment #2—10 Minutes:

Front 5	*Whip and Free Safety*	*Cornerbacks, Stud, Rover*
Option and trap reads	Option and trap reads	Jam coverage techniques

Segment #3—10 Minutes:

Front 5	*Defensive Backs and Backers*
Zone and counter trey reads	1-on-1 vs. out, curl, post, post corner, and dig routes

Segment #6—10 Minutes:

Front 5	*Defensive Backs and Backers*
Pass runs—lanes and techniques	7-on-7 vs. out, curl, post, post corner, and dig routes

Segment #7—15 Minutes:

Front 5, Backers, Free Safety	*Cornerbacks*
Read drill vs. zone, CT, trap, and option	Shed 7 run support techniques

Segment #8—10 Minutes:

Team Adjustment Period: Versus ace and two-back sets
Coverage: Cover 1
Front five: Moe, Toe, Me, Tee, Nat, Nam

Diagram 17-2

Grading Player Performance

Each position coach is responsible for grading his player's performance. This can be done on Saturday prior to preparing the scouting report or at some other agreed upon time. The following factors should be tallied during this process:
- Solo tackles
- Assisted tackles
- Hurried throws
- Quarterback sacks
- Fumbles recovered
- Fumbles forced
- Takeaways
- Interceptions
- Batted balls
- Loafs

Each player should receive a grade. Opinions vary as to how this should be done. The most effective system is a plus/minus system. If the player assumed the proper alignment and employed the correct techniques, he receives a plus. If he didn't, he receives a minus. Distinction is made between plays that directly involve the player and plays that did not. Plays directly involving a player are referred to as critical plays. In grading critical plays, the coach will circle the player's plus or minus grade. Non-critical plays will not be circled. Critical plays will be averaged separately from non-critical plays. Each player will, therefore, receive two grades: a critical play grade and a non-critical play grade. The critical play grade is obviously the best indicator of each player's performance.

Scouting Reports

The following method for breaking down film and preparing a scouting report is old-school, but it's proven to be thorough, effective, and expeditious.

Normal Agenda for Saturday

- Every defensive coach is involved. No one sits leisurely with his feet on his desk and watches film. Everyone has a specific task.
- For visual learners, it may be useful to diagram each play on a sheet of paper rather than using the HUDL procedure of recording each play using words. In this case, the final report will consist mostly of pictures accompanied by information about how many times the run, pass, draw, screen, or formation shown was used.

- One coach is responsible for compiling the jersey numbers of the opponent's starting offense, along with substitutions. He notes any significant changes that may occur with situational personnel groupings. After all films have been viewed, he is responsible for researching MaxPreps®, and getting the name, height, weight, and statistics for each player. He then prepares a page or two that will be included in the report that details all of this information.
- Another coach is responsible for compiling the following tendency information:
  - ✓ Total percentages of runs, passes, screens, and draws
  - ✓ Percentage runs, passes, screens, and draws toward the wideside of the field
  - ✓ Percentage runs, passes, screens, and draws toward the shortside of the field
  - ✓ Percentages of runs, passes, screens, and draws toward the right and left
  - ✓ Percentage of runs, passes, screens, and draws towards and away from the opponent's bench
  - ✓ Percentage of runs toward and away from a tight end
  - ✓ Percentage of runs, passes, screens, and draws executed in the four zones of the field: the red zone (from the 20-yard line to the opponent's goal line), the open zone (from the 50-yard line to the opponent's 20-yard line), the cautious zone (from the team's own 20-yard line to the 50-yard line), bad zone (from the team's own goal line to the 20-yard line)
  - ✓ Down-and-distance percentages for runs, passes, screens, and draws:
    ⇨ First-and-five
    ⇨ First-and-10
    ⇨ First-and-15
    ⇨ Second-and-short (1–3)
    ⇨ Second-and-medium (4–6)
    ⇨ Second-and-long (7–10+)
    ⇨ Third-and-short (1–3)
    ⇨ Third-and-medium (4–6)
    ⇨ Third-and-long (7–10+)
    ⇨ Fourth-and-short (1–3)
    ⇨ Fourth-and-medium (4–6)
    ⇨ Fourth-and-long (7–10+)
    ⇨ First-and-goal
    ⇨ Second-and-goal
    ⇨ Third-and-goal
    ⇨ Fourth-and-goal
  - ✓ After viewing all of the film, this coach prepares two pages that are included in your report that details all of this information.

- The last coach notes all of the different blocking schemes used by the opponent. This information is especially important in understanding the opponent's pass protection schemes and determining how to pressure their quarterback. He is also responsible for collecting all newspaper articles associated with the opponent and posting them on the bulletin board.
- Next, all of the plays are sorted according to formation, and a page is prepared illustrating the percentages of runs, passes, screens, and draws from each formation.
- All of the runs and passes are then sorted. The pass plays are given to the defensive back coach, and he prepares pages illustrating every pass and the number of times it was thrown. The same thing is done with each running play.
- After all of the final report pages have been assembled, copies are made (which usually consists of a 10- to 15-page report), and each coach reports the details of his findings to the entire staff, and a discussion should follow.
- After discussing the report, suggestions can be made regarding any strategies and tactics that might be needed.
- In some instances the game plan may be finalized.
- Following the discussion, index cards are prepared that will be needed to illustrate the opponent's plays to the scout team during practice.
- Monday's practice is then planned.

Sunday's Agenda

If the game plan has been finalized on Saturday, there is no need to meet on Sunday. If a Sunday meeting is necessary, it should held at a time that is convenient for everyone. Sunday's meeting should be well organized and focused with no time wasted.

APPENDIX A
Motivation

Good coaches motivate their players. All coaches search for ideas that they can use as themes to inspire or motivate their players. Sometimes, it's a quote; other times, it's an anecdote, a poem, or a picture. The following are 101 devices that I have used throughout my career. Hopefully, other coaches may find some or all of them useful.

#1

> "I've earned respect thanks to basketball. And I'm not here just to hand it to the next person. Day in and day out, I've seen people take on the challenge to take what I've earned. I've got something that people want. And I don't ever want to give it away. Whenever the time comes when I'm not able to do that, I'll just back away from the game."
>
> —Michael Jordan

#2

> "You are in the presence of a true competitor when you observe that he or she is indeed getting the most joy out of the most difficult situations. That is when they focus better and function better."
>
> —John Wooden

#3

> *"I found this sandbank by the Pearl River near my hometown, Columbia Mississippi. I laid out a course 65 yards or so. Sixty-five yards on san is like 120 on turf. But running on sand helps you make your cuts at full speed. I try to pick the heat of the day to run in, but sometimes that sand will get so hot you can't stand in one place. It'll blister your feet. You get to the point where you have to keep pushing yourself. You stop, throw up, and push yourself again. There's no one around to feel sorry for you."*
> —Walter Payton

#4

Bob Ladouceur became the head football coach at De La Salle High School in 1979. Prior to 1979, De La Salle was one of the worst teams in Northern California. On his first official day as head coach, he found antiquated suspension helmets, hand-me-down pants, and frayed jerseys in a pile so huge that he was unable to open the door to the equipment closet. Not only was there no weight room, there wasn't a free weight on campus. An old Universal machine sat in the corner of the locker room. Its cables were frayed and it was in dire need of reconditioning.

Today De La Salle High School is the winningest football program at any level of competition in the history. They travel coast to coast and play the best programs in America. They are always ranked in USA Today's Top 25—usually they're #1. They've had the longest winning streak in the history of football-over 200 consecutive wins

#5

> *"If a team is to reach its potential, each player must be willing to subordinate his personal goals to the good of the team."*
> —Bud Wilkinson

#6

> *"Talent is God-given. Be humble. Fame is man-given. Be grateful. Conceit is self-given. Be careful."*
> —John Wooden

#7

> *"Nothing in the world can take the place of Persistence. Talent will not; nothing is more common than unsuccessful men with talent. Genius will not; unrewarded genius is almost a proverb. Education will not; the world is full of educated derelicts. Persistence and determination alone are omnipotent. The slogan 'Press On' has solved and always will solve the problems of the human race."*
> —Calvin Coolidge

#8

"The difference between a successful person and others is not a lack of strength, not a lack of knowledge, but rather in a lack of will."

—Vince Lombardi

#9

"I've missed more than 9,000 shots in my career. I've lost almost 300 games. 26 times, I've been trusted to take the game winning shot and missed. I've failed over and over and over again in my life. And that is why I succeed."

—Michael Jordan

#10

"Most people have the will to win; few have the will to prepare to win."

—Bob Knight

#11

"It doesn't matter whether you win or lose—until you lose."

—Joe Namath

#12

"It's fine to celebrate success but it is more important to heed the lessons of failure."

—Bill Gates

#13

"The ultimate measure of a man is not where he stands in moments of comfort and convenience, but where he stands at times of challenge and controversy."

—Martin Luther King, Jr.

#14

"Build up your weaknesses until they become your strong points."

—Knute Rockne

#15

The Winner is always a part of the answer
The Loser is always a part of the problem.

The Winner always has a program
The Loser always has an excuse.

The Winner says, "Let me do it for you"
The Loser says, "That's not my job."

The Winner sees an answer for every problem
The Loser sees a problem in every answer.

The Winner says, "It may be difficult but it's possible;"
The Loser says, "It may be possible but it's too difficult."

—Unknown

#16

"One thing I believe to the fullest is that if you think and achieve as a team, the individual accolades will take care of themselves."

—Michael Jordan

#17

"Success comes in a lot of ways, but it doesn't come with money and it doesn't come with fame. It comes from having a meaning in your life, doing what you love and being passionate about what you do. That's having a life of success. When you have the ability to do what you love, love what you do and have the ability to impact people. That's having a life of success. That's what having a life of meaning is."

—Tim Tebow

#18

"You cannot attain and maintain physical condition unless you are morally and mentally conditioned. And it is impossible to be in moral condition unless you are spiritually conditioned. I always told my players that our team condition depended on two factors: how hard they worked on the floor during practice and how well they behaved between practices."

—John Wooden

#19

"The road to Easy Street goes through the sewer."

—John Madden

#20

"Football is an honest game. It's true to life. It's a game about sharing. Football is a team game. So is life."

—Joe Namath

#21

Harlem

What happens to a dream deferred?

Does it dry up
like a raisin in the sun?
Or fester like a sore—
And then run?
Does it stink like rotten meat?
Or crust and sugar over—
like a syrupy sweet?

Maybe it just sags
like a heavy load.

Or does it explode?

—Langston Hughes

#22

"Champions aren't made in gyms. Champions are made from something they have deep inside them—a desire, a dream, a vision. They have to have last-minute stamina, they have to be a little faster, they have to have the skill and the will. But the will must be stronger than the skill."

—Muhammad Ali

#23

"Anything worth having in life is hard to get, and the things that are easy to get or achieve generally don't mean much."

—Ty Murray

#24

"The Green Bay Packers never lost a football game. They just ran out of time."

—Vince Lombardi

#25

"Love is the force that ignites the spirit and binds teams together."

—Phil Jackson

#26

"Nobody who ever gave his best regretted it."

—George Halas

#27

"To succeed ... You need to find something to hold on to, something to motivate you, something to inspire you."

—Tony Dorset

#28

Indispensable Man

*Sometime when you're feeling important;
Sometime when your ego's in bloom
Sometime when you take it for granted
You're the best qualified in the room,
Sometime when you feel that your going
Would leave an unfillable hole,
Just follow these simple instructions
And see how they humble your soul;
Take a bucket and fill it with water,
Put your hand in it up to the wrist,
Pull it out and the hole that's remaining
Is a measure of how you'll be missed.
You can splash all you wish when you enter,
You may stir up the water galore,
But stop and you'll find that in no time
It looks quite the same as before.
The moral of this quaint example
Is do just the best that you can,
Be proud of yourself but remember,
There's no indispensable man.*

—Saxon White Kessinger

#29

"In basketball—as in life—true joy comes from being fully present in each and every moment, not just when things are going your way. Of course, it's no accident that things are more likely to go your way when you stop worrying about whether you're going to win or lose and focus your full attention on what's happening right this moment."

—Phil Jackson

#30

"If you train hard, you'll not only be hard, you'll be hard to beat."
—Herschel Walker

#31

"The principle is competing against yourself. It's about self-improvement, about being better than you were the day before."
—Steve Young

#32

"A football game is just 60 minutes, but I'm training six, seven hours in every day. So, going for 60 minutes becomes easy."
—Ray Lewis

#33

"Much can be accomplished by teamwork when no one is concerned about who gets credit."
—John Wooden

#34

Don't Quit

*When things go wrong, as they sometimes will,
When the road you're trudging seems all uphill,
When the funds are low and the debts are high,
And you want to smile, but you have to sigh,
When care is pressing you down a bit,
Rest, if you must, but don't you quit.*

*Life is queer with its twists and turns,
As every one of us sometimes learns,
And many a failure turns about,
When he might have won had he stuck it out;
Don't give up though the pace seems slow–
You may succeed with another blow.*

*Often the goal is nearer than,
It seems to a faint and faltering man,
Often the struggler has given up,
When he might have captured the victor's cup,
And he learned too late when the night slipped down,
How close he was to the golden crown.*

Success is failure turned inside out—
The silver tint of the clouds of doubt,
And you never can tell how close you are,
It may be near when it seems so far,
So stick to the fight when you're hardest hit—
It's when things seem worst that you must not quit.

—Unknown

#35

"Talent is cheaper than table salt. What separates the talented individual from the successful one is a lot of hard work."

—Stephen King

#36

Winners Are People Like You*

Winners take chances.
Like everyone else,
they fear failing,
but they refuse
to let fear control them.

Winners don't give up.
When life gets rough, they hang in
until the going gets better.
Winners are flexible.
They realize there is more than one way
and are willing to try others.

Winners know they are not perfect.
They respect their weaknesses
while making the most of their strengths.

Winners fall, but they don't stay down.
They stubbornly refuse to let a fall
keep them from climbing.

Winners don't blame
fate for their failures
nor luck for their successes.
Winners accept responsibility
for their lives.

*Used by permission of the author

*Winners are positive thinkers
who see good in all things.
From the ordinary, they make
the extraordinary.*

*Winners believe in the path they
have chosen
even when it's hard,
even when others can't see
where they are going.*

*Winners are patient.
They know a goal is only as worthy
as the effort that's required
to achieve it.*

*Winners are people like you.
They make this world
a better place to be.*

—Nancye Sims

#37

"Adversity causes some men to break, others to break records."
—William Arthur Ward

#38

"Football is a game played with arms, legs and shoulders but mostly from the neck up."
—Knute Rockne

#39

"Today I will do what others won't, so tomorrow I can accomplish what others can't."
—Jerry Rice

#40

"It takes 20 years to build a reputation and five minutes to ruin it. If you think about that, you'll do things differently."
—Warren Buffett

#41

"Success is a lousy teacher. It seduces smart people into thinking they can't lose."

—Bill Gates

#42

"The price of success is hard work, dedication to the job at hand, and the determination that whether we win or lose, we have applied the best of ourselves to the task at hand."

—Vince Lombardi

#43

"The main ingredient of stardom is the rest of the team."

—John Wooden

#44

"People who work together will win, whether it be against complex football defenses, or the problems of modern society."

—Vince Lombardi

#45

"Winning takes talent, to repeat takes character."

—John Wooden

#46

"It's the little details that are vital. Little things make big things happen."

—John Wooden

#47

"The fight is won or lost far away from witnesses—behind the lines, in the gym and out there on the road, long before I dance under those lights."

—Muhammad Ali

#48

"Pressure is something you feel when you don't know what the hell you're doing."

—Peyton Manning

#49

"The Enemy of the best is the good. If you're always settling with what's good, you'll never be the best."

—Jerry Rice

#50

"Confidence doesn't come out of nowhere. It's a result of something ... hours and days and weeks and years of constant work and dedication."

—Roger Staubach

#51

"Once you've done the mental work, there comes a point you have to throw yourself into the action and put your heart on the line. That means not only being brave, but being compassionate towards yourself, your teammates and your opponents."

—Phil Jackson

#52

"Teamwork is not a preference; it is a requirement."

—John Wooden

#53

"There is an old saying about the strength of the wolf is the pack, and I think there is a lot of truth to that. On a football team, it's not the strength of the individual players, but it is the strength of the unit and how they all function together."

—Bill Belichick

#54

"When it's too hard for them, it's just right for us!"

—Marv Levy

#55

"As we look ahead into the next century, leaders will be those who empower others."

—Bill Gates

#56

"Don't measure yourself by what you have accomplished, but by what you should have accomplished with your ability."

—John Wooden

#57

"Ability is what you're capable of doing. Motivation determines what you do. Attitude determines how well you do it."

—Lou Holtz

#58

"The ideal way to win a championship is step by step."

—Phil Jackson

#59

"'We've got to bring it up a notch now that we're in the finals?' I had no idea what those guys were talking about. If I had been a football player whose goal was to win the Super Bowl, I would have stepped it up a notch the moment the ball was kicked off in the first game of the season, and I wouldn't have let up until they were handing out championship rings. That was the way I rode. 'I don't have another level,' I told the reporter. 'I give it all I have every time I'm out there. That's all I know. If I had to take it to another level to win, I'd be out of luck, because this is the only level I've got.'"

—Ty Murray

#60

Invictus

Out of the night that covers me,
Black as the Pit from pole to pole,
I thank whatever gods may be
For my unconquerable soul.

In the fell clutch of circumstance
I have not winced nor cried aloud.
Under the bludgeonings of chance
My head is bloody, but unbowed.

Beyond this place of wrath and tears
Looms but the Horror of the shade,
And yet the menace of the years
Finds, and shall find, me unafraid.

It matters not how strait the gate,
How charged with punishments the scroll.
I am the master of my fate:
I am the captain of my soul.

—William Ernest Henley

#61

"If you truly expect to realize your dreams, abandon the need for blanket approval. If conforming to everyone's expectations is the number-one goal, you have sacrificed your uniqueness, and therefore your excellence."
—Hope Solo

#62

"The reason of football is not to be the best but to be the best team."
—Barry Sanders

#63

"Without self-discipline, success is impossible, period."
—Lou Holtz

#64

"Be more concerned with your character than your reputation, because your character is what you really are, while your reputation is merely what others think you are."
—John Wooden

#65

"The only place success comes before work is in the dictionary."
—Vince Lombardi

#66

"The thing about football—the important thing about football—is that it is not just about football."
—Terry Pratchett

#67

"Most of what I really need to know about how to live, and what to do, and how to be, I learned in kindergarten. Wisdom was not at the top the graduate school mountain, but there in the sand box at nursery school.

"These are the things I learned. Share everything. Play fair. Don't hit people. Put things back where you found them. Clean up your own mess. Don't take things that aren't yours. Say you are sorry when you hurt somebody. Wash your hands before you eat. Flush. Warm cookies and cold milk are food for you. Live a balanced life. Learn some and think some and draw some and paint and sing and dance and play and work every day."
—Robert Fulghum

#68

"We should not have to push you to work hard, you should work hard because you want to be a great player."

—Bob Knight

#69

"The main thing is winning. Stats aren't that important, but I think in the end things will work themselves out."

—John Harbaugh

#70

"If you work harder than somebody else, chances are you'll beat him though he has more talent than you."

—Bart Starr

#71

"Before we can talk about a championship, we have to practice like a championship team."

—Mike Singletary

#72

"Don't let what you cannot do interfere with what you can do."

—John Wooden

#73

"I love practicing every day … I'm still learning."

—Peyton Manning

#74

"If you accept the expectations of others, especially negative ones, then you will never change the outcome."

—Michael Jordan

#75

"Difficulties break some men but make others. No axe is sharp enough to cut the soul of a sinner who keeps on trying, one armed with the hope that he will rise even in the end."

—Nelson Mandela

#76

"You can't live a perfect day without doing something for someone who will never be able to repay you."

—John Wooden

#77

"Only a man who knows what it is like to be defeated can reach down to the bottom of his soul and come up with the extra ounce of power it takes to win when the match is even."

—Muhammad Ali

#78

"One of the most important things for a player to have during drill work is an imagination. He must imagine that it is a game-like situation."

—Bob Knight

#79

"Winning isn't everything, but it beats anything that comes in second."

—Paul "Bear" Bryant

#80

"You're the only one that can put pressure on yourself. ... No one else can put pressure on you. It's self-inflicted. For me, I just want to go out and play football."

—Maurice Jones-Drew

#81

"My attitude is that if you push me towards something that you think is a weakness, then I will turn that perceived weakness into a strength."

—Michael Jordan

#82

"Setting a goal is not the main thing. It is deciding how you will go about achieving it and staying with that plan."

—Tom Landry

#83

"Expectations are a form of first-class truth: If people believe it, it's true."

—Bill Gates

#84

"I hated every minute of training, but I said, 'Don't quit. Suffer now and live the rest of your life as a champion.'"

—Muhammad Ali

#85

"Whether you think you can or you can't, you're probably right."

—Henry Ford

#86

"Wisdom is always an overmatch for strength."

—Phil Jackson

#87

"The person who sends out positive thoughts activates the world around him positively and draws back to himself positive results."

—Norman Vincent Peale

#88

"The reason of football is not to be the best, but to be the best team."

—Barry Sanders

#89

"Like life, basketball is messy and unpredictable. It has its way with you, no matter how hard you try to control it. The trick is to experience each moment with a clear mind and open heart. When you do that, the game—and life—will take care of itself."

—Phil Jackson

#90

"There are 11 people out there playing defense. What makes a difference is how those 11 people play. That's what defense is about. It's about team defense. You are always trying to isolate it into one player, one situation or one thing, and it just doesn't work that way."

—Bill Belichick

#91

"I have always adhered to two principles. The first one is to train hard and get in the best possible physical condition. The second is to forget all about the other fellow until you face him in the ring and the bell sounds for the fight."

—Rocky Marciano

#92

"Someone's sitting in the shade today because someone planted a tree a long time ago."

—Warren Buffett

#93

"I learned that courage was not the absence of fear, but the triumph over it. The brave man is not he who does not feel afraid, but he who conquers that fear."

—Nelson Mandela

#94

"If you're trying to achieve, there will be roadblocks. I've had them; everybody has had them. But obstacles don't have to stop you. If you run into a wall, don't turn around and give up. Figure out how to climb it, go through it, or work around it. One thing I believe to the fullest is that if you think and achieve as a team, the individual accolades will take care of themselves."

—Michael Jordan

#95

The six most important words: I admit that I was wrong.
The five most important words: You did a great job.
The four most important words: What do you think?
The three most important words: Could you please ... ?
The two most important words: Thank you.
The most important word: We.
The least important word: I.

—Unknown

#96

"If a tie is like kissing your sister, losing is like kissing your grandmother with her teeth out."

—George Brett

#97

"You play the way you practice."

—Pop Warner

#98

"There is no 'I' in team, but there is in win."

—Michael Jordan

#99

"Failure is a detour, not a dead-end street."

—Zig Ziglar

#100

"It's not whether you get knocked down; it's whether you get back up."
—Vince Lombardi

#101

If you think you're beaten, you are;
If you think you dare not, you don't;
If you'd like to win, but think, you can't
It's almost a cinch you won't.
If you think you will lose, you're lost;
For out in the world we find,
Success begins with a fellow's will,
It's all in the state of mind.
If you think you're outclassed, you are
You've got to think high to rise
You've got to be sure of yourself before
You can win a prize.
Life's battles don't always go
To the stronger of faster man
But sooner or later the one who wins
Is the one who thinks he can.

—Walter D. Wintle

APPENDIX B
One Dozen Suggestions for Longevity in the Coaching Profession

I've been a football coach for 45 years, and I'll probably continue to coach until they put me in the hole that will become my "permanent residence" and throw dirt on my face. After 42 years in the classroom, I stopped teaching school two years ago. I now volunteer to coach wherever the wind leads me. In 2012, I coached at a school in the Navajo Nation that had previously won only five games in seven years. In 2013, I coached at a university in Ensenada, Mexico. I'm not sure where I'll coach in 2014, but I know that if I'm still living above ground that it will be somewhere.

I continue to coach because I believe that football is more than a game. It has taught me some of the most important lessons that I've ever learned, lessons that I don't believe I could have learned in any other setting. Football taught me to work hard, to endure physical pain, and to "suck up my guts" when the going got tough. It instilled mental toughness and taught me that no matter how tough life got, that I could spit in adversity's face and deal it an uppercut to the jaw. It enabled me to exceed my mental and physical expectations. Most importantly, football taught me the importance of being involved in a team—something that is bigger and more important than myself. This is something that we have seemingly forgotten in America. Today, too many of us are focused on only one person: ourselves. This is evident in our families, religions, corporations, government, and relationships with foreign countries, and our environment.

You may not want to coach as long as I have, but for those of you that do, the following 12 suggestions may assist you in achieving longevity as a football coach.

Don't forget the one that really loves you.

If you're a young coach and you're planning to get married, make sure that your future spouse knows in advance exactly what a coach's life is like and how that lifestyle will affect her life. She needs to know that a coach's life is not glamorous. It is long hours, hard work, and frequent disappointments. She needs to understand that she'll have many "friends" when your team is winning, but those same "friends" may post a For Sale sign on her front lawn when you're not. She needs to know that she may move many times during her lifetime. There are not a whole lot of women to whom this type of lifestyle appeals, so if you're lucky enough to find a woman willing to give you her love and put up with your job, make sure you give her all of the love that she deserves. A good wife is any man's greatest treasure. Make sure you reciprocate by being a good husband, and if you're lucky enough to be blessed with children, give them the time and love that they deserve.

Keep yourself healthy and in good physical condition.

Too many coaches are negligent in this area. They don't take time to exercise and eat healthy. They get out of shape, become sluggish, and eventually end up with a multitude of health problems. This not only affects their ability to coach with enthusiasm and vigor, but causes them develop a negative attitudes. And, if they live long enough, they end up having a crippled lifestyle when they reach retirement age.

Don't worry about things over which you have no control.

Some coaches think that the only way to win is to work 18 to 20 hours a day and give attention to every little detail. Those that do usually end up in a divorce court with ulcers, heart problems, a blown prostate, and premature burnout. Some of the game's most successful coaches regularly ate dinner with their families; Vince Lombardi and Bud Grant are two examples. Sometimes we lose perspective of reality and forget what Lombardi told us: "Football is a simple game; it's about blocking and tackling. The perfect name for the perfect coach would be Simple Simon Legree." Many problems that occur during the season are totally out of our control, and worrying about them won't make the problems any better. Enjoy the journey, and roll with the punches. The sun will rise tomorrow.

Be positive.

My five-year-old grandson recently told me that he had already been awarded five trophies. He then asked me how many trophies I had. I told him that I never received a trophy until I was in high school and began winning boxing tournaments. He had a hard time understanding that. Today kids are rewarded for almost everything they do. Through the years, I've found that most players respond better to positive reinforcement, and that negative reinforcement usually ends with negative results. An old cowboy once gave me some great advice when he said, "Ya cain't make a thoroughbred run faster by hittin' it with a baseball bat."

The only certainty is uncertainty.

This is true not only in football but also in life. It's a reality that all living creatures have to deal with.

Don't follow the crowd.

My friend Al Baldock always stressed the importance of "daring to be different," which has proven to be some of the best advice I have ever received. Geronimo didn't fight like the Calvary. His tactics kept them in a state of constant confusion; consequently, it took one-third of the United States Calvary (5,000+ men) to force Geronimo and his band of 34 Chiricahua renegades to surrender. David didn't fight Goliath in hand-to-hand combat as Goliath had expected. Instead, David defeated Goliath at long distance with a sling shot. No coach will defeat opponents with superior talent by imitating other coaches who are blessed with extremely talented players. One of the real shortcomings of our profession is that we have a tendency to imitate rather than innovate. Dare to be different!

Delegate responsibility.

Many people today believe that in order to foster a sense of ownership, every member of a group must voice his opinion, and each opinion must be valued. People who believe this often spend a lot of time in lengthy staff meetings talking and listening, but accomplishing very little. When a coach asks his staff how they think wind sprints should be run the next day, the question frequently begins an argument that lasts until 1:00 a.m. Sometimes it's a lot more efficient for a head coach to say, "Clyde, you're in charge of wind sprints. You've got seven minutes; work 'em hard." Giving everyone something to be responsible for, but not making everyone responsible for everything, often saves time and energy.

Don't be influenced by either failure or success.

Rationalizing, blaming, or making excuses never change the numbers on the scoreboard. Winners analyzes their mistakes and then makes plans to avoid those mistakes in the future. Also beware of the disease complacency, which may infect you and your team following success. You succeeded because you worked hard and made good decisions. After a win or a successful season, enjoy the moment, but get back to work ASAP!

Don't forget the people you're serving.

It's not about X's and O's or numbers on the scoreboard; it's about your players. Sometimes, we forget that they're the only reason why we're coaching. Treat them right, and never forget the words of Eddie Robinson: "Coaching is a profession of love."

Study the game.

Bear Bryant once said that all coaches should study the game all ways and always. Al Baldock also told me that if a coach studied football intently his entire life that he might be able to learn 15 to 20 percent of it. Football is a fascinating science that is in a constant state of evolution. Study everything that you can about it, but never forget that in the final analysis, it's about blocking and tackling.

Don't fall in love with a particular philosophy.

John McKay often said that there is only one good play in football. He called that play the "pitch play." The pitch play occurs when a player crosses the goal line and pitches the ball to a referee. Your job is to stop the pitch play. How you do this will vary many times during your lifespan as a coach. Always keep an open mind: "there are many roads to Rome."

Work hard, be humble, and keep your mouth shut.

A great young coach and good friend, Tony Sanchez, head coach at UNLV, once told me that this advice is the reason for his success. It's great advice for any coach—even an old relic such as myself.

About the Author

Leo Hand has coached championship teams at both the high school and college levels during his 46 years of coaching. As a head high school coach in California, he coached teams that were ranked in *USA Today*'s Super 25 and won 81 percent of their games, a state championship, and numerous league championships. During his tenure as the offensive coordinator at Los Angeles Harbor College, the Seahawks posted an 8-3 record, were ranked number 27 in the United States, and won a K-Swiss Bowl—at a school that hadn't been to a bowl game in 20 years. A former Golden Glove boxing champion and linebacker at Emporia State University, Hand holds a master's degree from the College of Saint Thomas. Hand and his wife, Mary, have nine children, 17 grandchildren, and one great-grandchild.